D0873627

The
MINISTRY
of
GOD'S WORD

WATCHMAN NEE

Living Stream Ministry
Anaheim, California • www.lsm.org

© 1993 Living Stream Ministry

All rights reserved. No part of this work may be reproduced or transmitted in any form or by any means—graphic, electronic, or mechanical, including photocopying, recording, or information storage and retrieval systems—without written permission from the publisher.

First Edition, June 2000.

ISBN 0-7363-0629-3

Published by

Living Stream Ministry
2431 W. La Palma Ave., Anaheim, CA 92801 U.S.A.
P. O. Box 2121, Anaheim, CA 92814 U.S.A.

Printed in the United States of America

06   07   08   09   10   11   /   11   10   9   8   7   6   5   4   3

CONTENTS

PREFACE

The Ministry of God's Word contains eighteen lessons given by Watchman Nee to his co-workers in a training at Kuling between 1948 and 1949. The chapters are divided into four sections. The main subject is the ministers of God's word and their ministry. The structure and divisions of the book are well organized, and the content is rich and unique. May the Lord bless the reader with the light and revelation contained in these pages.

SECTION ONE

THE MINISTER

CHAPTER ONE

THREE KINDS OF MINISTERS

Acts 6:4 says, "But we will continue steadfastly in prayer and in the ministry of the word." The phrase *ministry of the word* can be translated as "service of the word." The work of serving men with God's word is known as the ministry of the word, and the persons who are involved in this service are called ministers of the word. *Ministry* refers to the work, while *minister* refers to the person. The ministry of the word occupies a very important place in God's work. The announcing of God's word and the ministry of this word to men follow specific principles, and God's servants should learn these principles well.

Throughout the Old and New Testaments, God spoke. He spoke in the Old Testament. He also spoke in the New Testament at the time of the Lord Jesus and through the church. The Bible shows us that the most important work of God on earth is the speaking out of His word. If we remove His word from His work, there is practically nothing left of His work. The main item of His work in this world is His speaking. Without the word, there would be no work. As soon as His word is removed, His work becomes a void. We must realize the place that God's word occupies in His work. As soon as we remove His word from His work, the latter ceases. God's work is carried out through His word. In fact, His word is His work. His work is occupied with nothing but His word.

How did God release His word? It is amazing and unusual to realize that God's word is released through man's mouth. This is why the Bible speaks not only of God's word but also of the ministers of the word. If God did all of His speaking directly, there would be no need of any ministers of the word.

However, He chose to speak through man. This brings in the matter of the ministers. We must be clear before the Lord that God's work is conveyed through His word and His word is released through man. This immediately brings us to the crucial place of man in God's work. God does not release His word through any means other than man's mouth. He needs ministers of the word, and He needs men to convey His word.

Throughout the Old and New Testaments, we find three kinds of people. Simply put, three kinds of ministers of the word are involved in spreading God's word. In the Old Testament God's word was released through the prophets, that is, through the ministry of the prophets. When the Lord Jesus was on earth, God's word became flesh, and there was the ministry of the Lord Jesus. In the remainder of the New Testament, God's word was released through the apostles, that is, through the ministry of the apostles.

THE OLD TESTAMENT MINISTERS OF THE WORD— THE PROPHETS

In the Old Testament God selected many prophets to speak His word. These prophets received visions and spoke. Even men like Balaam spoke for God. Balaam was a prophet. His prophecy was one of the greatest prophecies in the Old Testament (Num. 23—24). The prophets in the Old Testament, who were the ministers of God's word, spoke when God's word came upon them. Balaam prophesied when the Spirit of God came upon him; that is, he involuntarily spoke what the Spirit told him to speak. His own feelings and thoughts were temporarily suspended by God. The revelation and utterance that he received from God were totally unrelated to his own condition; they were simply spoken out from his mouth. He had no share in God's word. His opinions, feelings, and thoughts were not involved at all. In other words, God used his mouth as if it were His own. Balaam is a typical example of an Old Testament minister of the word. The Holy Spirit would give words, and God would give the utterance. Under the constraining and restraining power of the Holy Spirit, God's word was released through the Old Testament minister's mouth. There was no possibility of a mistake. God used men, but these men were merely conveyers of the word. The human element was kept to a minimum in these revelations. Nothing of man was added to the divine utterance. Man's role was merely that of being a mouthpiece.

In the Old Testament we also see men like Moses, David, Isaiah, and Jeremiah, who were used by God to speak for Him in their work. However, they were more than just mouthpieces for God; they were slightly more advanced than Balaam or some of the other prophets. Most of Moses' writings were words given by God. He spoke according to the instructions of God, but in a sense his speaking was in the same principle as Balaam's speaking. When Isaiah saw vision after vision, he recorded these visions in his writings. In a sense his writings also were in the same principle as Balaam's speaking. God put words in Balaam's mouth, and God also put words in the mouths of Moses and Isaiah. In principle they all experienced the same thing, but there was also a difference between Moses and Isaiah on one side and Balaam on the other side. When Balaam spoke on his own behalf, he uttered something according to his own sentiments. This kind of speaking was wrong, and it was condemned by God. When he spoke under divine inspiration, he spoke God's word. When he spoke out of himself, the result was sin, error, and darkness. Moses was different. Even though most of his speaking was ordered by God, when he nevertheless spoke according to his own feeling in the presence of the Lord, his speaking was acknowledged by God and recognized as part of the divine speaking. This means that Moses was more of an instrument of God than Balaam. The same can be said of Isaiah. Most of Isaiah's prophecies came from visions he received directly from the Lord. However, there are instances in the book of Isaiah which indicate that he was speaking out of himself. David and Jeremiah spoke according to their own feelings even more than Moses and Isaiah. They were more akin to the ministers of the New Testament. In principle, however, they were the same as the Old Testament prophets who spoke only when God's word came upon them.

THE MINISTER OF THE WORD IN THE GOSPELS—
THE LORD JESUS

The Lord Jesus was the Word becoming flesh on earth. He is God's Word. He put on the flesh and became a man of flesh. Everything He did and said formed part of God's word. The service of the Lord Jesus was the service of God's word. In Him, God's word was released in an entirely different way than it was released through the Old Testament prophets. In the Old Testament God merely used man's voice to deliver His word. Even John the Baptist, the last of the prophets, was merely a voice in the wilderness. God's word was merely conveyed through his voice. But the Lord Jesus was the word itself becoming flesh on earth. In other words, He was the word embodied in the flesh; He was the word becoming a man. We could say that here was a man, and we could also say that here was God's word. When God's word came upon man in the Old Testament, the word was the word and man was man. The word was merely being conveyed through man's voice. Although there is a slight variance in the cases of Moses and David, in principle, man's voice was merely a carrier during the Old Testament age. But when the Lord Jesus came, the word no longer came upon a man, with the word remaining the word and the man remaining man. God's word put on human flesh; the word became a man. No longer was God's word released through man's voice as a carrier, but the word put on a man. The word had human feelings, thoughts, and opinions, yet it remained God's word.

When man's opinion was added to God's word in the Old Testament, the word ceased to be God's word. As soon as human feelings, thoughts, and opinions were added to God's word, it was no longer God's perfect, pure, and unadulterated word. God's word was damaged. The purity of God's word could only be maintained when it was not contaminated with any human feelings, thoughts, or opinions. When God's word was released through Balaam's voice alone, it was a prophecy. But when Balaam put in his own feelings and opinions, the word was no longer just God's word; God's word was altered. This was the Old Testament. In the case of the Lord Jesus, however, God's word was conveyed not only through a man's voice but through his thoughts, feelings, and opinions as well. Man's thought became God's thought, man's feeling became God's feeling, and man's opinion became God's opinion. This was the ministry of the word which God secured in the Lord Jesus. The Lord Jesus served as a minister of the word under an entirely different principle from the Old Testament ministers. The Old Testament ministers of God's word were principally serving God with their voice. With some people God used more than just their voice; they acted more in the principle of the New Testament. Yet, in reality, they were still standing on Old Testament ground. But in the case of the Lord Jesus, He was the very Word of God. God's Word became flesh. Hence, we can say that the feeling of the Lord Jesus was the feeling of God's word, His thoughts were the thoughts of God's word, and His opinions were the opinions of God's word. The Lord Jesus was God's very word becoming flesh. God does not want His word to remain the word alone; He wants His word to take on human resemblance. He is not satisfied with just the word alone; He wants His word to become flesh. This is the greatest mystery in the New Testament. God is not satisfied with the word alone; He wants His word to be a personified word that carries human feelings, thoughts, and opinions. The Lord Jesus was such a minister of the word.

In the person of the Lord Jesus, God's word was no longer something objective; it became something subjective. In such a word we find human feelings, thoughts, and opinions. Yet the word remains God's word. Here we discover a great scriptural principle: It is possible for God's word to not be influenced by man's feeling. Even with the presence of human feeling, God's word is not necessarily contaminated. The question is whether or not such human feeling is up to the standard. This does not mean that every time human feeling is present, God's word is damaged. There is no such thing. This is a very profound subject! Here we discover a tremendous principle: The human element does not have to obstruct God's word. In the Lord Jesus we find that when the Word became flesh, the thought of that flesh became the thought of God. Originally, we could only say that the thought of the flesh was the thought of man. But in the New Testament age, the word has became flesh. In other words, the word became a man; the thought of this man was the thought of God's word. In the Lord Jesus, we find human thought that is up to the standard. There is one kind of human thought which, when added to God's word, does not contaminate it but instead completes it. God's word was not hindered by the human element of the Lord Jesus. On the contrary, it was fulfilled through the thoughts of the Lord Jesus. In the Lord Jesus we find God's word reaching a higher level than that which is found in the Old Testament. Matthew 5:21 says, "You have heard that it was said to the ancients..." This was Jehovah's word to Moses. It was Moses' direct inspiration from God. But the Lord Jesus continued in verse 22, "But I say to you..." Here we see the Lord speaking from Himself; He was saying things according to His own thought and opinion. But this speaking did not overturn God's sovereignty; it complemented His sovereignty. It did not overturn God's word; it attained a height that was unreachable in the Old Testament.

Here we see the very characteristic of the Lord Jesus as the minister of God's word. In Him God's word was made full. In this sinless man, there was not only a voice but feeling and thought as well. In the Lord Jesus, God's word was no longer merely a revelation; it became the very Lord Jesus Himself. God's word was no longer conveyed through human voice alone; it became a man. It was personified. God's word has been joined to man's word, and man's speaking has become God's speaking. The meaning of God's word being joined to man is that His word has been joined to man's word. This is a most glorious fact! When Jesus of Nazareth spoke, God spoke! Here was a man whose words were unmatched both before and after His time. No one ever spoke like Jesus of Nazareth. He was absolutely without sin. He was God's holy One, and He was completely of God. God's word was in Him, and He was the human embodiment of God's word. God's word was Him, and He was God's word. When He spoke, God was speaking. Here was a minister of the word, in whom God's word was altogether subjective. God's word was a very subjective entity in Him. It was so subjective that He Himself was the very word of God.

In the Old Testament we find prophets who spoke for God. In the Gospels we find the Lord Jesus whose very person was God's word. At the time of the prophets in the Old Testament, we could only point to the prophets when they opened their mouths and say, "Here is God's word." But with the Lord Jesus, we could point to His very person and say, "This man is God's word." His feeling was the feeling of God's word, and His thought was the thought of God's word. When He opened His mouth, there was God's word, and there was still God's word when He did not open His mouth. His very person was God's word. The minister of God's word has advanced from revelation to personification. With the Old Testament prophets, God's word was a matter of revelation. But in the Lord Jesus, God's word is a matter of personification. In the Old Testament the word and the person were two different things. The word was the word, and the person was the person. The word was channeled through man, yet the man remained just a man. But in the Lord Jesus, God's word became flesh. A man became God's word. When this man spoke, God was speaking. He did not need any revelation, because He was God's word. He did not need God's word to come to Him externally before He spoke the divine word, because His very speaking was God's speaking. He did not need more of God's word, because He Himself was God's word. When He spoke, God spoke. When He felt something, the feeling was the feeling of God's word. His opinion was God's opinion. In this man, God's word was not affected or limited by human factors. When this man opened His mouth, the pure word of God came out. Although He was a man, God's word did not suffer any loss in passing through Him. In fact, God's word was fully expressed through Him. This was the ministry of Jesus of Nazareth.

THE NEW TESTAMENT MINISTERS OF THE WORD— THE APOSTLES

There is another kind of minister of the word in the New Testament—the apostles. The ministry of the word in the

Old Testament was completely objective. The ministry of the word in the Lord Jesus was completely subjective. In the Old Testament the ministry of the word was realized when the word came upon a man and the man's voice was used as a carrier. In the Lord Jesus the ministry of the word was not through the visitation of the word but through the embodiment of the word as a man. The word took on not only the human voice but human thoughts, feelings, and opinions as well. Everything that belonged to this man was being employed by the word, because every aspect of this man was in harmony with God's word. This man is the Lord Jesus.

When we come to the apostles in the New Testament ministry of the word, we find a ministry with the same nature as that of the ministry of the Lord Jesus. We also find the element of the Old Testament revelation mingled with the nature of the Lord Jesus' ministry. The difference between the New Testament ministry of the word and the Lord's ministry of the word is this: In the case of the Lord Jesus, who was God's word becoming flesh, first there was God's word and then there was flesh to match this word. All of the feelings, thoughts, and consciousness of this man were in harmony with God's word. In the case of the New Testament ministry of the word, however, first there is the flesh. We all have the flesh. In order for this flesh to become a minister of the word, it has to be transformed to match the requirement of God's word. This means that the thoughts, feelings, and opinions of the flesh have to be transformed. The flesh has to match God's word. Hence, we can say that the New Testament ministry of the word is different from both its Old Testament counterpart and from the Lord's ministry. The Lord Jesus' ministry was one hundred percent subjective; He Himself was the word. The New Testament ministry, on the other hand, is the ministry of the prophets plus the ministry of the Lord Jesus. There is the visitation of God's word, the revelation of God. But there are also human feelings, thoughts, and opinions. Collectively, we can call these aspects the human elements. The New Testament ministry of the word is divine revelation plus human elements.

Men chosen by God in the New Testament are different from the Lord Jesus, who is God's "holy thing" (Luke 1:35) and God's Holy One. In Him there is not a hint of any mixture; His word was God's very word. With the men chosen by God in the New Testament, we have a different story. In addition to depositing His word into their being, God had to deal with the persons themselves; He had to build them up. On the one hand, God put His word into such persons. On the other hand, He dealt with them. God used their thoughts, feelings, and characteristics, yet at the same time He dealt with them. God dealt with the New Testament ministers of the word in their experience, speaking, feeling, thoughts, opinions, and characteristics. He dealt with them before He used them to express His word. A New Testament minister of the word not only has God's word and not only releases God's word with his human voice but expresses God's word through his human life in its full dimensions. God is pleased to put His word into a man and to allow such a man to express His word. The Lord Jesus is the word becoming the flesh, while the New Testament ministers are those who express the word in a flesh that has been dealt with by God.

HUMAN ELEMENTS WITHIN DIVINE INSPIRATION

Some presume that no human element can ever be contained in divine inspiration. They think that once the human element is involved, the divine inspiration is no longer divine. This is wrong. Those who think this way do not understand the nature of inspiration. God's inspiration does contain human elements. In fact, His word is expressed through human elements. Although the human elements in the prophetic ministry of the Old Testament were minimal, one cannot say that they were completely absent. At the least God used the human mouth to convey His message. The Lord Jesus was the Word becoming flesh. All the human elements within Him were God's word. Today in the New Testament age, God secures ministers of His word by expressing His word through human beings with human elements.

If one reads the New Testament carefully, it is clear that Paul frequently used words that Peter never used. John used some words that Matthew never used. Some words are found only in Luke's writings, while others are found only in Mark's writings. In studying the Bible, we find that every writer has his special characteristics. The Gospel of Matthew is different from the Gospel of Mark, and the Gospel of Mark is different from the Gospel of Luke or the Gospel of John. Paul's Epistles were written in one style, while Peter's Epistles were written in another style. John's Gospel and Epistles contain the same subject; they are related. For example, the first sentence of the Gospel of John says, "In the beginning...." The first sentence of his first Epistle says, "That which was from the beginning...." One speaks of the beginning, and the other speaks of that which was from the beginning. The book of Revelation, which was also written by John, echoes his Gospel and Epistles and contains the same style. Moreover, we can observe that every writer uses idiomatic expressions which are distinctly his own. Luke was a doctor. In describing sicknesses, he freely used medical terms. The other three writers of the Gospels only described these ailments in general terms. The book of Acts was written by Luke as well, and we find the same free use of medical terminology. Every Gospel has distinctive terminologies and themes. For example, Mark is unique in its use of the word *immediately,* Matthew, in the use of the phrase *the kingdom of the heavens,* and Luke, in the use of the phrase *the kingdom of God.* All these are unique characteristics of the writers. Every book of the Bible is impregnated with the marks of its writer, yet every book remains very much the word of God.

The New Testament is full of human elements, yet it is all God's word. Every writer has his own style, expression, and characteristic, and God uses these characteristics to express His word through them. His word is not damaged by this process. There are human marks and human characteristics, yet it is still God's word. This is the ministry of the New Testament. In the New Testament ministry God entrusts His word to man, and He uses man's very own elements to express His word. He does not make man a tape recorder, recording His speaking verbatim and then playing it back objectively. God does not want to do this. The Lord Jesus has come, and the Holy Spirit has carried out His work in man. The goal of His work is to keep the human elements and yet at the same time not damage the divine speaking. This is the foundation of the New Testament ministry. The Holy Spirit modulates, regulates, and operates on man to the degree that his elements remain, yet God's word is not sacrificed; rather, it is complemented. If God's word is void of human elements, it means that man has become a tape recorder. Today God's word contains human elements and is, in fact, complemented by human elements. We know that speaking in tongues is a gift from God. However, Paul did not encourage everyone to speak in tongues in the meeting, because when a man speaks in tongues, his mind is unfruitful (1 Cor. 14:14, 27-28). In other words, the human mind is not involved. This is more in the principle of the Old Testament ministry; it is different from the New Testament ministry. When a man speaks in tongues, his mouth conveys an unintelligible, divine utterance. But God wants human elements in His New Testament ministry. By the restriction, regulation, and operation of the Holy Spirit, everything of man can be used by God, and God can release His word through man. It is truly God's word, yet at the same time it is full of human elements. A New Testament minister of God's word must be possessed by God to such an extent.

Consider the example of a musician. He may be very skillful with the piano, organ, and violin. He can play the same tune on different instruments. Every instrument has its own characteristics, and the music it produces bears distinctive characteristics. A man can tell whether the sound is from a piano or a violin. The tune is the same, but the sounds are different. Every instrument bears its own distinctive sound quality. The piano has its own quality, as do the organ and the violin. Every instrument is different, yet all the characteristics added together bring out the sentiments and ethos of the music. There is an analogy between this and the New Testament ministers. Some are like the piano, while others are like the organ or violin. The tune may be the same, but different sounds are produced. One man releases God's word, and we find his own human elements in the word. Another man releases God's word, and we find his own human elements in the word. Everyone whom God uses has his own human elements. Under the regulation, direction, and perfection of the Holy Spirit, the human elements do not become a hindrance to God's word. Instead, they glorify it in the process of releasing it.

Since God's word must pass through man and must pick up the human elements, those who have never experienced God's dealing cannot expect their human elements to be of any use. If a man's own elements are questionable to God, God cannot release His word through such a man. Such a one cannot serve as a minister of God's word, and God cannot use him. In the Old Testament God used a donkey to speak for Him. This, however, is the age of the New Testament, and the New Testament ministry of the word is different from that of the Old Testament. In the New Testament God's word is expressed through human elements. This is why God is very selective; He decides whom He can use and whom He cannot use. If our human elements are not properly dealt with, we cannot be a minister of the word. We do not have the option of conveying God's word like a tape recorder. God needs to see changes in us. If we cannot come up to God's standard, He cannot use us. If we want to be a channel of God's word, we need much calibration and adjustment. If God set aside our human elements, it would be a simple matter to convey His word. But God wants the human elements, and the very persons whom He will use become a big issue. Some human elements are contaminated with defilement, carnality, and traces of the fall. God cannot use these; He has to put them aside. Some people have never been broken by the Lord. Others have a mind that is full of crooked guile. Some argue with God, while others are never dealt with in their mind or their emotion. They remain stiff-necked. God's word can never be released through these ones. Even if they receive God's word, they cannot pass it on. Even if they force themselves to pass it on, they will not be able to do so effectively. The basic consideration of a New Testament minister of God's word is his very condition before the Lord.

Today God does not want His word to remain His word alone; He wants His word to be spoken through man's mouth in a way that it is seen as man's word. What God wants is a word that is truly divine yet at the same time human. In reading the New Testament, can we find one word that was not written down by man? The outstanding characteristic of the New Testament, from the first page to the last, is that it is a record of man's speaking. It is absolutely human; nothing can be more human than its speaking. At the same time, however, it is absolutely divine; it is one hundred percent God's word. God is not satisfied with just the expression of His word; He wants His word to be expressed through man's word, so that the word which is released is truly human and at the same time truly divine. This is the New Testament ministry of the word.

In 2 Corinthians 2:4 Paul said, "For out of much affliction and anguish of heart I wrote to you through many tears." In writing to the Corinthians, Paul was serving them God's word. He wrote out of much affliction and anguish of heart. He was delivering God's word through many tears. Here was a man whose entire being was into his speaking. His whole being constituted his speaking. His writing was full of his human feelings. When God's word came to him, he was filled with affliction and anguish of heart, and he wrote through many tears. While he was writing, his human elements were mingled with God's word, and he released God's word this way. His human elements enhanced God's word and made it all the more God's word. Paul was not void of feelings and thoughts. He was not like a tongue-speaker, who receives a word and passes it on without the mind having any effect upon the word itself. Paul wrote God's word with much feeling and exercise of thought. As God's word was uttered, he was in much affliction and anguish of heart, and he wrote through many tears. This is a New Testament minister of the word.

God's word is expressed through man, the entire man. As such, man's characteristics, idiomatic expressions, tone of voice, and subjective experiences before God all flow through the word. Through the word we can find the extent to which a man has been taught by God, disciplined by God, and tested by God. When God's word comes to man, it can be expressed through man's human elements without damaging God's word.

It does not have to be contaminated. This is what it means to be a minister of the word in the New Testament. A New Testament minister of the word is one who has been taught by God for many years and one whom God can freely use. When the word reaches such a man, it can flow through him freely. The divine word will suffer contamination only if the human elements which interact with God's word are fleshly or natural.

Only when God's word has been impregnated with the human elements is such a word complete. Do not be mistaken; God's word is not just one commandment or ten commandments. The Bible shows us clearly that there is a human flavor and human elements within God's word. God has put His word into man and entrusted man to speak His word. Moreover, He requires that man's condition be right so that He can include man in His speaking. The basic principle of God's speaking is the principle of the Word becoming flesh. God is not satisfied with having His word alone; He wants His word to become flesh, to become part of man's word. This does not mean that God's word has been downgraded to the status of being just man's word. It means that God's word has been seasoned with man's flavor. However, it is preserved as His pure word. It is truly man's word and at the same time truly God's word. It is genuinely God's word and at the same time genuinely man's word. The New Testament ministry of the word is man speaking God's word. In reading the book of Acts as well as 1 and 2 Corinthians, we find men speaking God's word. In reading 1 and 2 Timothy, Titus, and Philemon, we also find a man speaking God's word. God's word is manifested through man's word and expressed through human elements. It is man speaking, yet God recognizes it as His word.

If this is the case, how great is the responsibility of those who speak God's word! If a man makes a mistake or if he introduces unclean elements into his speaking, God's word will be contaminated and will suffer loss. We must realize that the critical factor in speaking God's word is not the amount of Bible knowledge one possesses. It is useless if all one has are empty doctrines and a knowledge of the Bible.

It is possible for these to remain completely objective matters to a person. A man can preach all he wants about these things yet remain absolutely separate from them. We cannot be like the Lord Jesus, who was the word becoming flesh. However, as ministers of the word, we should realize that God's word is expressed through our flesh; He needs our flesh. This is why our flesh needs to be dealt with by God. Daily we have to have transactions with God; we need to experience His dealings. If we are short in any way, God's word will be damaged as soon as it passes through us and mingles with our own words.

Do not think that anybody can speak God's word. Only one kind of person can speak God's word—the one who has passed through His dealings. The greatest challenge to a speaker of God's word is not the appropriateness of the subject or the choice of words but the very person of the speaker. If the person is wrong, everything else will be wrong. May God teach us the genuine way to serve in the ministry of the word. We must remember that preaching is not a simple matter; it is serving God's people with God's word. May the Lord be merciful to us. Because our whole being is involved with the word, any unsuitable elements in our thoughts, expression, and attitudes, and any shortcoming in our training and experience will unconsciously damage His word. Our very being must be dealt with by the Lord. If we are dealt with by the Lord, His word will not suffer our contamination when we serve as His ministers. We will be able to release His word in a pure way. We can see this in Paul, Peter, Matthew, Mark, Luke, and John, and we can see this in many servants of the Lord. Human elements are present in God's word. But while human elements are present, they do not express the flesh. On the contrary, one finds glory in its expression. This is amazing—God's word becomes man's word, and man's word becomes God's word.

Chapter Two

THE CONTENT OF THE WORD
AND THE TRANSMITTING OF THE WORD

The Bible shows us that God transmits His word in a way that transcends all human concepts. According to our concept God can spread His word and make His speaking known in at least two ways.

First, He could create something in nature similar to a tape recorder that would convey His word to man. If man can invent a tape recorder, God certainly can create something in the universe which would faithfully convey His word verbatim. With such a device, every word of God could be captured. Then every so often, it could be turned on and God's word could be played back to man. If God were to convey His word to man this way, there would be no possibility of mistakes; everyone could hear God's pure word. God, however, has not chosen to do this.

Second, God could commission the angels to spread His word. The Bible tells us that angels can carry God's messages to man. However, the occurrences of this are rare. In every case, God did so because there was no other recourse. The use of angels was an exception; it was not God's ordinary way of communicating with man. If God had intended to use angels as His messengers, He could have dictated His words as ordinances, like the Ten Commandments. Such documents or ordinances would not have any tint of human experience; they would contain no human error. Some may think that this kind of speaking would eliminate many theological arguments, debates, and heresies. They think that if God's word were to be spelled out line after line, man would have no problem understanding it. It would be a simple thing if God spelled out His word in five or six hundred clauses that resembled the law. But our God would not do this. Some people wish that the Bible had been written as 1,189 well-organized dogmas instead of 1,189 chapters. When a man picked up such a Bible, he would have a manual of Christianity, which would tell him all about Christianity at a glance. God, however, has not chosen to do this.

If God used something like a tape recorder to transmit His word, there would be very little chance of error, and God could continually repeat His word. His word would not become rare, and no one could say that His vision was fading. His word could continue to go forth on the earth. But the basic problem with such a word is that it does not carry any human element with it, and only God could fully understand it. Even though the word would be of God, there would be no ground for mutual communication; there would be no connection between God and man. God would only be speaking God's word, and man would not understand it. If God's word does not contain human characteristics, it would be the same as thunder to us; we would not know what it meant. Clearly, God could never speak to us in this way.

Furthermore, God does not organize His word into doctrines and ordinances. While there are doctrines in God's word, His word is not merely written for man's understanding. Many people like to pick out the doctrinal parts of God's speaking. They cherish these parts. Many unbelievers find the Bible tasteless, being full of common words such as *we, you,* and *they.* To them the Ten Commandments are much more interesting. Man always wants to arrange God's word into sections, with some parts being spoken by angels, some parts being spoken by God, and some parts being revealed through thunder and lightning, with no human element whatsoever. But we must remember that God's word always bears the mark of human traits. This is a characteristic of the word of God. No book is as personal as the Word of God. In writing his Epistles, Paul repeatedly used the personal pronoun *I.* We ordinarily avoid using the personal pronoun *I* too often in a letter, lest our letter become too personal. But the Bible is full of human elements. God selected men to be ministers of His word, and He wants His word to contain human elements. This is a basic principle.

THE CONTENT OF THE WORD

Here we must explain what human elements are. As far as content is concerned, the Bible is full of human elements. If we remove the human elements from the Bible, not much is left of it. Human elements occupy a crucial place in the word of God. For example, the book of Galatians speaks of God's promise by referring to the story of Abraham. If we removed Abraham's story from the Bible, we would not understand what God's promise is. The Lord Jesus is the Lamb of God that redeems man from sin (John 1:29), and the Old Testament speaks of men repeatedly offering sacrifices of bulls and goats. From Abel's sacrifice in Genesis to the book of Leviticus with its many offerings, we find men offering sacrifices to God again and again. This is a picture of the Lord Jesus becoming the Lamb of God to propitiate for sinners. Consider the example of David in the Old Testament. He fought in battles and won. He obeyed God, and he was a man after God's heart. He prepared materials for God's house, and Solomon built the temple with the gold, silver, and precious stones that David had prepared. We see David, and we see Solomon. These two show how the Lord Jesus fought the battle, how He won, how He ascended, and how He was enthroned. If the story of David and Solomon were taken away, we would not be able to see the Lord Jesus fully. The Bible says that the Lord Jesus is greater than David and Solomon (Matt. 22:43-44; 12:42). Before the Lord Jesus came, there first had to be a David and a Solomon. Otherwise, we would not see anything. Consider the example of Moses leading the Israelites out of Egypt through the wilderness. The details of this history are recorded in the Bible, including how Joshua led the Israelites into the land of Canaan and how they overcame the thirty-one kings of Canaan. If the stories of Moses and Joshua were taken away, there would be very little left of the books of Exodus, Numbers, and Joshua. If we did not have the book of Joshua, it would be hard to understand the book of Ephesians. These examples show us that human elements are present throughout the Word of God.

One characteristic of God's word is that it is full of human elements. God's word is not released through thin air; it is released through man. God reveals His word through man and events related to man. This makes His word simple, understandable, and comprehensible. Whenever God speaks, He speaks so that man can understand. God's word is not merely something that God utters, but something that man can understand. It is not merely supernatural; it is also very natural. It is not merely spiritual; it is also human. Through its human composition we can understand what God is doing and, therefore, what He is saying. The book of Acts provides very little doctrine; it is primarily a record of the acts of the apostles under the leading of the Holy Spirit. Peter's actions became part of God's Word, and Paul's actions also became part of God's Word. The beginning of the church in Jerusalem became part of God's Word, and the beginning of the churches in Samaria and the church in Antioch also became part of God's Word. These events are not merely history; they are part of God's Word. Through history, man acted out God's word. By means of history, man declared God's word. The Holy Spirit reveals God's word through man by means of history. God's Word is full of human elements. This is a characteristic of the Bible. It is not a book of creeds. It is a book of man acting out God's word. When God's speaking is being carried out, acted out, and lived out by man, we have the word of God.

One basic principle of the Scripture is the principle of incarnation. If a man does not understand incarnation, that is, the principle of the word becoming flesh, it will be hard for him to understand the word of God. God's word is not abstract. It is not spiritual to the point that all human flavor is suppressed. God's word is not that distant; it does not remain in an unseen, untouchable, and unapproachable realm. "In the beginning was the Word....He was in the beginning with God" (John 1:1-2). Yet this Word became flesh and tabernacled among men, full of grace and reality (v. 14). This is God's word. His word tabernacles among men. We have to remember that the incarnation of the Lord Jesus unveils the basic principle of the ministry of God's word. If we want to understand the ministry of God's word, we have to understand the Lord Jesus' incarnation. What is the ministry of the word? It is the word becoming flesh. It is absolutely heavenly, but it is not in heaven; rather, it is on earth. It is one hundred percent heavenly, but it is not without the flesh; rather, it is embodied in the flesh. It is truly heavenly, but it is not devoid of human elements; rather, it is manifested through men. It is very heavenly, but at the same time, it is seen and touched by men. This is the testimony of the apostles. First John 1:1 says, "...which we have heard, which we have seen with our eyes, which we beheld and our hands handled...." God's word can be seen, beheld, and handled.

Consider the matter of holiness. Before the Lord came, no one knew what holiness was. Today, however, holiness is no longer abstract, because we can see holiness lived out on earth in the Lord Jesus. Holiness walked among men. When we see the Lord Jesus, we know what holiness is. The word becoming flesh means that holiness has become flesh. We did not know what longsuffering was. But today we see long-suffering in the Lord Jesus. God is love, but we did not know what this love was like. Today this love can be seen in Jesus of Nazareth. We may think that a spiritual man does not smile or cry or that he must be devoid of all feeling. Yet when we see Jesus of Nazareth, we know the meaning of being spiritual.

If all we had was God's holiness, we would not know what holiness is. But now we can understand what it is because we have the holiness of the Lord Jesus. If all we had was the love of God, we would not know what love is. But now we can understand what it is because we have the love of the Lord Jesus. If all we had was the longsuffering of God, we would not know what longsuffering is. But now we can understand what it is because we have the longsuffering of the Lord Jesus. If all we had was the glory of God, we would not know what glory is. But now we can understand what it is because we have the glory of the Lord Jesus. If all we had was God's spirituality, we would not know what spirituality is. But now we can understand what it is because we have the spirituality of the Lord Jesus. This is the meaning of the word becoming flesh. When the word became flesh, glory became flesh, love became flesh, and longsuffering and holiness became flesh. When we touch this flesh, we touch God. Jesus' love is God's love. His glory is God's glory, His holiness, God's holiness, and His spirituality, God's spirituality. If all we had was God, we would not know these things. But now that we have seen the Lord Jesus, we can understand all these things.

The principle of incarnation is a fundamental principle. God's work on man and His communion with man are governed by the basic principle of incarnation. Although we do not have incarnation in the Old Testament, we do see God moving in this direction. Although the incarnated One has ascended to the heavens now, God still operates according to this principle. God's work in man and His fellowship with man are absolutely based on the principle of incarnation. Today God is no longer an abstract God, an ethereal God, or a hidden God. He has been incarnated; He has come forth. Many times when we preach the gospel, we like to declare that our God has come forth. In the Old Testament He did not come forth. Psalm 18:11 says that "He made darkness His hiding place." Today God is in the light; He has come forth. He has revealed Himself in the light, and we can see Him. When God was hiding in darkness, we could not see Him or know Him. But today He is in the light, and we can see Him and know Him. He has come forth. He has come forth in the person of Jesus His Son. Incarnation is a very basic principle. The content of God's word is full of human elements.

THE TRANSMITTING OF THE WORD

Since God's word is full of human elements, He also includes man in the transmission of His word. Since God's word is full of human elements, God cannot use a tape recorder, thunder, lightning, or angels to communicate His word. Human elements must be involved in the communication of His word. Because the content is so full of human elements, God must convey it through human elements. It is not a matter of receiving a voice from God and then sending this voice out. God's word has to pass through our spirit and even our mind, feelings, and understanding and then be converted into our own words before it can be released. This is what it means to be a minister of the word. It is not a matter of receiving His word with one hand and sending it out with the other. That is not the ministry of the word. If we receive a word from God and send out the same word verbatim, we are acting merely as a recording machine. God does not want us to transmit His word like a machine. He wants us to receive the word and then dwell on it, feel it, be bothered by it, rejoice over it, and chew on it before sending it out.

John 7:37 says, "Now on the last day, the great day of the feast, Jesus stood and cried out, saying, If anyone thirsts, let him come to Me and drink." If I am thirsty, I can go to the Lord and drink. But the matter does not stop there. In verse 38 the Lord said, "He who believes into Me…out of his innermost being shall flow rivers of living water." When I am thirsty, I can go to the Lord Jesus and drink. But if others are in need, can I simply pour a drink for them? No, God's Word says that after a man takes a drink, the water goes into his innermost being and then rivers of living water flow out of his innermost being. The ministry of the word is God's word coming into us and then flowing out from our innermost being to quench others' thirst. This indirect route constitutes the ministry of the word. It is not a matter of how many verses we can recite or how many messages we can deliver. It is a matter of the living water making an indirect turn and flowing out of our innermost being. The need for a turning within our innermost being and a subsequent flowing out from within our inner being tells us that a price is involved. Sometimes the living water flows into us but cannot flow out. At other times, it ceases to be living after coming into us. Still at other times, many impurities from our inner being are carried with it when it flows out. When this happens, we do not have the ministry of the word.

The ministry of the word has nothing to do with well-prepared sermons. When the word comes into us, it grinds and churns within us. When it passes through us in this way, human elements are added to the word. The word is not contaminated or damaged; it is enhanced. This is the meaning of having the ministry of the word. The Lord is making us channels of living water; water has to flow out from our very being. Our innermost being is the channel. In order for the living water to flow out of us, our very being has to be proper. If we are not proper, God's word cannot come out from us. We should not think that the power of a message comes from intelligence or eloquence. No, intelligence and eloquence are not the point. The point is whether or not our human elements will enhance and complete God's word when it passes through us. Does the word become human while still being divine, or do we damage God's word when our human elements are added to it? This is the basic question that faces a minister of the word.

A big problem with many people is that the living water ceases to be living when it passes through their innermost being! This is why we emphasize the discipline of the Holy Spirit. If a man does not see the importance of being dealt with by the Lord and if his habits, character, and living are not dealt with, he will be useless as far as God's word is concerned. If a man thinks that being a minister of the word is merely a matter of eloquence and cleverness, he is far from the truth! In fact, nothing can be farther from the truth! God's word must first come to us, pass through us, fill us, and even bother us, grind us, rub us, and deal with us. We must first suffer these trials and pay this price before we can be brought to the clear realization of God's word. In this way God's word is added to us little by little. It is assembled in us and woven into us stitch by stitch like a quilt. Then when the word comes out of us, it will involve the release of the spirit, not just the repetition of words. The water that comes forth will be clear and pure, fully proceeding out from God. We will only enhance its perfection; we will not mar its perfection. We will only add to its holiness, not diminish it. As we are released, the living water will be released. As we are speaking, God will also be speaking. This is the meaning of the ministry of the word.

The ministry of the word is like a combined flow of two rivers; it is not a single river. In order for this to happen, the Holy Spirit needs to operate in us. We need the Spirit to direct our environment to discipline us in many ways. When the Holy Spirit works on us, breaks us, dismantles us, and molds us, we are formed into a channel through which the living water can flow. Our outer man has to be broken and dismantled by God; it needs to be thoroughly and drastically dealt with by God. Our spirit will acquire the understanding, and the Holy Spirit will have the freedom to release God's word through us only after the Holy Spirit has accomplished such a work. God's word will take up our human element, yet it will not be contaminated by our human element. Instead, His word and our word will be a combined flow of two rivers.

We must always bear in mind the meaning of the ministry of the word. The ministry of the word means the outflow of God's Spirit in His divine word through man. It is not the independent release of God's Spirit in His word but the release of His Spirit in His word in conjunction with man. This is the significance of the ministry of the word. It is something that contains God's word as well as man's ministry. God's word is present in this utterance and so is man's ministry. God's word first comes to man. Man's ministry is then added to this word. The two are released together. If there is only God's word without man's ministry, we do not have the release of His word.

Some people think that they can successfully transmit God's word as long as they pick up a few phrases here and there. However, it is never that simple. The ministry of the word is a combined flow; it is not a single flow. A single flow will not work. God does not operate this way, because this is a fundamental contradiction to the principle of the ministry of the word. We must realize that God's word cannot be released without man's word; He has to use man. As far as our disposition and nature are concerned, we are stubborn, defiled, and rebellious. It is easier for God to use a donkey than it is for Him to use us, yet He still prefers man. In His ministry of the word and in the release of His word, God has a desire for man's element to be involved. God has chosen man to release His word. We must remember that God's word is present only where there are ministers of the word. Without ministers of the word, we cannot have God's word. God must secure ministers before He can release His word; without ministers, there cannot be the word. We will be hoping in vain if we expect God to release His word without providing proper ministers for Him. God's ordained way is to put His word first into ministers, those who have experienced the dealings of the Holy Spirit. We all agree that God's Spirit is in His word. But His Spirit is also in us. In other words, God's Spirit is both in His word and in the ministers. God's Spirit is within the word. But if only this word is released, His Spirit will not do anything. He will only work when the word resides in and is combined with the ministers. The seven sons of Sceva tried to cast out demons in the name of the Jesus whom Paul preached, but they could not cast them out. Not only did the demons remain, but they even prevailed over two of the sons (Acts 19:13-16). The sons had the right words, but the Spirit did not do anything. It is not enough simply to speak the right words. There is also a need to be proper persons, proper ministers. God's Spirit must first join Himself to the ministers. Then the living water will flow as His Spirit is released through the word.

Let me repeat: God's word does not operate independently; it is expressed through human elements. Man is the channel, the channel of God. It is impossible to try to overturn this principle by presuming that God's word alone is sufficient and that there is no need to consider man's condition. Without the operation of God's Spirit behind His word, the word will be a useless, empty shell. The crucial issue today is the ministers. The focus is on the ministers. The ministers must have the Spirit. God's Spirit must accompany His ministers before the word will become effective. As a consequence, the fundamental problem is with the ministers of the word. The ministry of the word is not merely a matter of the word. If one emphasizes the word without emphasizing the ministers, what he has will not be the word. Such a word will be a loss, and it will not be a ministry.

The problem today lies entirely with the ministers. There is no scarcity of vision, light, or God's word. The problem today is that God cannot find proper ministers. Many times God's light ceases to be visible to others when it is put into our mouth. Many people speak about the Holy Spirit in their messages, but others do not touch the Holy Spirit. On the contrary, they touch the flesh. Many people speak about God's holiness, but others do not sense any holiness in them. They only touch a frivolous spirit. Some speak about the cross on the platform, but others can sense that they have never passed through any dealings. There is not even a trace of the cross in them. Some like to speak of love, but only temper, rather than love, is expressed through them. All of these cases speak of a basic problem—something is wrong with the ministers. If all the preaching on this earth today were in the principle of ministry, the church would be very rich. It is unfortunate that there is very little of God's word despite all of the preaching! This is the basic problem in the church today. Without ministers, there is no inspiration and no revelation. With many people, the more they preach, the further their speaking is from being an inspiration, from being the release of any light, and from being qualified to be called revelation. The problem is with the preachers; they are not the ones whom God can use. God cannot use such men, yet He does not want to speak alone. This is a problem. He has the word, yet He does not want to release this word by Himself. He does not want to be the minister of the word; He wants man to be the minister of His word.

Brothers, God will not speak by Himself. If ministers cannot speak His word, what will be the condition of the church? The church is desolate, poor, and in ruin because human elements have not come up to the standard of God's word. If God can find a person who has been dealt with by Him, who is broken, and who is prostrate on his face, God's word will flow through him. We are looking all the time for God's word, but He is looking all the time for men whom He can use. We are looking for God's word, while He is looking for ministers.

If we are unwilling to be dealt with, we will not be able to work for God. We must not think that such dealings are optional. We should not presume that, after hearing a certain number of messages, we can release the same word. No! If a person is not proper, his message will not be proper. Man can hinder God's word. The Holy Spirit is not released through the word alone. When God's word comes to us, we must be free from all hindrances. We must be broken, and we must bear the mark of the cross. Our spirit must be a smitten spirit. God can only use such persons, and the Holy Spirit will only flow through such persons. If the Holy Spirit is locked within us, the hindrance and frustration is our outer man, our emotion, and our temperament. When such things are present within us, surely God's word cannot flow through us. Even if we deliver a wonderful sermon, in reality it is nothing but words, teachings, and doctrines; there is not the word of God.

God's word has to penetrate our whole being—our feelings, our understanding, our heart, and our spirit. It has to flow in and out of us; it has to be identified with us, and then it must be released from us as a result of grinding, crushing, and pressing. If our emotion is misaligned, if our mind is impaired, or if our understanding, heart, and spirit are even slightly off, we will damage God's word. Not only will our word be flawed, but the church will suffer as well. We will damage God's word and affect the church. This is the way of the ministry of the word, and this is where our problem lies. We have to learn to allow God's word to pass through us without any hindrance or contamination. If God is merciful to us, we will find light in this matter.

CHAPTER THREE

PAUL'S COURSE AND HIS MINISTRY

We have discussed already the nature of God's word. God's word contains many human elements, yet it nevertheless remains God's word. It is not corrupted by the human elements. The word remains eternal, excellent, transcendent, divine, holy, and pure. We have also seen that the ministry of the word consists of the release of this human-impregnated word through human faculties such as the memory, understanding, thoughts, heart, spirit, and utterance. This is the reason that it is so important for a minister of the word to be proper before God when he preaches the word. If his condition is not proper, God's word will be corrupted.

Let us consider Paul, who was very much used by the Lord in the New Testament. We will see the ways he served as a minister of God's word.

ONE

Paul said, "I have finished the course" (2 Tim. 4:7). The word *course* in Greek refers to a journey. Paul's course was based on an itinerary; it was marked in advance. God assigns a definite course for everyone. This course is marked and calculated in advance. It is marked not only as to its direction but also as to its distance. Paul obtained mercy from God and was able to run on his assigned course. He finished his course at the proper moment. When it was time for his departure from the world, he said, "I have finished the course." I believe God placed this course before Paul on the day that he believed in the Lord.

We know that God begins His work on a person long before he is saved. Paul said the same to the Galatians: "But when it pleased God, who set me apart from my mother's womb

and called me through His grace, to reveal His Son in me
that I might announce Him as the gospel among the Gentiles,
immediately I did not confer with flesh and blood" (Gal.
1:15-16). In the first part of this passage Paul said, "God,
who me apart from my mother's womb and called me
through His grace." This shows that Paul was set apart from
his mother's womb. Then he told us that he became a minister
of God's word. While he was yet in his mother's womb, God
set him apart, and his course was assigned. When he was
saved, he embarked on this course. This shows that the
preparation and initiation of a minister is determined by God
when he is still in his mother's womb.

Every experience we had before we were saved was under
God's sovereign arrangement. God gives us our distinctive
characters, our temperaments, our inclinations, and our
virtues. God prepares all of these things. No one goes through
any experience by accident. Every experience is part of God's
sovereign arrangement. No person inherits a character trait
by accident; everything is under God's sovereign hand. He
made provisions long ago for our natural abilities and
experiences, and He has prepared us for our future commission. Paul was set apart from his mother's womb. His course
was set long ago by God. Even his profession before his con-
version was set by God.

Peter was fishing when he was called. His lifetime work
involved bringing men to the Lord (Matt. 4:18-20). The keys to
the kingdom of the heavens were given to him; he was the one
who opened the door (16:19). He opened the door at Pentecost,
and he opened the door at the house of Cornelius. We should
pay attention to the fact that it was the fisherman who
brought in the men.

John was also a fisherman. But when he was called, he
was not fishing; he was mending the nets (4:21-22). The
Gospel of John was the last of the four Gospels to be written.
In his Gospel he unveiled the matter of eternal life. If we
only had the first three Gospels and if John had never mended
what was lacking in these three, we would not know what
eternal life is today. Moreover, John's Epistles were written
decades after Peter's and Paul's Epistles. By that time the

Gnostics had brought in their philosophies. John turned men back to the matter of the eternal life. He showed us the condition and expression of a man who is born of God. In the early days of apostasy, we had a mender who mended the net with eternal life. John's Revelation is the last of the sixty-six books of the Bible. Without this book, the Bible would not be complete; many things would not have a proper conclusion. John mended the net and completed the Bible with Revelation. This shows us John's ministry—the ministry of mending.

Let us turn back to Paul. God had set a course for him. Even his profession was foreordained by God. He was a tent-maker; he was not a weaver. He sewed and stitched with fabric, and he made dwellings fit for traveling. His ministry came after the work of the Lord Jesus and the work of Peter. Paul's ministry stands between Peter's work and the work of the future kingdom. The kingdom has not yet come. In the meantime, men are being saved and are building up the church. Paul's ministry was in the principle of tentmaking; he put material together and built it into a habitable dwelling. His work was not to produce the fabric—a kind of raw material. His work involved tents—which serve as habitable dwellings. Paul's profession was something arranged by God.

A minister of God's word is set apart from his mother's womb. For this reason, no one should act foolishly before the Lord. Everyone should understand God's sovereign arrangement in his environment. God's sovereign hand is behind everything—his environment, his family, and his profession. God has no intention to annul these human elements; He has no intention to remove them. God does not want us to act unnaturally. He does not want us to be pretentious or legal in any way. He wants us to be like simple children. Yet at the same time, He wants to break our outer man. The Spirit of God can reconstitute all of our human elements. At the same time, our very self (not the human elements), which is made up of our natural "shell," i.e., our natural life, together with our emotional and intellectual life, must be broken by Him. God has to break these things. The outward man must be broken and torn down. But this does not mean that God will set aside the human elements completely.

The biggest problem is that we do not know at which point this work begins and where it ends. We do not know how much of what we have in us is permitted to stay and how much is hated by God and in need of being broken. As soon as we function in our ministry, whoever has been taught by God will have an inner registration of a pure or a defiled service. This is not a simple pathway to take. Everyone has to submit to God's discipline; everyone has to submit to the cross. The cross has removed everything that God condemns and hates, and it has broken down everything that needs to be broken down. A man must learn submission; he has to tell the Lord, "I have many problems within me. I do not know how to deal with them all. I ask for Your shining, for the killing of Your light. Deal with me according to Your light. Deal with me to such an extent that my human elements will not become a hindrance to Your work but a means to express Your work." Paul's entire life, from beginning to end, was under God's hand. His salvation was a pattern to others (1 Tim. 1:16). First, God's light subdued him; he fell before the Lord. This was a strong salvation. Immediately after he stood up, God's word came to him, and it never stopped. He wrote most of the Epistles of the New Testament. God was pleased to release His word continually through Paul. He was indeed a great minister under God's hand.

TWO

Let us turn our attention to Paul's Epistles to the Corinthians, in particular to the manner in which he fulfilled his ministry of the word. A brother once said that of all the books of the Bible, the Corinthian Epistles, and in particular 1 Corinthians 7, show us the peak of human experience. This is right. Paul's experience proves this. Consider the following examples:

Verse 6 says, "But this I say by way of concession, not by way of command." The phrase *this I say* clearly indicates that this was Paul's own word.

Verse 7 says, "Yet I wish all men to be even as I am myself." Such a wish was Paul's own wish. Verse 6 presents Paul's own word, while verse 7 speaks of his own wish. He did not say that God commanded such or that God ordained such. Verse 7 continues, "But each has his own gift from God, one in this way, the other in that." God works in different ways. But it seems as if Paul was giving his own opinion. He was hoping that all would be even as he was.

Verse 8 says, "But I say to the unmarried and to the widows, It is good for them if they remain even as I am." This was again Paul's own word.

Verse 10 says, "But to the married I charge, not I but the Lord, A wife must not be separated from her husband." Paul first said that he *charged* them, but then he said that it was not him but the Lord who charged them. We can only find such expressions in 1 Corinthians 7. On the one hand, Paul charged, and on the other hand, he said that it was not his charge but the Lord's charge.

Verse 12 says, "But to the rest I say, I, not the Lord." This is Paul's word again. Verses 12 through 24 are all Paul's word; they are not the Lord's word. How could Paul have dared to say such a word? How could he have been so bold? By what authority was he speaking these words? In the following verses he presents the basis for his speaking.

Verse 25 says, "Now concerning virgins I have no commandment of the Lord." Paul did not lie. He honestly confessed that he did not have a commandment of the Lord. "But I give my opinion as one who has been shown mercy by the Lord to be faithful." Here was the opinion of one who had been shown mercy by the Lord, one who was empowered by the Lord to be faithful. God had done a profound work in him and had made him a faithful one. He was able to claim that God's mercy had made him a faithful person, that it had done so much work in him that he was now able to express his opinion. Here we do not find the Lord's commandment. Instead, we find Paul's opinion, that is, his view concerning a certain matter. All the words were Paul's. He told the Corinthians how he felt.

Verse 26 says, "I consider then that this is good because of the present necessity." Paul said that this was his opinion.

Verse 28 says, "I am trying to spare you." This was again Paul's opinion.

Verse 29 says, "But this I say, brothers." This is Paul's word.

Verse 32 says, "But I desire you to be without care." This is Paul's word.

Verse 35 says, "But this I say." This is again Paul's word.

Verse 40 says, "According to my opinion." This is Paul's opinion.

In verse 17 Paul said, "And so I direct in all the churches." He said this not only to the Corinthians but to all the churches. He charged all the churches with the same things.

Brothers and sisters, how marvelous this is! This is the opposite of our common understanding. In John 8:28 the Lord said, "As My Father has taught Me, I speak these things," and in 12:50 He said, "Even as the Father has said to Me, so I speak." Yet Paul was bold to tell others that his words were his own opinions, views, and even his charge to the churches. This is either the loftiest experience or the worst experience. Thank God that this *is* the loftiest experience. No place in the Bible is as high as 1 Corinthians 7. After his words in this passage, Paul concluded by saying, "I think that I also have the Spirit of God" (v. 40). Here we reach the highest peak. Paul was clear that he did not have God's commandment; he was clear that he did not have a word from the Lord. His speaking was merely based on the mercy that had been shown to him. He had no other basis. His only basis was God's compassion and mercy to him. But after he spoke, he could say that he thought he had the Spirit of God.

This is the "human element" which we discussed earlier. This is an outstanding and stark example of man's elements being employed in God's word. Here was a man who was disciplined, restricted, and broken by the Lord to the extent that he could speak even when he was very clear that the Lord had not said anything. Yet in the end, his word became the word of the Holy Spirit. Paul was giving others his own opinion. Yet in the end his opinion was the opinion of the

Holy Spirit. Paul said that it was his thought and his opinion. Yet in the end it was the intention of the Spirit of God. Here was a man under the Lord's Spirit and His operation so much that when he spoke, the Holy Spirit was speaking. What a great difference this is from the donkey of Balaam! Balaam's donkey could speak God's word only when the word was put into its mouth. When God's word was taken away, only the donkey was left. In contrast, here was a man who had followed the Lord, received mercy from Him, and been faithful for years. In the end his speaking became the Spirit's speaking. Paul made it clear that it was his opinion. But in the end it was the Lord's opinion. God had worked in him to such an extent that he could almost speak God's word without having God's word. What is this? This is a minister of the word.

With many servants of the Lord, God's word can be found in them only when a word is put into their mouth, and when it is not placed in their mouth, they do not have any word. Yet Paul had reached the stage where he had God's word whether or not it was put into his mouth. Here was a man so trained that he could earn the Lord's trust. Here was a man so trained and trusted by God that his speaking became God's speaking. We cannot do anything about this except to plead for mercy. Brothers, we cannot be just a donkey. We cannot be satisfied with God's word just being placed in our mouth. If this is our condition, it means that we ourselves have nothing to do with God's word. Paul was a man who had much to do with God's word. Even his own opinions became God's opinions. The little thoughts that he had became the thoughts of the Holy Spirit. He was so one with the Spirit of God! His very speaking represented God's speaking. He indeed reached the highest peak.

A minister of the word is not merely one who transmits God's word. He must be a person who has a certain relationship with God's word. He has God's thoughts and opinions, and he has reached the stage where his desires become God's desires. He does not act in a certain way because he comes to a separate realization of God's desire in a certain matter. Rather, he is restricted by God to such an extent that God trusts his thoughts and ideas. God can acknowledge his thoughts and ideas as His own. This is what we have been saying for years; it is what we call the constituting work of the Holy Spirit. God constitutes Himself into us. He works and wroughts Himself into us. The golden lampstand was made of beaten work (Exo. 25:31). We must remember that something is given to us by the Lord on the one hand, while God is beating the same thing into us on the other hand. We are like an unshaped piece of gold. God is beating us blow by blow until we are formed into the shape of a lampstand. The Holy Spirit not only puts the divine word in our mouth but also beats such a word into our being until we are conformed to God's defined shape. This is not a matter of whether or not we have God's word in our mouth but a matter of whether we have been beaten to the point where God can entrust His word to us. Paul was constituted by the Lord to such an extent that his opinion was considered trustworthy; the Lord worked in him to such an extent that his thoughts were trustworthy enough to convey God's word. When God's word is placed in such a man and he is called to be a minister of the word, there is no danger of corruption.

A minister of the word is a person in whom God can confide His trust and faith. Ministry of the word means that there is not only the word but the man, the very person who serves as the minister of the word. Such a person has been so perfected that God's word will not suffer damage or misunderstanding through him. He is a person whom God can use, one who can serve as a minister of the word. A minister of the word is one who is so constituted by God that God can entrust him with His very opinions, thoughts, and desires. His own human elements can be involved in the speaking; they will not cause any problem to the divine word. Brothers and sisters, do not think that we are contradicting what we have preached in the past. In the past we pointed out that human ingredients are forbidden in God's work. Why then do we now say that God's word contains human elements? We are not admitting every kind of human element; we are saying that only certain kinds of human elements can be involved in God's word. Those who have such elements will find God's word flowing out of them freely. God can freely trust them.

We should spend a little more time to consider Paul's word. He said that he had obtained mercy to be faithful. Mercy is of God, and the result of mercy is faithfulness. This means that God did some constituting work in Paul. He worked in Paul to such an extent that Paul's very being resembled God's word. Because of this, Paul could release God's word wherever he went. Paul could say "I wish," "I say," or "I direct in all the churches" because he was a person who had met God; he knew God. When he spoke his word, it was God's word that came out. We have to remember that God's word is not released in a supernatural way; it is released through man and with human elements. If the person is not right, God's word cannot be released, and such a person cannot be a minister of the word. Never think that a man can preach a message just by memorizing it. God's word has to make a turn within man before it can be released. If you are not the proper person, God's word will be damaged as soon as it goes through you. As soon as man's frivolity and carnality come in, God's word is defiled. A man must reach the point where God's constituting work is well formed in him. Then the Lord's word can pass through him without suffering loss on account of his person.

In 1 Corinthians 7 God's word did not suffer any loss in Paul. Here was a man who was mature. If he spoke according to his own opinion, we are assured that this opinion was right. If he said something, we have the confidence that what he said was right. When he directed all the churches to do certain things, we have the assurance that this direction was right. Here was a man who was directing others, yet God's word was coming through him; he was not acting independently. Here was a man whom God could trust. He had reached the pinnacle. A minister of the word must attain such a height before God's word can be released through him. The measure of discipline and restriction one receives from the Lord determines the degree of purity of God's word that is released through him. The degree of brokenness before the Lord determines the degree of purity of one's speaking. The less one receives and learns from the Lord, the more likely God's word is defiled and contaminated when it is released through him. The more restriction, discipline, blows, and breakings one receives, the purer God's word is when it is released through him. The ministry of the word is based on the ministry a person possesses before the Lord. If our ministry before the Lord is a failure, our speaking is a failure as well.

THREE

Let us turn to 1 Corinthians 14:29-32, which says, "And as to prophets, two or three should speak, and the others discern. But if something is revealed to another sitting by, the first should be silent. For you can all prophesy one by one that all may learn and all may be encouraged. And the spirits of prophets are subject to prophets." Prophethood is the highest ministry among all ministries of God's word. The Holy Spirit gives the word to the prophets, and the same Spirit is within the prophets. It is the spirits of the prophets which enable the prophets to speak God's word. But something else is also mentioned: A speaker has to watch to see if others have also received God's word. If they have, then he has to allow them to speak. Although the first one may have God's word in his mouth, he should stop and allow others who have received a revelation to speak. If four or five persons have received a revelation, they should not all speak; at most two or three should speak, while the rest should keep quiet, because the spirits of prophets are subject to prophets. When the Holy Spirit is upon a person and he is serving as God's minister of the word, the spirit of such a person is subject to him. "The spirits of prophets are subject to prophets"—this is God's own word.

Here we find a basic principle: In releasing God's word, the Holy Spirit decides what should be spoken, but the prophets decide when and how the word should be spoken. In a meeting, if two or three have received a revelation and are speaking, the fourth and the fifth should shut their mouths even though they have also received a revelation. Although the word they have received is from the Holy Spirit, they have to decide when they should release it. They cannot speak whenever they want. If someone else receives a revelation while they are speaking, they have to stop and allow the other to speak. Hence, the word is given by the Spirit, but the time and way it is delivered is determined by the prophets. The spirits of prophets are subject to prophets. When the Spirit of God wants you to speak, you should bear in mind that your spirit is subject to you. The time and way to speak is determined by the prophets. One does not speak whenever the word comes to him.

The responsibility of the ministers of the word is great. Much of the responsibility rests on the shoulder of the ministers, not on God. If the ministers are not proper, God's word will suffer loss. The words may be the right words, but the attitude of the speaker may be wrong or the timing may be wrong. As a consequence, God's word will suffer loss. If we are not proper, we cannot release a proper word. Or if we are not trustworthy, the word will fail even while it is still in us. If the spirits of prophets are subject to prophets, how great is the responsibility of the prophets! It is relatively easy to speak when the word comes upon us. It is also easy to stop speaking when the word does not come upon us. But when the Lord gives us the word, we still have to decide how and when we should speak such a word. If we have never been dealt with or restricted by the Lord and if there is no constitution of the Holy Spirit or knowledge of His way in us, His word will suffer damage in our hands. The Lord entrusts His word to us, and we have to consider how and when we should deliver it. This is a tremendous responsibility, and we must not regard it lightly.

We should realize that the ministry of the word means that God has entrusted His word to man. This word is not a replay from a tape recorder, but a word that is placed within man. It gives room for man to consider the way and time for it to be delivered. The spirits of prophets are subject to prophets. The Lord intends that such spirits be subject to the prophets. The time and way for the word to be delivered is entirely the responsibility of the prophets; they are not the responsibility of the Spirit. If a prophet has not experienced the proper dealings, discipline, and restriction, his spirit will run wild, and trouble will result. The critical issue today is not related to whether one is a prophet but to what kind of person a prophet is. The distinction is not between prophets and non-prophets but between one prophet and another prophet, that is, the difference between one prophet and another. Putting it in another way, what is the difference between Jeremiah and Balaam? We must be clear about this basic principle before the Lord. Today there is the need for God's word, and there is the need for the ministry of the word. Without God's word, there is no ministry of the word, and without a proper person, there is also no ministry of the word.

One basic problem in the church is the lack of proper ministers of the word. This does not mean that God's word is rare or that the vision or light is unclear. It means that there is a shortage of men whom God can use. God desires that the spirits of prophets be subject to prophets. Who are the prophets to whom the spirits of the prophets will be subject? Can the spirits of prophets be subject to those who walk according to their own will, who give ground to the flesh, and who are stubborn in their mind and emotion? If a man does not bear the mark of the cross in his spirit, he is a wild and proud man. He may have suffered years of discipline, but he is not yet defeated. The Lord's smiting hand may have been on him once, twice, or even ten times, but he is still not defeated. In spite of the Lord's repeated chastisement, he is still unyielding. Such a man proves himself to be a useless vessel. Is the problem before us a shortage of vision, light, or the word? No. It is a shortage of prophets whom God can use.

A characteristic of Paul was God's ability to use him and God's willingness to entrust him. If God cannot use a person, He cannot entrust His word to him. If God entrusts His word to you and charges you to speak, how are you going to speak? You have to speak according to what you are. When God lets you speak His word, your mind will frustrate God's word if it is not working properly. If your emotion is improper, your emotion will contaminate God's word. If your motive is not proper, your motive will damage God's word. If your opinion is not proper, your opinion will contaminate God's word. If your spirit is not proper, you will give others the impression of an improper spirit even though all of your words may be correct. The fundamental problem today is that God's word has suffered much in the hands of man! His word has suffered much loss in the hands of man! This is why God cannot entrust His word to man.

The more we are dealt with by the Lord and the deeper His dealing touches our being, the closer we are to having a revelation. When a man's emotion, mind, will, and spirit are all dealt with, the Holy Spirit puts His word in that person's mouth, and his utterance is an inspiration, a revelation. The inspiration that the Bible refers to occurs when human elements are kept under the control of the Holy Spirit and are barred from going off on their own tangents. When the word is put into the mouth of such a person, the resulting ministry of the word is a revelation, an inspiration. This is why we say that the more dealings we receive, the more inspiration we will have. Our mind, emotion, and will all have to pass through God's dealings. Even our memory has to pass through God's dealings. Moreover, our understanding is very much related to God's word. Hence, our understanding must pass through God's dealings as well. Our hearts need to be dealt with. Our motives also need to be dealt with. God has to work on our entire being. We have to remember that a minister of the word cannot be constituted without paying a price. We should not think that constitution can occur without the paying of a price. Can a man become a minister of the word simply because he has a quick mentality? No. We should never have the mistaken thought that human wisdom, knowledge, or eloquence can add anything to God's word. We have to be smitten, pressed, and dismantled. All of those who know the Lord realize that His hand is very heavy upon those whom He uses. The purpose of His hand is to make a person a useful vessel. The Lord has to break and dismantle us before we can become a minister of the word. Being a minister of God's word does not come without the paying of a price.

Some people have gone through years of dealings, perhaps ten, twenty, or even thirty years. During all those years, the Lord's hand has been upon them. He has dealt with them again and again and has worked on them over and over again. Are we so dull? Are we so sleepy? It is impossible for us to remain as we are and hope to participate in the ministry of the word. We need to prostrate ourselves before the Lord and say, "I am a useless vessel. I have to go on. I have to be smitten and broken to the point where I can become useful in Your hand. Otherwise, I have no way to accomplish anything for You." Once we reach this point, the Lord's word will be released through us freely.

In summary, the Holy Spirit puts God's word into us. It is His responsibility to tell us what we should speak. But He leaves the decision of how and when we should speak to us. God entrusts us and believes in us. His charge is that the spirits of prophets be subject to prophets. How grave is the responsibility of the prophets! The way of the ministry of the word is the way of releasing God's word through man's mind and man's word. If our contribution is not up to the proper standard, God's word is no longer His word. This brings in serious consequences! It is easy for God to speak from the heavens. It is easy for Him to speak through the angels. But He loves us and has chosen us. It is indeed unfortunate if we become an obstacle to Him everywhere and in everything. We are often proven to be useless vessels. In order for God to secure ministers of the word, we have to beg for mercy. We have to say to the Lord, "I will not let You go unless I receive mercy from You." If we do not receive mercy from Him, His word will stop with us. Today the entire responsibility rests upon our shoulders.

We have preached the word for more than ten or twenty years, but how much of what we have preached has been the utterance of God's word? We claim that we are preaching God's word, but how much of God's word truly has been preached? The basic principle of the ministry of the word is the principle of incarnation, the word becoming flesh. The word cannot skip the flesh. Where there are ministers, there is God's word. Where there are no ministers, God's word is not found. If we do not find the ministers, we do not find God's word. There must be ministers before there can be God's word. How great is the responsibility of the ministers before the Lord. If we are ministers, we have to realize that the responsibility is on our shoulders. God must secure ministers before He can speak. Without ministers, God cannot speak. Today God does not speak directly to man, the heavens do not speak directly to man, and the angels do not speak directly to man. If man does not open up his mouth, no one will hear God's word, and His word will be locked up. During the past two thousand years, God's word was released whenever He found some men. Sometimes He would find one man, and His word would be released in a mighty way. If God finds some ministers today, His word will be released in a mighty way once again. If the church will stand on new ground and if it will satisfy God to become His vessel, God's word will once again be released in a mighty way. But if we stand still, God will have no way to go forward on this earth. Let me repeat: It is the ministers who bring in God's word. Without the ministers there is no word. The spirits of prophets are subject to prophets. We must be uplifted to Paul's standard. When we speak God's word, we should have the feeling that both we and the Lord are speaking. Then we will see the riches. God's word is indeed rich. May He be merciful to us and grant us the word. May we see many ministers of the word being raised up.

CHAPTER FOUR

THE HIGHEST POINT
IN THE MINISTRY OF THE WORD

ONE

Besides the Lord Jesus, who is the very Word of God becoming flesh, there are two kinds of ministers in the ministry of the word. In the Old Testament there is one kind, and in the New Testament there is another. In principle, the Old Testament ministers were completely objective in nature; they did not have any subjective experience of their own. Although Jeremiah, Isaiah, and many other Old Testament prophets had many subjective experiences, these experiences pertained to their personal history only; they were not experiences in the principle of the ministers of the word. As a rule, God only needed to place His word in man's mouth, and man only had to speak this word verbatim. This constituted a person an oracle of God. Man would receive God's word on the one hand and release this word on the other hand. Under this rule, even Saul was considered as one of the prophets (1 Sam. 10:10). Balaam was another prophet. God's word and those who spoke His word had little relation to each other. Man was like a water pipe; water flowed into one end and flowed out from the other end. The pipe remained the pipe with little relation to the water itself. With this kind of speaking, the only thing that was required to preserve God's revelation was for man to be accurate. This was not too difficult.

But the ministers of the New Testament are different. If a New Testament minister matches God's goal, his ministry is more glorious than that of the Old Testament ministers. If he does not match God's goal, however, he is more dangerous than the Old Testament ministers. In the New Testament God entrusts His word to man. He places it before man and allows man to deliver it according to his own thoughts, feelings, understanding, memory, and words. If man delivers the word in a pure way, this ministry is many times more glorious than the Old Testament ministry. It is a most glorious thing for man to be involved in God's word without changing or contaminating it. But if there is even a slight problem or flaw on the part of the speaker, God's word suffers.

Some may wonder why God uses such a cumbersome method to release His word. This question is similar to those asked by unbelievers when they ask why God did not remove the tree of the knowledge of good and evil at the beginning, and why God did not create a man who could not sin. If God had done this, there would have been no danger of sinning, and God would have spared Himself the trouble of redemption. The answer to these questions can be applied equally to the question concerning ministers of the word. God does not want His creatures to be like a robot, something that does not have its own choice and which moves around only as a dutiful machine. It would be easy for God to create a machine that follows His directions completely. This would involve no effort on man's part. Of course, it also would not give any glory to God. This kind of obedience and virtue is worth little. This kind of a man would never err or sin, yet he also would not have any holiness of his own. He could be pushed around like a machine. This is not what God wants. He desires a people who can discern the left from the right, who can choose good as well as evil, right as well as wrong. If the creature created by God chooses submission to God of his own volition, his choice gives God more glory than the obedience of a machine. God has given man a free will to choose between good and evil. If he chooses good, God gets the glory. Although the possibility of choosing evil is a risk, the decision to choose good is a great glory. This is why God did not create a dutiful machine. He did not create a machine that was only capable of performing good. Instead, He created a man with a free will who could choose between good and evil. God wants man to choose good and obedience of his own volition. This gives glory to God.

The same principle can be applied to the ministry of the word in the New Testament. There are numerous obstacles for God to speak His word through man. For God to speak directly by Himself poses no difficulty. Neither is there much problem for God to speak through angels. Even using a donkey poses less of a problem than speaking through man because a donkey is not as complicated as a man. A donkey does not form obstacles in its mind, understanding, memory, motive, and spirit. A donkey does not have these problems. If God's word were placed in its mouth, it could repeat the word accurately. But using a donkey is something exceptional for God. God used a donkey to release His word only when the prophet failed. He has no intention for the donkey to replace the prophet; He still wants man to be His prophet. God wants to use man. Man was created especially for God's use. When God created the world, His intention was not to have a submissive machine. In the same way, God is not after a machine that can preach. He is not after something without a will. He is after men who possess a free will. It seems as if He took a big risk when He chose man to be a minister of His word. But God would rather do this than not. God entrusts His word to man, a complicated man, one full of sin, defilement, and weakness. There are also the problems of the outward man, the natural man, and the carnal man. All these are factors against God. Yet God still entrusts His word to man. He wants to gain the greatest glory through overcoming the greatest difficulties. If God can break through these great obstacles, He will secure the greatest glory.

God desires to speak through man. Yet man can be both good and evil. Man can convey God's word in a pure way, or he can damage God's word. Obviously, therefore, God has to do a great and thorough work before He can entrust His word to man and before man can convey His word in a proper way.

TWO

First Corinthians 7 shows us that Paul was chosen by God to be a minister of His word. God perfected him to such an extent that his ministry became the very utterance of the divine inspiration. His speaking was so accurate that not a

single word missed the mark. His word not only contains
God's word, but it is so accurate that every sentence and
phrase hits the mark. How did he acquire this ministry? He
acquired it by being thoroughly dealt with by God. God worked
on him to the point that his thoughts, words, decisions, and
opinions were all approved by God; they were all right and
accurate in His eyes. With Paul, there was not the accuracy
of a machine but the accuracy of a person. With Paul, we
can see how God puts His word in man and how He releases
it through man. He does not speak His word through man
in the way of a verbatim repetition. If the release of God's
word were merely a matter of man repeating God's utterances
word for word, such a task would be easy. But God does not
release His word this way. Instead, He puts His word in man;
man has to search it out with his mind. God puts His light
in man, and man has to capture this light with his mind.
God lays His burden in man, and man has to express this
burden through his own word. It is man who exercises his
thought; it is man who searches and speaks. Yet when the
word is released, God acknowledges it as His own word.

The New Testament ministry of the word is not one in
which God dictates His message word by word and then man
repeats it word for word. When His word is revealed to man
in the New Testament, its light first shines into man's spirit
as a flicker. This creates a burden within man's spirit for the
word. This light can fade away quickly, and man must catch
its glow by exercising his own mind. He has to "fix" this light
with his own thoughts or else the light will seemingly
disappear. He has to fix the light with his thoughts. He has
to inquire of God for utterance that he may receive one or
two sentences that crystallize his light. He may ponder, and
a phrase may come to him. Then he may write down the
phrase, or he may have a certain feeling, judgment, or opinion
concerning a certain matter, and he may speak it out. While
he is relating his feelings, inward judgment, and opinion, the
burden within his spirit is released. The more he speaks, the
more the light within his spirit that has been captured with
his mind is released. At a certain point, the burden is fully
released. He has spoken his own words, expressed his own

thoughts, feelings, and opinions. But after he has finished his speaking, God acknowledges these words to be His own.

Do you see how vastly different this is from the creed-like declarations of man's imagination? You are doing the speaking, the writing, and the considering. But because you have been so thoroughly dealt with by God, your speaking is acknowledged by God as His own word. This is the meaning of the ministry of the word. What is hidden within you is only a light, a burden. But you have your opinions, proposals, and feelings. While you are brooding over your opinions, feelings, thoughts, and judgments, God gives you a few words or sentences to enunciate your inner registration. When you utter these words and sentences, God acknowledges this as His word. For this reason, a man has to climb to a great height before he can be considered as a minister of the word. If there are flaws in his mind, emotion, or feeling, he cannot be a minister of the word. Unless his very person has passed through God's dealings, his opinion will not be trustworthy. When his opinion is expressed, God will not recognize it as His own word. Many times you can tell that a brother's word does not meet this standard as soon as he opens his mouth. You can tell that what he has are only his own words; they are not God's word.

God puts so much trust in His ministers that He would give them a light, a burden, or an impression and would leave it up to them to grasp and sense the utterance and to make suggestions and proposals concerning it. Although such suggestions and proposals are their own, God puts His trust in their activities. He believes in His own ministers. God wants to operate in man to such an extent that man is like Him in his opinions, thoughts, feelings, and views. If our desire can be one with God's desire and we can love what God loves, never deviating in any way, our speaking will always be accompanied by the Spirit's presence. On the one hand, we will be saying something from ourselves. On the other hand, God's Spirit will carry our word along. As we speak, He will bear our word onward. This is the preaching of the New Testament prophets. This is the ministry of the word in the New Testament.

THREE

Let us again consider Paul's condition in 1 Corinthians 7.
Verse 6 says, "But this I say by way of concession, not by way
of command." Paul was saying that even though he agreed
with the proposition, the matter did not originate from him
as a command. He was very clear concerning the degree of
activity within him. He agreed with the matter, but he would
not make this a command. We have to observe the fineness
and tenderness in Paul's inner registrations. He made a very
clear distinction here. He was not only clear that the proposition was acceptable; he also was clear that it was not a
command that he initiated but a concession to others' ideas.
When we come to verse 40, we see that this was the word of
the Spirit of God. The Spirit of God gave His consent to Paul's
word. Paul felt that such a proposal was acceptable, and then
the Spirit felt the same. God was fully involved in Paul's
tender feelings. When we were on the subject of God's authority, we pointed out the tremendous significance of the Lord
Jesus entrusting His name to us. In the same way God has
entrusted His word to us. This is also a tremendous matter.
Suppose a person is troubled by difficulties and seeks our
help. We may say to a young brother, "Go and say something
to this man." The young brother may say, "I do not know what
to say." We may respond, "You can say anything. Whatever
you say can be counted as our words. You can say whatever
you want to him, and we will acknowledge it as our opinion."
This would be a tremendous charge, but it could result in
great damage. If there is any problem with the brother, we
could not trust him in this way.

This is what happens to ministers of the word today. God
does not piece His message together word by word, hand it
over to us, and then ask us to memorize it. It would not be
difficult for us to memorize a message. It would merely require
God to say a word or a sentence and then for us to repeat the
same word or sentence. If a message has six hundred words,
our responsibility would be over if we could recite all six
hundred words. But God does not want us to convey His
message in this manner. His intention is to put His word into

us, that is, for us to take it in as living water and then to let it flow out of us. He gives us a light, a burden, and then a few clear words to speak to others. Those who can be used will be useful to Him, and those who cannot be used will not be useful to Him. It is as if the God of heaven has commissioned us to speak for Him on earth, yet the same God allows us to say whatever we want to say. Of course, those who know God would not dare say anything rashly.

The responsibility of a minister of the word is not a small one. When a man stands up to speak for God, he has to draw from his feelings, thoughts, and opinions. He has to have the proper judgments and proposals. Therefore, his responsibility is very great. If his feelings are wrong, his speaking will be wrong. If his thoughts, proposals, and opinions are wrong, his speaking will also be wrong. If his mind, feelings, opinions, and judgments are untrustworthy or if his heart and his spirit are unreliable, his words will be unreliable. If this is so, how can he call himself a minister of God's word? This presents a fundamental problem. A man must be so thoroughly dealt with by God that his feelings become fine and tender. His feelings must represent God's feelings. While these feelings certainly belong to him and are independent of outside influence, they are attached to God at the same time. Paul's word in 1 Corinthians 7 is not a small matter.

In 1 Corinthians 7:7 Paul said that he wished. The same Greek word is used again in verse 32. This shows us Paul's inward condition. Within him there was a wish for something. He wished to see the Corinthians be the same as he was. By the time we come to verse 40, we find that this was actually the wish and desire of the Spirit of God. Paul's wish was God's wish. His desire was God's desire. Since this was the case, how careful Paul must have needed to be when he exercised his wish. If he wished wrongly, what would have happened? God's word would have been confused. Paul's wishing was a delicate feeling in his spirit. If he had made a mistake in his wishes and desires, what would have happened? God had full control over the delicate feelings of this man. This is the reason that when he wished for something, it was actually the Holy Spirit who was wishing.

Here was a man whose feelings were under God's hand. The Lord was able to put His trust in Paul's feelings. Brothers, can the Lord use our feelings? Can He trust us? We need to be broken. Without this, the Lord cannot trust our feelings. Paul's feelings were fully under God's hand; God could trust his feelings. They were dependable and accurate. In verse 12 Paul said, "But to the rest I say, I, not the Lord." He did not have the clear registration that the Lord was speaking. He made it clear that he was speaking, not the Lord. In the end, however, he said that he had the Spirit of God. What a marvel that Paul could reach such a stage!

In verse 25 he clearly conveyed his feelings before the Lord. He said, "Now concerning virgins I have no commandment of the Lord, but I give my opinion as one who has been shown mercy by the Lord to be faithful." Here was a man who had been following the Lord for many years. The Lord had shown him mercy again and again. This mercy had made him faithful. He was a steward of God, a minister of Christ, a steward of the mysteries of God. What is required of a steward is faithfulness (4:1-2). What was Paul faithful to? He was faithful to his ministry. He was a steward of the mysteries of God, a minister of the word of Christ. God had entrusted mysteries to him; He had placed His word in his hands. The main requirement of a minister of the word is faithfulness. Since Paul had obtained mercy from the Lord to be a faithful minister, he could tell others of his opinions. He did not receive any commandment from the Lord, but he expressed his wish. He had received mercy to be a minister and to exercise stewardship over God's word. Yet God had not given him a commandment, and he would not dare say anything by himself. However, based on the numerous times that he had exercised stewardship over God's mysteries, and through the numerous times he had served as an oracle for God's word, he could tell others his opinion concerning certain matters. He had received mercy from God and had been in touch with spiritual things and had handled similar matters repeatedly in the past. He had learned some lessons before God and had picked up something little by little. In this instance he did not have a commandment from the Lord, yet he told the Corinthians something based on what he had seen and learned throughout the years. He dared not say that his word was the Lord's commandment. He only told them his opinion. Yet in the end, God acknowledged this opinion. God recognized Paul's opinion as being His own. What a glory! We have to praise the Lord for this! Here was a man who had obtained mercy to be faithful and whose opinion was fully acknowledged by the Lord.

FOUR

This leads us to an important question which needs our attention. What is the work of the Holy Spirit within man? What do we know about His engraving work in man? We must realize that the Spirit of God not only resides in man but is doing an engraving and constituting work in man. This constituting work of the Holy Spirit is something that can never be erased. The Holy Spirit is in man and is one with man. Now He is engraving something into man. We should never consider that the Holy Spirit's indwelling is like a guest taking hospitality in someone else's house, residing for ten or twenty years and then leaving everything in the same condition when he leaves. No. The Holy Spirit does an engraving, building, and constituting work in man. Little by little the Holy Spirit constitutes the Lord's character in man. Even a house takes on the characteristics of its occupants after a while. The enduement of gifts upon a person may not produce any change in the person, but the indwelling of the Holy Spirit will surely manifest heavenly character traits when the Spirit bears fruit in man. The very fruit of the Spirit is the changes that are produced in a man's character. God reconstitutes man's character through the work of the Holy Spirit. When the Spirit operates in man's mind, He changes man's mind. When the Spirit operates in man's feelings, He changes man's feelings. When the Spirit operates in man's opinions and judgments, He changes man's opinions and judgments. The Holy Spirit works and constitutes something in man. The result of this work is a change in man's character.

Paul did not serve as a minister of God's word merely because he afforded the Spirit the freedom to speak through him. The Spirit actually took up his very character. The fruit of the Spirit in the Divine Trinity is the very product produced in man's character. The Spirit operates in man, a little today and a little more tomorrow, engraving and trimming more and more each day, until a certain character emerges. This character is distinctly man's, yet at the same time, it is distinctly a work of the Spirit. The character fully belongs to man, yet at the same time, it is fully begotten of the Holy Spirit; it is the result of the Spirit's work in man. When the Spirit builds up something in man, there is a transforming change in man from glory to glory.

We must realize that transformation is a basic truth as well as a fundamental experience in the Bible. Philippians 3 speaks of one kind of fundamental experience, and 2 Corinthians 3 speaks of another kind of fundamental experience. We readily admit that our flesh will never change. But at the same time, we believe that the Lord will transform us; He will create a new character in us. The Spirit of the Lord does not reside in us like a man residing in a house; He is in us as our life. It is unthinkable that the Lord could dwell in a man, being his life for ten or twenty years, yet the man would remain unchanged. When the Lord's Spirit abides in us and becomes our life, our mind, feelings, judgments, and opinions all have to change. Our heart and spirit have to change. Formerly there was nothing within us except the flesh. Now the cross has dealt with the flesh and overcome it. There is a new constitution and new fruit in our feelings, thoughts, and judgments, as well as in our heart and spirit. What then is the constitution of the Spirit? It is what results from God's building and constituting work within man. This will never go away. We should realize that the Lord's work within man is always solid, firm, and unchanging.

Paul received mercy from the Lord again and again. The Lord continued to work in him until he became a faithful one. His faithfulness refers to his attitude towards his ministry. He admitted that he did not have the Lord's commandment, yet he told the Corinthians his opinion. His opinion was the result of the constitution of the Holy Spirit. Paul's words were no ordinary inspiration; they were the issue of an inward constitution by God. In the end, these words of constitution became words of inspiration. This is amazing! When a man is under the inspiration of the Holy Spirit, he is conscious of God's word. When a man speaks under the constitution of the Holy Spirit, he may not have the consciousness that God is speaking. He may feel that he is speaking and expressing his own opinion. But because the constitution of the Holy Spirit has been wrought into him, his words become the words of the Holy Spirit. This is the reason that Paul said, "I think that I also have the Spirit of God." We need the constitution of the Holy Spirit. We need the Spirit's engraving work upon us. We need Him to work on us to the extent that our opinions, words, thoughts, and feelings no longer contradict God's word. When this happens, we are qualified to be a minister of God's word.

The character which the Holy Spirit constitutes within man is different from person to person. Paul's preaching carried his distinctive features. Peter's message carried his distinctive flavor. His Epistles are very different in style from Paul's Epistles. John's writings are also different from others' writings. Everyone has his own style. The styles are personal. Yet it is an amazing fact that the Spirit would take up the style of those who have been constituted by Him. If the sixty-six books of the Bible were all one style, the Bible would be very dull indeed. God's glory is manifested in man's various styles. This can only happen when there is the constitution of the Holy Spirit. A word may be uttered in different ways, but it remains the word of the Holy Spirit. When a man submits to the discipline of the Holy Spirit, he is given the freedom to express his characteristics. No two items in God's creation are identical. Every blade of grass is different. Every tree is different. No two faces are identical. The glory of one star is different from the glory of another star. In the same way, the constitution of the Holy Spirit is different in different people. Paul was full of the love of the Spirit, and so was John. But those who have been taught by God know that the Spirit's love as manifested in Paul was different from that which was manifested in John. They each expressed the love of the Holy Spirit, but in a different way. God does not need uniformity. Everyone has his own characteristics, and the constitution of the Holy Spirit is different in everyone.

Brothers, do not misunderstand me. I am not saying that we can all follow the example of 1 Corinthians 7. In the whole Bible, only 1 Corinthians 7 presents such a noble example. If the Lord has no leading for us to speak in this way, however, it is a gross error for us to speak this way. First Corinthians 7 shows us the kind of person Paul was. This helps us to understand the books of Ephesians, Colossians, Romans, and Galatians. First Corinthians 7 reveals the person of Paul; it shows us the person who wrote Ephesians, Galatians, etc. We know that the book of Colossians is very high, but 1 Corinthians 7 tells us about the person who wrote Colossians. Romans contains a clear exposition of the gospel, but 1 Corinthians 7 tells us about the person who wrote Romans. This is what makes 1 Corinthians 7 precious.

In this chapter we clearly see a man whose feelings, thoughts, opinions, and words were worthy of God's trust. When God's word was put into him, this word became the highest revelation; it did not suffer any corruption. If we did not have 1 Corinthians 7, we could only know what the Holy Spirit had done through Paul; we would not know what the Holy Spirit had done in Paul. First Corinthians 7 shows us a man whose feelings, thoughts, and words are all trustworthy. When God's word came upon this man, there was no frustration to the word, just as there was no frustration during those times when God's word was not active in such a person. If we are not trustworthy, we become a frustration even when we have God's word. The Lord cannot commit His revelation and light to some because they are not trustworthy. He cannot acknowledge them as ministers of the word because their thoughts, feelings, opinions, and words are not trustworthy.

Brothers, some of Paul's Epistles, like Romans, Galatians, and Colossians, show us high revelations. His Epistle to the Ephesians even shows us the highest revelation. Yet in the two Epistles to the Corinthians, we find the kind of person to whom God would commit His revelation. Paul was qualified to receive these revelations because of the kind of person he was. If we only had his other Epistles, without having 1 Corinthians 7, we would not know the kind of person Paul was. He was a faithful and trustworthy person. That is the reason that God's revelation did not suffer any corruption in him. In fact, there was so much glory in his constitution that his style was adopted to perfect God's word. Paul's personality and idiomatic expressions all contributed to God's word; they made the latter more glorious and rich. What a glory that man can be used by God and that his human elements can be used by Him without compromising the perfection of God's word, but instead enhancing its glory, riches, and perfection!

May God be merciful to us so that He can use us and release His word through us. No need is greater today than the need for the word. May all the brothers see that there is a pathway that must be followed in order to be a minister of God's word. We have to beseech God to grant us much light, word, and inner dealings. We need deep and profound dealings. We need to be molded deeply, inwardly, and thoroughly. Even our most delicate feelings have to be faithful to God. When these feelings are expressed, they will be regarded as the Lord's very own feelings. When our inclinations are expressed, they will be regarded as the result of the work of the Holy Spirit. Our own love and patience will flow out, yet this love and patience will be the fruit of the Holy Spirit. This fruit will be the result of the frequent, deep, and thorough work of the Holy Spirit in us. Through His operation in us we can bear this fruit. When we are constituted with the Holy Spirit, fruit is expressed in a spontaneous way. Brothers, as the Holy Spirit performs His work in us and as we are being reconstituted by the Spirit, our feelings spontaneously become the Spirit's feelings, our thoughts become His thoughts, and our opinions become His opinions. When this happens, God will commit His word to us and allow us to transmit it to others. Others will acknowledge it as God's word, and God will receive the greatest glory.

The fundamental question today is whether or not God can commit Himself to us. We have to see that the problem is not with His word but with the ministers. Without the ministers, there is no word of God. Today God is still speaking just as He did in earlier days. He has no intention of annulling the prophetic ministry in the church. Neither does He have the intention of removing the teaching ministry or the evangelistic ministry from the church. The biggest problem today is the scarcity of ministers. Whether or not there is ministry in the church and whether or not this ministry can be multiplied depend on us; the responsibility is on our shoulders. May we awake to the fact that the poverty and darkness of the church are related to us. May we pledge to the Lord solemnly, "Lord! I am willing to be broken. Break me so that Your word can get through in me." May the Lord be gracious to us.

Section Two

The Word of God

CHAPTER FIVE

THE BASIS OF THE WORD

ONE

We have seen that being a minister of God's word is not a simple matter. Not everyone can speak God's word. The basic question concerning a minister of God's word relates to his person. Now we want to turn our attention to another matter—God's Word itself. When we talk about the ministry of God's word, we are not saying that God has other words unrelated to the Bible. We are not saying that a person can add a book to the sixty-six books of the Bible. Nor are we saying that a man can receive a revelation or introduce a ministry that is not found in the Bible. We believe that God's word is complete in the Old and the New Testaments. We do not need to add any words to what already has been recorded in the Bible. Yet at the same time we have to realize that a knowledge of the Bible alone does not qualify one to preach God's word. Everyone who desires to be a minister of God's word must realize what God's Word is. If he does not know what God's Word is, he cannot be a minister of His word.

The sixty-six books of the Bible were written by approximately forty people. They all used their own individual, idiomatic expressions; each one adopted his own style. Each writer used his own special terminology, and his writing contained his own feelings, thoughts, and human elements. When God's word came to these writers, their personal elements were taken up by God. Some were used to a greater extent while others were used to a lesser extent, but everyone was used by God, everyone received revelation from Him, and everyone was a minister of His word. God's Word is like a piece of music, and these many people were like many instruments. An orchestra contains many instruments, and every instrument has its own distinctive sound. When the whole orchestra plays, however, all the sounds blend together in a harmonious way. When the sounds reach our ears, we can distinguish between the sound of the piano, violin, trumpet, clarinet, and flute, but we do not hear a jumble of chaotic sounds. Instead, we hear one harmonious piece of music. Every instrument has its own characteristic and personality, yet all are playing the same music. If there are two pieces of music, there will be clashes and confusion. The same can be said of the ministers of the word. Every minister has his own personal characteristics. Yet each one is speaking God's word.

The Bible is not a chaotic collection of writings. From its first page to its last, it is an organic whole. Although one minister may say one thing and another minister may say something else, their ministries, when combined together, form an organic whole. There are approximately forty writers of the Bible. Although this number is quite large, their message is unified; there is no confusion or fragmentation. The Bible may reflect a few dozen instruments, but it is only one piece of music. Anyone who tries to add another tune becomes obviously conspicuous. As soon as the tune reaches our ear, we know that it has the wrong kind of sound. God's Word is one unified whole. The sounds may be different, but there must not be any dissonance. We should not presume that as long as there is sound, it is good enough. We should not think that anyone can stand up, say a few words, and claim to be speaking God's word. God's Word is a unified whole from beginning to end. The ministries of the word in the past belong to this undivided entity, and the present ministries of the word also belong to this undivided whole. No foreign element can be added to it or form part of this whole. God's word is the Lord Jesus Himself; it is one, and it is living. If we try to add anything to it, we will not have God's word, but confusion, apostasy, and discord. What we have will not be God's word.

The Old Testament contains thirty-nine books. Historically speaking, the book of Job was probably written first. But Moses' Pentateuch is placed at the beginning of the Bible. It is a wonderful thing that all of the writers of the Bible who came after Moses did not write independently; they built upon the writings that were before them. Moses wrote the Pentateuch without reference to the writings of others. But Joshua's writings were based on Moses' Pentateuch. In other words, Joshua's ministry of God's word was not an independent one; his service as a minister was based on his knowledge of the Pentateuch. Following Joshua, other writers, such as the authors of the books of Samuel, also based their writings on Moses' books. This means that other than Moses, who was divinely called in the beginning to write his five books, all subsequent ministers of God's word functioned upon the basis of the preceding words of God. The remaining books of the Old Testament were written with earlier writings as their basis. Although subsequent writers wrote differently, they all based their word on preceding words. All of the ministers of God's word after Moses speak on the basis of the divine word that precedes them. God's Word is one whole entity, and no writer can take his own course. Those who come later always speak on the basis of the word of those who preceded them.

When we come to the New Testament, the only new revelation that we find is the mystery of the Body of Christ. Ephesians tells us that the Body is composed of the Jews and the Gentiles. Other than this, nothing is new; everything is based on Old Testament teachings, and everything that is in the New Testament can be found in the Old Testament as well. The Old Testament contains almost all of the doctrinal revelations. Even the new heaven and new earth are found in the Old Testament. One version of the Bible capitalizes all of the New Testament quotations of Old Testament passages. If one reads through it, he will find that many things in the New Testament were actually spoken first in the Old Testament. Some passages in the New Testament are clear, direct quotations of the Old Testament. Other passages are not direct quotations, yet the writers clearly make references to passages in the Old Testament. This is like our preaching; sometimes we quote the Scripture by merely making reference to the chapters and the verses. At other times we recite the entire verse, and those who are familiar with the Bible will know its reference. There are over fifteen hundred references to the Old Testament in the New Testament. We have to remember that the ministry of the word in the New Testament is based on the divine utterance in the Old Testament. There is no independent speaking.

If a person stands up today and declares that he has received an independent revelation, we immediately can condemn this revelation as being untrustworthy. Today no one can receive God's word apart from the Bible. Even the New Testament cannot exist independently by itself. Paul's word cannot exist independently by itself. One cannot cut off the Old Testament and keep only the New Testament. Neither can one cut off the four Gospels and keep only Paul's Epistles. We must realize that all subsequent words are based on preceding words; they are light derived from preceding words, not independent, separate words. Independent, separate words can only be words of heresy; they cannot be God's word. We must understand what the ministry of the word is. All ministries in the Bible relate to one another. No one can receive a revelation that is completely independent of and unrelated to other revelations. No revelation can be completely isolated from other revelations or without reference to other revelations. The twenty-seven books of the New Testament are based on the Old Testament. Subsequent ministers always receive supply from preceding ministers.

TWO

We must condemn all independent revelations and independent ministries. Second Peter 1:20 says, "No prophecy of Scripture is of one's own interpretation." The word *own* also can be translated as *private*. It qualifies the word *interpretation*. This means that God's prophecy cannot be interpreted just according to its immediate context; it cannot be interpreted from just the passage itself. For example, Matthew 24 cannot be interpreted by reference to just Matthew 24; we have to consider it in the light of other passages of the Scripture. We cannot interpret prophecy by the prophecy itself. We cannot interpret Daniel 2 by reference to just Daniel 2, or Daniel 9 by just Daniel 9. If we interpret a text by the text itself, we are making a "private interpretation." We have to remember that God's Word is one undivided whole. In order to speak God's word, we have to realize first of all that it is an undivided whole. None of the Bible can be privately interpreted; it cannot be interpreted according to the immediate text alone. It has to be interpreted in conjunction with many other passages. Today we have the Bible before us; we cannot release any independent so-called "word of God" which is unrelated to God's established Word. If our speaking does not match God's established Word, what we have is heresy and a deception of the devil.

The first ministers of the word spoke independently for God. They spoke independently because there was no minister of the word before them. But the second group had to build its speaking upon the speaking of the first group. Its speaking should have been only a repetition and an amplification of the first group. When the third group comes along, it should build its speaking upon the first and second groups; it cannot speak independently either. The light which God gives can only be a further application of that given to the first and second groups. God may give new visions and new revelations, but these visions and revelations are based on words that He has already spoken. Here is where the virtue of the Bereans comes in. They examined the Scriptures to see if what they had heard was indeed so (Acts 17:10-11). God's Word does not change from day to day. It is an undivided whole, ever unchanging from beginning to end. It builds upon itself little by little. God is building something that He Himself is after. The men in the Old Testament and the New Testament who received further light did not receive any independent revelations; their revelations were all based on the first revelation in the Old Testament. That first revelation continued. From one revelation more light developed; men's eyes were opened more and more, until we have both the Old Testament and the New Testament. A person becomes a New Testament minister of God's word by receiving visions of God's word in the Old Testament. Anyone who wants to be a minister of the word today must consider God's word in view of the Old Testament and the New Testament; he cannot have God's

word apart from them. This is a very important principle. A
minister of God's word today is not independent, just as the
ministers of His word in the former days were not independent. All ministers of the word depend on God's previously
spoken word. No one can receive revelation apart from the
Bible. Anyone who receives a revelation apart from the Bible
is receiving heresy, something which is absolutely unaccept-
able.

Among God's children there is a big misunderstanding
concerning the Old Testament and the New Testament. Some
think that these two testaments contradict each another. They
think that the law and grace contradict one another. But in
reading God's Word, can we find the Old Testament contradicting the New Testament or the law contradicting grace? If
we read the Epistles to the Romans and Galatians, we will
find that there is no contradiction. In fact, Galatians shows
us that the two testaments compliment each other. Many
people have the wrong notion that the law and grace contradict
each other, because they notice that God deals with men in
one way in the Old Testament and in another way in the New.
They think that the Old Testament and the New contradict
each other because God appears to men differently under the
law and under grace. They do not realize that the New
Testament is an advancement of the Old Testament, not a
contradiction of it. Grace is an advancement of the law, not
a contradiction of it. We should realize that the New Testament is a continuation and further development of the Old
Testament; the two do not contradict each other at all.

Paul tells us that grace did not begin in just the New
Testament age. In reading Galatians, we find that the "promise" was given when God called Abraham. In other words,
God preached the gospel to Abraham and told him to wait
for Christ, through whom blessing would come upon the whole
world. At the time God granted Abraham grace, the law had
not come in yet. Galatians tells us clearly that God did not
give Abraham the law but a promise, which was the gospel
(3:8). In Galatians Paul says that our gospel is based on
Abraham's gospel and that our grace is based on the grace
that Abraham received. The promise we have received is based

on the promise given to Abraham, and the Christ we have received is the very seed of Abraham (vv. 9, 14, 16). Paul clearly shows that both the Old Testament and New Testament follow the same line.

Why then do we have the law? In Galatians Paul says that the law was something that was "added" (3:19). In the beginning God gave man grace; He gave man the gospel. But because sinners did not know or condemn their sins, they were unable to receive grace and the gospel. With the coming of the law, man's sin was exposed and condemned. But Galatians tells us that even after man was condemned, God still gave him the gospel and the promise. In other words, God does not give us grace at one time and the law at another time. He does not give us the promise at one time and demand work from us at another time. God's work does not change from beginning to end. Galatians shows us that the grace we receive today is not without precedence; it is the same grace that God gave to Abraham. Because we have become the descendants of Abraham, we are able to inherit this grace and enjoy God's promise. Hence, the beginning promise, the intervening law, and the accomplishment of Christ's gospel today are all along the same line. God's Word is one undivided whole; there are not two lines. It is progressive, not contradictory.

God first gave Abraham the promise. Then He gave the Israelites the law. Are these two contradictory? No. They do not contradict each other. On the contrary, this shows a progression. Today we find God dealing with us according to grace once again. Does this mean another contradiction? No. It is a progression. The way God deals with men becomes clearer and clearer as time goes on. God's promise to Abraham cannot be annulled by the law which came four hundred and thirty years later (Gal. 3:17). Four hundred and thirty years after He gave Abraham the promise, God gave man the law, not for the purpose of annulling the promise but in order to fulfill it, because one will receive the promise only after becoming conscious of his sins. By shutting up all under sin, God is able to grant man the grace which He dispenses through His Son (vv. 21-22). The Old Testament is progressive and advancing. The New Testament follows the Old Testament, and it is also progressive. The New Testament does not contradict the Old Testament. God's Word remains one undivided whole. Subsequent ministries of the word expand and develop former revelations and instructions of God; they are neither independent nor contradictory.

A minister of the word today must know what God has spoken in the Old Testament and the New Testament. It is clear that the ministers of the word who wrote the New Testament were acquainted and familiar with the Old Testament. It is also clear that today's ministers must also be well acquainted with the Old Testament and the New Testament. We must be familiar with the word of the ministers before us. Only then can our words match those of the Old and the New Testaments; only then will our speaking not be independent speakings. The ministry of the word today is not a matter of receiving some independent words from God and speaking such words to men. The ministry of the word today involves a knowledge of what God has spoken in the Old Testament and the New Testament enhanced by renewed light and revelation. When we speak such a word to men, it is God who speaks it. The New Testament ministers of the word spoke on the basis of the Old Testament. When we stand up to speak today, we have to remember that we have plenty of words in the Old Testament and plenty of words in the New Testament already. When the first group of men stood up to speak God's word, they did not have any spoken word from God to serve as their basis. When the second group of ministers was raised up, they could only quote as much of the Scripture as the first group had released. When the third, fourth, and subsequent groups were raised up, they could quote more, and they had a broader basis to build upon because more of God's word had been released. Today we have advanced further and have reached a much richer place. All of the words of the Old Testament have been released, and all of the words of the New Testament have been released. We can find all the words that God has spoken in the Old Testament and the New Testament. At the same time, all of these words are here to judge us. If we are off, these words will tell us that we are speaking from ourselves, not by the

Spirit. If our word does not match that of the Old Testament and the New Testament, we can know with certainty that we are off. The Bible is the word of God. Hence, if we do not know the Old Testament and the New Testament, we cannot be a minister of the word. Everyone who desires to be a minister of God's word must at least have a practical knowledge of the Bible; he should be so familiar with the Bible that he can apply it at will. If he is not familiar with the whole Bible, he cannot apply it at will, and he cannot be a minister of God's word. If he has never seen any new light from the written word, he has no basis for his speaking; he does not know when he has veered off in his speaking. This is the reason that we have to familiarize ourselves with the Bible. Otherwise, we will face great obstacles when we try to serve as God's minister of the word.

We are not saying that a knowledge of the Bible alone qualifies a person to be a minister of the word. We are saying that a minister of the word must familiarize himself with the Bible. If we have never heard the word God spoke in the past, we cannot receive any revelation now. Revelation begets revelation; they are not independent of each other. God's revelation is first contained in the Word. When His Spirit shines through the Word, more revelation is produced, and more light is seen. The glow becomes brighter. This is the way revelation comes to us. God does not give us revelation from nothing. He does not do such a thing. He always brings light out of some existing word, and then expands on this light. Time after time when this light is revealed, it becomes brighter and brighter. This is the way God's revelation works. If we have no past revelations from God, His light will not have the means to shine to us. Today God does not grant revelation to men in the way He did to the first men. This is a fundamental governing principle. When God first revealed Himself to man, He spoke without any previous words as His basis. But today all of God's progressive words and progressive revelations are based upon His spoken words and revealed revelations. He adds by building upon the foundation. Anyone who is not familiar with God's spoken word is not qualified to be His minister of the word. Without such a basis, God cannot give us any light.

THREE

Psalm 68:18 speaks of the Lord Jesus dispensing gifts at the time of His ascension. This is the Old Testament basis of Paul's development in chapters one and four of Ephesians. Ephesians 1 tells us that the Lord Jesus ascended to the height and is seated at the right hand of God the Father (v. 20). Then chapter four tells us that in His ascension, the Lord Jesus led captive those who were taken captive by His enemy and gave gifts to men (v. 8). If we look back a little, we will find that this is exactly what Peter said on the day of Pentecost. He said, "Therefore having been exalted to the right hand of God and having received the promise of the Holy Spirit from the Father, He has poured out this which you both see and hear" (Acts 2:33). Both Peter's word concerning the outpouring at Pentecost as well as Paul's word in Ephesians concerning the ascension and the giving of gifts for the building up of the church were based on a knowledge of the light revealed in Psalm 68. God did not give Paul direct light. He put this light in Psalm 68 and then revealed it to Paul. In order for anyone to receive this light, he must know Psalm 68. We should remember that God concealed this light in Psalm 68. Then one day He opened up this passage and revealed this light to men. Men became clear concerning this truth. Peter and Paul were men of revelation, but they did not receive revelation in an independent way.

The book of Hebrews unveils the meaning of many sacrifices in a clear way. It shows us that the Lord Jesus is the unique sacrifice. If a man does not understand the Old Testament sacrifices, he will not understand how the Lord Jesus offered Himself as a sacrifice. God's light is contained in the Old Testament sacrifices. The writer of the book of Hebrews understood the Old Testament revelations. Otherwise, he could not have written the book of Hebrews. God's light is contained in the Old Testament. In other words, God's light is contained in Abraham, Isaac, Jacob, Joseph, Moses, Joshua, Samuel, David, and Solomon. If we do not see these men, we will not see light. This is like saying that light is in the candle. Without the candle we do not have the light. Light is expressed through the lamp and the lampstand. Without the lamp and the lampstand, there is no light. We must realize that the words of the Old Testament and the New Testament are the containers of God's light. If we do not understand these words, we cannot meet today's need. God's Word is one undivided whole. This Word is the very place where God's light is stored and out from which the light shines.

Take for example Galatians 3:6, which says, "Abraham believed God, and it was accounted to him as righteousness." This is a quotation from Genesis 15:16, which is quoted two other times in the New Testament—in Romans 4:3 and James 2:23. While it is used only once in the Old Testament, it is quoted three times in the New Testament. Three words are crucial in this verse—*believed, accounted,* and *righteousness.* This word was in the Old Testament. God's light was contained in it. When Paul wrote Romans 4, he highlighted the word *accounted.* Those who believe are *accounted* righteous. In Galatians 3, Paul quoted the same passage again, but this time the emphasis was not on accounting but on believing. He said that those who *believe* are justified. When James spoke of this passage, his emphasis was neither on accounting nor on believing, but on *righteousness.* One has to be righteous. God's light was released in three different aspects, from three different sources. When you read Romans 4, you find God's light which was concealed in Genesis. When you read Galatians 3, you also find God's light which was concealed in Genesis. When you read James 2, you can find the same thing—God's light, which was concealed in Genesis. If Paul had never read Genesis 15, or if he had read it and forgotten about it, or read it without receiving revelation from it, this word would never have been written.

A man who is careless, frivolous, and capricious about God's Word cannot be a minister of the word. A minister of the word must dig out all the facts in the Bible. He should even find out all the fine points in the Word of God. He must first get into the facts of God before he can receive the light of God. Without God's light, one can see nothing. But without the facts revealed in the Bible, there is no means whereby one can receive the light. If there is no lamp, there cannot be light. However, if one has a lamp but does not light it, there is no light either. The light must shine through the lamp. Without the lamp, there can be no light. We need God's established Word before we can speak His word.

Habakkuk 2:4 says, "The righteous one will live by his faith." This verse is also quoted three times in the New Testament—in Romans 1:17, Galatians 3:11, and Hebrews 10:38. This verse also has three important words—*righteous, faith,* and *live.* Romans 1 pays attention to "righteous"; it is *the righteous* who live by faith. Galatians 3 pays attention to "faith"; a man lives by *faith.* Hebrews 10 pays attention to "live"; the righteous shall *live* by faith. God's light is contained in the Old Testament. But in the New Testament, this light is released through the same verse, once here, once there, and once in another place. Hence, revelation is the release of light based on God's spoken word. This light is not independent; it has a basis.

FOUR

Let me repeat: other than the mystery of the Body of Christ, which is composed of Jews and Gentiles, and which is depicted in Ephesians, the New Testament contains nothing new. Everything in the New Testament is a further development of the Old Testament. The basic principle to remember is that God's light is contained in His Word. In order to learn to serve the Lord and be a minister of His word, we have to learn to know His Word. Not everyone who is familiar with the Bible can serve as a minister of the word, but those who are not familiar with the Bible will have less of a chance to become a minister of the word. We cannot be lazy in our knowledge of the Bible. In order to know the Bible, there is the need for spiritual familiarization. It is not enough just to memorize or read through the Bible. We must read it before the Lord. We need the light, and it must become a shining book to us. We have to study the words contained in this book in the presence of God, and we have to allow these previously spoken words to speak to us once again. If a man has never touched God's word in the Bible, he can never touch God's light. The present-day word is contained in the New Testament words, just as the New Testament words are contained in the Old Testament words. We have to realize that just as Paul and the other apostles derived their speakings from Moses and the prophets, we also derive our speaking from Paul and the apostles. We have to learn to receive a further word through receiving the apostles' words.

All the revelations we have today represent further light upon previously spoken words. The first time God spoke, He spoke directly to men. Since that time, we receive further words through existing words; our words are built upon existing words. The basic principle today is to receive the word through the Word and to build words upon the words of the Bible. We do not receive God's word independently or autonomously. If we do not receive our word from existing words, we are not qualified to be a minister of the word. We should go to God's Word according to the pattern of the apostles, not according to the fashion of the scribes and Pharisees. We should all find light from the Word and produce more words from the Word. The first grain of wheat was created by God, but all subsequent grains are begotten. One grain begets many grains. From the one grain, many grains are produced, and many grains bring in many more grains. The first grain was from God; it was created. It was not preceded by anything; it was unprecedented. God's word works according to the same principle. The first word was created by God; it was unprecedented. From this word more advancements were made and more words were spoken. The first word God spoke was unprecedented. Today this word in us has produced more words. Once we have the established word in us, more words are produced. Each generation finds the word becoming clearer and more abundant. Today we cannot expect God to create a grain from nothing and then to sow with such a grain. In the same way, we cannot expect God to create a word out of nothing. We can only receive words that are based on God's established words; we can only receive light that is based upon existing light and revelation that is based upon existing revelation. This is the way of the ministers of the word today. If anyone goes beyond this limit, he is a heretic.

Brothers and sisters, do not allow anyone to lightly claim that he is an apostle or a prophet. If a man goes beyond the boundary of God's established, spoken Word in his speaking, his speaking is heretical and devilish. If a man is not careful with his speaking, he will get into great trouble. Today light is contained in the previously received light, the word is contained in the Word, and revelation is contained in the past revelations. Anything that comes from the Bible is right; anything that does not come from the Bible, but from other sources, is wrong. All the speakings we have today come from past speakings. Today is not the day of creation. Today's principle is the principle of begetting. Revelation begets revelation, light begets light, and word begets word. Today we are learning to speak step by step. Eventually, we hope that we will have the ministry of the word.

CHAPTER SIX

INTERPRETATION BY THE HOLY SPIRIT

We have to take note, for our own sake as well as for the sake of others, that the word released by ministers of the word today cannot be independent from those that are found in the Bible. All of God's subsequent words are based on His original words. All of the words of the New Testament are based on the words of the Old Testament. Hence, all of our speaking today must be based on the speaking of the New Testament and the Old Testament. God's word is one living and organic whole. If a man claims that his word is independent, separate, and distinct from the New Testament and the Old Testament, that it bears no correspondence to God's past words, and that it is not based upon them, we can say with certainty that this is heresy; it must be the doctrine of the devil. Today God still has ministers of the word. These ministers are building their ministry upon a certain foundation; they do not speak capriciously.

We need to go one step further. The words released by the ministers of the word must be based on God's previously spoken words on the one hand; however, God must explain and interpret these words to the ministers on the other hand. The ministry of the word must not just have God's word as its foundation; God Himself must open and explain this word as well. Hence, not everyone who bases his speaking on God's word is a minister of His word. Neither can a person claim to be a messenger of God's word simply because he has equipped himself with God's previous speakings. A man may be well-versed in the Old Testament, but this does not mean that he can write the New Testament. In the same way, this does not mean that a person who is familiar with the New Testament can be a minister of the word today. God's word must be the foundation, but God must also furnish the explanation. God must explain His word to His ministers before they can have the ministry of His word. We should set aside all words that do not have a proper foundation. But even when a word is based on the proper foundation, this does not necessarily mean that we can accept it. We must check whether or not it has God's interpretation.

God's previous words can only be interpreted by God Himself. We cannot trust in our good mind, good memory, or diligence in the Word. We cannot take God's previously spoken word as it is and make it God's present ministry of the word. A man who memorizes the one hundred fifty psalms in the book of Psalms may not be able to expound the psalms. Similarly, a man who memorizes the Song of Songs may not be able to interpret the Song of Songs. A man cannot expound the book of Isaiah simply because he has memorized it or expound the book of Daniel just because he has spent fifty years studying it. Those who do not base their speaking on God's previously spoken word cannot be His spokesmen, but those who do are not necessarily ministers of the word either. Those who speak without the basis of God's word are disqualified. But this does not mean that those who speak with such a basis are accepted. There were many scribes and Pharisees who were very familiar with the Old Testament, but none were ministers of the word. Today some people may have studied the Bible very thoroughly, but this does not mean that they are ministers of the word. Ministers of the word are those who are familiar with God's Word and those to whom God has also explained and opened up the Word. A minister of God's word must first possess a proper foundation. Next he must have the proper interpretation. Otherwise, he cannot be a minister of God's word.

How does God explain His word? How did He interpret the Old Testament words to the New Testament ministers? In the New Testament there are at least three kinds of interpretation. The first is the interpretation of prophecies. The second is the interpretation of history. The third is interpretation by synthesis of a few passages of the Scripture. In reading the Old Testament, the New Testament ministers had these three kinds of words before them. The first was prophecies, the second was history, and the third was a combination of various passages. All three required the interpretation of the Holy Spirit.

INTERPRETATION OF PROPHECIES

Let us take the Gospel of Matthew as an example and consider how Matthew served as a minister of God's word. The Holy Spirit took full control of Matthew when he related the story of the Lord Jesus. Matthew 1:23 is a quotation of Isaiah 7: "'Behold, the virgin shall be with child and shall bear a son, and they shall call His name Emmanuel.'" While Matthew was writing his Gospel, the Holy Spirit was enlightening him. It was not a matter of how much time Matthew had spent studying. Of course, I do not mean that Matthew did not study the Old Testament. He had been a tax collector, but he probably spent much time later studying the Old Testament. This is the reason that the Holy Spirit could remind him of quotations. This is why he could quote, "'Behold, the virgin shall be with child and shall bear a son, and they shall call His name Emmanuel.'" But what does this word mean? The Holy Spirit had to explain and interpret this word to Matthew. He had to show Matthew that it referred to the birth of the Lord Jesus. Up to a certain point, God was with us. Prior to that day, God was not with us in quite the same way. Now God is with us through the Lord's appearance on earth. This is an interpretation by the Holy Spirit. We must be familiar with God's past speaking, but we also must have the interpretation of the Holy Spirit. Only the Holy Spirit can ascertain the meaning of God's word for us.

Matthew 2:15 speaks of the Lord Jesus coming out of Egypt. Here Matthew quotes Hosea 11:1. If we read Hosea 11:1 by ourselves, we might not realize that this passage refers to the Lord Jesus. But through the Holy Spirit's interpretation, Matthew realized that these words refer to the Lord Jesus.

Matthew 2:18 says, "'A voice in Ramah was heard, weeping and great lamentation: Rachel weeping for her children, and she would not be comforted, because they are no more.'" This is a quotation of Jeremiah 31:15. In reading Jeremiah 31:15 we would not have the thought that this refers to Herod's intention to kill the Lord Jesus. But through the interpretation of the Holy Spirit, we find the meaning of this passage.

Matthew 3:3 says, "For this is he who was spoken of through Isaiah the prophet, saying, 'A voice of one crying in the wilderness, Prepare the way of the Lord; make straight His paths.'" In reading Isaiah 40:3 we would not have the thought that this refers to John the Baptist. The Holy Spirit had to interpret this for Matthew and show him that this refers to John the Baptist.

Matthew 4:13 speaks of the Lord Jesus in Capernaum, which is within the borders of Zebulun and Naphtali. In verses 15 and 16 Matthew quotes the word of Isaiah 9:1-2: "In order that what was spoken through Isaiah the prophet might be fulfilled, saying, 'Land of Zebulun and land of Naphtali, the way to the sea, beyond the Jordan, Galilee of the Gentiles: The people sitting in darkness have seen a great light; and to those sitting in the region and shadow of death, to them light has risen.'" In reading Isaiah 9, we would not have the thought that this referred to the Lord Jesus. It takes the Holy Spirit's interpretation to show us that this refers to the Lord Jesus. This shows us that it is not enough for God's minister of the word to just have His word; the Holy Spirit must interpret His word to us. When we have the interpretation of the Holy Spirit, we can claim God's Word as our basis. Without the interpretation of the Holy Spirit, the Word is closed to us and, as such, can never become the basis of our speaking.

In Matthew 8 the Lord Jesus healed many who were sick and cast out many demons. Verse 17 quotes Isaiah 53:4, saying, "So that what was spoken through Isaiah the prophet might be fulfilled, saying, 'He Himself took away our infirmities and bore our diseases.'" The word of Isaiah 53 was opened to Matthew. This opened word served as the basis of his speaking. The ministry of God's word is based on God's past speaking. Yet this speaking has to be opened to the ministers before they can use it as the basis of their speaking. Without such an opening, the use of any quotation is a kind of artificial application. It is a misfit at best; it is not the ministry of the word. The opened word affords a person the ministry of the word. Hence, there is the need for not only a foundation but also the proper interpretation.

In Matthew 12:10-16, the Lord Jesus healed a man with a withered hand, saying to him, "Stretch out your hand." The man stretched out his hand, and it was healed. When the Lord left that place, many followed Him, and He healed them all, charging them not to make Him known. At this point Matthew quotes Isaiah 42:1-4: "In order that what was spoken through Isaiah the prophet might be fulfilled, saying, 'Behold, My Servant whom I have chosen, My Beloved in whom My soul has found delight. I will put My Spirit upon Him, and He will announce justice to the Gentiles. He will not strive nor cry out, nor will anyone hear His voice in the streets. A bruised reed He will not break, and smoking flax He will not quench until He brings forth justice unto victory. And in His name will the Gentiles hope'" (Matt. 12:17-21). It was the Holy Spirit's interpretation that linked Isaiah 42 with Matthew 12. Such an interpretation afforded Matthew the ministry of the word.

Ministry of the word requires the Holy Spirit's interpretation of God's Word. Such interpretation is veiled from ordinary men as it was from the scribes and Pharisees. God has to explain this Word to us before we can speak His word. Matthew did not serve as a minister of the word capriciously; his speaking was based on the writings of the Old Testament. How could he base his speaking on the Old Testament? First, he must have studied the words of the Old Testament well, and then the Holy Spirit must have explained and opened these words to him before he could take them as the basis of his speaking. This is what ministry of the word means. Ministry of the word is based on the Spirit's interpretation of God's Word. Without this there is no ministry of the word. There are many quotations from the Old Testament in the book of Matthew, not a few of which were made by the Lord Jesus Himself. The above examples, however, were quoted by Matthew. He told us that what was happening was a fulfillment of what Isaiah or other prophets had said. We know that Matthew was a tax collector. Yet it is precious to find that he was able to quote from the Old Testament. He was not a scribe or a Pharisee like Paul, yet he had the ministry of the word. He had the words of the Old Testament as his basis, and the Holy Spirit had interpreted these words to him. He needed the Spirit's interpretation before he could have the ministry of the word. Without the Spirit's interpretation, there could not have been the ministry of the word. With this interpretation, he was able to use the Old Testament words as his basis. Without this interpretation, he could not have used such words as his basis. It is not enough to just have the Scripture; the Scripture must be opened to us by the Holy Spirit.

In chapter twenty-seven Matthew said something more. The Lord Jesus was about to leave the world, Judas had hung himself, and the high priest and the elders had taken the money which Judas received to betray the Lord and bought a field. In verse 8 Matthew said, "Therefore that field has been called the Field of Blood to this day." We have to pay attention to the fact that this statement was made by Matthew himself. Then he continued to say, "At that time what was spoken through Jeremiah the prophet was fulfilled, saying, 'And they took the thirty pieces of silver, the price of Him that had been priced, whom they of the sons of Israel had priced, and they gave them for the potter's field, as the Lord directed me'" (vv. 9-10). Matthew pointed out that this was a fulfillment of Jeremiah's word. When we read Jeremiah's word, it is not easy to see that it refers to the above instance. Yet God's Spirit explained this verse to Matthew, and he was able to make such an association. In him we see the ministry of the word.

INTERPRETATION OF HISTORY

First Timothy speaks of the history of Adam and Eve in 2:13-14: "For Adam was formed first, then Eve; and Adam was not deceived; but the woman, having been quite deceived, has fallen into transgression." Satan did not deceive Adam directly; his deception was aimed at Eve. He tempted Eve first, and then Eve tempted Adam. First Eve fell as a result of Satan's deception, and then Adam fell as a result of Eve's temptation. In the Old Testament we only have the record of this fact. But in the New Testament, the Holy Spirit opens up this fact to us and shows us that the woman should not be the head in the church; she should not dominate over the man. A pattern is shown, and a basic principle is established. Whenever the woman assumes headship, sin is brought into the world. This fact is part of the history of Adam and Eve. Yet when this fact is opened up, it becomes the basis of the ministry of the word.

In Romans 9 Paul spoke of the story of Abraham. He quoted from Genesis 21. Romans 9:7 says, "'In Isaac shall your seed be called.'" Verse 9 says, "'At this time next year I will come, and Sarah shall have a son.'" This is Old Testament history; it is Old Testament fact. Yet the Holy Spirit opened up to Paul the fact of Abraham's begetting of Isaac, and he was able to see its significance. He began to realize that "not all who are out of Israel are Israel; neither is it that because they are the seed of Abraham, they are all children" (vv. 6-7). Only those who are out of Sarah are the children. God's promise was to Sarah when He said, "'At this time next year I will come, and Sarah shall have a son'" (v. 9). This was God's promise. Isaac was born of God's promise. Only this son was reckoned as Abraham's descendant. Hence, only those who have believed in the Lord Jesus, who are born of God's promise, are the children of God. The Holy Spirit unveiled the history of Abraham's begetting of Isaac to Paul. When he saw this, he had the ministry of God's word. If Paul had read the story of Abraham and Sarah without the interpretation of the Holy Spirit, it would have remained just a story; he would not have had the ministry of the word. Hence, God's Word requires the interpretation of the Holy Spirit. Without the interpretation of the Spirit, one cannot use God's past words as the basis of his speaking, and he will not have the ministry of the word.

In the book of Galatians, the story of Isaac is expounded with more detail and clarity. Galatians 3:29 says, "And if you are of Christ, then you are Abraham's seed, heirs according to promise." Galatians 4:28 says, "But you, brothers, in the way Isaac was, are children of promise." This was Paul's word; it was his ministry of the word. Where did he derive his ministry from? He derived it from an Old Testament story. The Holy Spirit opened this story to him and showed him the key to this story, which was the promise. The key of the promise is found in Genesis 18:10: "I will certainly return unto thee according to the time of life; and, lo, Sarah thy wife shall have a son." This was a promise of God. It was to happen the following year, not that very day. This is the reason we can say that Isaac was born according to a promise. Like Isaac, we are also born according to promise. Thus, the matter becomes clear. Paul was able to minister God's word to His children because the Holy Spirit had interpreted this word to him. He had the ministry of the word. Hence, ministry of the word is based on the interpretation of the Holy Spirit. Without the interpretation of the Spirit, there is no release of the word. We need the interpretation of the Spirit for prophecy and for history. Every part of the Old Testament history requires the explanation of the Spirit. Without the interpretation of the Holy Spirit, there is no release of the word.

Another clear example can be found in Galatians 3:15, which says, "Brothers, I speak according to man, though it is a man's covenant, yet when it has been ratified, no one nullifies it or makes additions to it." Paul said that any man who makes a covenant cannot nullify it or make additions to it. This is true not only with God but even with man. Verse 16 then says, "But to Abraham were the promises spoken and to his seed. He does not say, 'And to the seeds,' as concerning many, but as concerning one: 'And to your seed,' who is Christ." This shows us how accurate Paul was. In Genesis God told Abraham that He would bless others through his seed. In this passage the Spirit of God explained this word to Paul. God would bless others through Abraham and his seed. What do we know about the word *seed* in Hebrew? This word is singular, not plural, in Hebrew. As soon as this fact dawned on Paul, he became clear. God's intention was not to bless the nations through the many descendants of Abraham. If that were the case, God's grace would have been for the

Jews only; only they could bring blessing to the whole world. But the word *seed* is singular in number. It refers to Christ. When God said that He was going to bless the nations through the seed of Abraham, He was referring to Christ. The fact is simple, involving one word being singular rather than plural in number. Yet behind this simple fact lies a very important truth. The Holy Spirit opened up this fact to Paul and showed him the meaning behind this fact. Once he became clear, he had the ministry of the word.

Let us consider another fact. Abraham believed God, and God reckoned him righteous. This is recorded in Genesis 15. Based on this Paul showed us that God does not justify man according to his righteousness but according to his faith. This is Paul's ministry. Abraham believed God, and God reckoned this faith as righteousness. Paul went on to show us that all of Abraham's descendants are justified the same way that Abraham was justified. Abraham was justified by faith, and all those who are justified by faith are sons of Abraham (Gal. 3:6-7). God justified Abraham out of faith; He reckoned Abraham righteous out of faith. Similarly, He justifies everyone who, like Abraham, possesses the same faith (vv. 8-9). Paul shows that Genesis 15 speaks not only of a fact or of history but of a principle, the principle of justification by faith.

We should remember that both Old Testament history and Old Testament prophecies are equally valuable. Some people think that the prophecies, ordinances, and teachings in the Bible are valuable but that the history is not. They consider the history as merely stories. But we must remember that all historical records in the Bible are part of God's word, in the same way that the teachings are God's word. If we show an unbeliever God's Word, he may take the book of Proverbs and throw out Genesis. But we know that the prophecies recorded in the Old Testament are God's word, and so are the teachings, the ordinances, and even the history. God's Word is one undivided whole, and the same principle governs all of its parts. Whether they are presented in the form of history or in the form of prophecy, they are equally God's word, and they equally require the Holy Spirit's interpretation. Prophecies require interpretation by the Holy Spirit, and the history also requires interpretation by the Holy Spirit. Many truths and revelations come from the unveiling of Old Testament history. In serving as a minister of God's word, Paul sometimes received the Spirit's revelation through Old Testament prophecies and sometimes through historical records. Once he saw the revelation, he had the ministry of the word. There is the need for the interpretation of the Holy Spirit. The Holy Spirit has to interpret the facts in the Old Testament to us before we can have the ministry of the word. Otherwise there is no ministry of the word.

INTERPRETATION BY SYNTHESIS

Both prophecies and history require the interpretation of the Holy Spirit. There is a third kind of interpretation—interpretation by synthesis. God assigns a special place for this kind of interpretation for His minister of the word. Consider how Peter served as a minister of God's word at Pentecost. On the day of Pentecost something wonderful happened: The Holy Spirit was poured out and the gifts came. On that day many people spoke in tongues; they spoke the languages of many people. On that day the one hundred twenty received what the Israelites had never received. Previously, the Holy Spirit would come upon one person. One or two or at the most a group of prophets would receive God's Spirit upon them. But on that day all one hundred twenty men and women received the outpouring of God's Spirit; they were filled as if they were drunk with new wine. This was unprecedented in the history of Israel. At that time God clearly put the key in Peter's hand. Among the eleven apostles, Peter clearly took the lead. He seized the opportunity to testify for the Lord, standing up to tell the Jews what had happened to them. Peter not only explained to the people what was happening that day; he also testified to them and exhorted them to receive the same thing. Peter was preaching. At Pentecost he was a minister of the word. He did not base his speaking on one passage but on three. He combined three passages together and received light through this synthesis. This was not an analysis but a synthesis. Three passages were put together. God not only explained this phenomenon to him, but three passages of the Scripture were put together to show the Jews what was really happening to them. Today, God's servants also see things by putting together various passages of the Scripture. Such a practice is in the principle of Peter's ministry at Pentecost.

On the day of Pentecost Peter put together and spoke from three passages—Joel 2, Psalm 16, and Psalm 110. His ministry of the word at Pentecost consisted of a synthesis of these three parts of the Scripture. The Holy Spirit combined the three passages together and interpreted the meaning behind them to him. This is interpretation by synthesis. With such a synthesized interpretation, men receive light from these passages. A minister of the word does not necessarily function through only one passage of the Scripture. Many times, the interpretation comes from a combination of passages. This principle of combination is even more common with the ministry of the word today. We need to put together many passages to find the meaning behind them.

For example, four things were used as objects of worship in the Old Testament: the golden calf, the bronze serpent, Gideon's ephod, and Micah's molten image (1 Kings 12:28-33; 2 Kings 18:4; Judg. 8:27; 18:14-31). If you want to give a message on various kinds of worship apart from God, you can combine these passages and speak something concerning them. Many subjects need to be studied synthetically.

Peter did a work of synthesis on the day of Pentecost. He spoke from Joel 2 on the outpouring of the Holy Spirit, from Psalm 16 on the resurrection of the Lord Jesus, and from Psalm 110 on the ascension of the Lord. He put these three things together. The Lord Jesus has resurrected. After His resurrection, He did not remain on the earth; He ascended to the heavens. The result of this ascension is the outpouring of the Holy Spirit. The Lord's ascension follows His resurrection. Death could not hold Him; He ascended to the Father and is waiting for His enemy to become His footstool. Today the Father has glorified Him, and the outpouring of the Holy Spirit is the proof of His glorification. While Peter was serving as a minister of God's word that day, the Holy Spirit interpreted these three passages of the Scripture to him.

With the interpretation of these three passages, he had a strong foundation for his speaking. The ministry of the word requires the Holy Spirit's interpretation of God's Word to us. We, in turn, have to take this interpreted word as the basis of our speaking ministry.

In Acts we find other examples of such synthesized teaching. For example, in chapter three, Peter's message was short, consisting of only a few sentences, yet he combined Deuteronomy with Genesis. In chapter seven Stephen's word, without a doubt, was a ministry of the word. It was, in fact, a very distinctive ministry of the word. His word was powerful, and there were few explanations in his message. He simply related to his audience the history in the Old Testament period by period, from Abraham's calling in Genesis 12 to Moses' time in Egypt to the Israelites' rebellion against God. He went from Genesis to Exodus to Deuteronomy and then quoted the words of Amos and Isaiah. He went on and on without much explanation. That speech enraged those who heard it, and they stoned him to death. This shows us that his ministry of the word was a very special one. There was no explanation; he merely related the history part by part. Such a message was pressed out of Stephen's spirit. Those who listened to it could not stand it. This synthesis was very powerful. In chapter thirteen Paul's word was in this same principle. While he preached in Pisidian Antioch, he quoted from 1 Samuel 13, Psalm 89, Psalm 2, Isaiah 55, Psalm 16, and Habakkuk. This was a synthesis. Based on this synthesis, Paul came to a conclusion and challenged the audience to accept Jesus of Nazareth as their Savior.

As the New Testament ministers read God's Old Testament word, they received three different kinds of interpretation from the Holy Spirit. The first was the interpretation of prophecy, the second was the interpretation of history, and the third was the interpretation of a combination of various passages. The Holy Spirit gave interpretations to all three kinds of words. We should pay special attention to words that are a combination of various passages. The book of Hebrews contains many words of this kind, and so do the books of Romans and Galatians. When the Holy Spirit instructed the apostles to speak on a certain topic, He selected many verses from the Old Testament and led them to speak what they ought to speak. We should realize that the same principle governs the ministers of the word today. Just as Peter, Paul, Matthew, and all the other apostles fulfilled their ministry by speaking according to the Old Testament, words with which the Holy Spirit had instructed them, we fulfill our ministry by speaking according to both the Old and New Testaments, as the Holy Spirit has also instructed us. The apostles did not speak carelessly; they were under the direction of the Holy Spirit. They spoke what God wanted them to speak based on the Spirit's interpretation of God's previous speakings. Today the ministers of the word must follow the same principle. Our basis should be the words of the New Testament and the Old Testament, words which the Spirit instructs us to speak and which He has interpreted for us. We should speak what God wants us to speak today based on these words. This is what it means to have the ministry of the word.

THE NEED FOR THE SPIRIT'S INTERPRETATION

Neither Matthew, Paul, Peter, nor any of the other ministers of the New Testament spoke their own words. None of them spoke independently or autonomously. All their speakings were based on the Old Testament.

Yet not everyone who reads the Old Testament can speak like Matthew, Paul, or Peter. One must have the interpretation of the Holy Spirit before he can have the ministry of the word. It is the Holy Spirit who enlightens, who explains the meaning of a word, who finds the facts in the Old Testament, who points out the highlights in these words, and who affords a person the basis for speaking.

All of the writers of the New Testament had their own ministry of the word. Today the same ministry is needed among us. If we want to be ministers of God's word, we have to study His Word earnestly. It is not enough to simply read with our mind. We have to ask the Lord's Spirit to show us the highlights in His written Word, to turn our attention to these facts, and to interpret them for us. A minister of the word must have a basis upon which to speak. We must never speak in an independent way. Nor should we presume that merely memorizing His Word is all that we need. We need the interpretation of the Holy Spirit.

We have to remember that the ministry of the word today is far richer than the ministry of the word seen in the writers of the New Testament. This is not to say that what we see today is more profound than what they saw. We know that God's Word was completed when the book of Revelation was finished. All of God's truths have been released. The highest and the deepest of all truths have been released. What we are saying is that as far as the riches are concerned, the ministry of the word today should be far richer than the ministries of the New Testament writers. The basis of the divine word upon which Paul spoke was the Old Testament writings only. But the basis of the divine word upon which we speak is the Old Testament writings plus Paul's, Peter's, and others' writings. The Bible we have in our hand today is bigger than the one Paul had in his hand. He only had thirty-nine books, but we have sixty-six books. Today God's servants should have a richer ministry of the word. There is so much more material for God's Spirit to use and so much more opportunity for God's Spirit to give interpretation that it is only right for there to be a greater abundance of the ministry of God's word today. There should not be any poverty at all; there should be more riches instead.

We need to study the Bible in a careful way, and we need the Holy Spirit to interpret the Scripture for us. In the past many people have spent considerable time in studying the Bible. The Holy Spirit has given us much light. Some have discovered the difference between words with articles and words without articles, such as the difference between *Christ* and *the Christ,* between *law* and *the law,* and between *faith* and *the faith.* This requires careful study. In the New Testament the title *Jesus Christ* refers to the Lord before resurrection, while the title *Christ Jesus* refers to the Lord after resurrection. Nowhere in the Bible is there reference to the believers being *in Jesus.* We only find the expression *in Christ.* These fine points require careful studying to dig them out. We have to allow the Lord's Spirit to speak to us, and we have to realize the accuracy of God's Word.

Many words in the Bible are not interchangeable. Many pronouns have special significance and cannot be replaced. Every time the Bible speaks of the blood, it refers to redemption, and every time it speaks of the cross, it refers to dealing with one's very person; the two are never confused. Every time it refers to the old creation, it speaks of the crucifixion of the cross, and every time it refers to the natural self, it speaks of the bearing of the cross. The two are never confused. We are the ones who are confused; God's Word is never confused. In regard to the operation of the Holy Spirit, the work of constitution is always inward, while the experience of the gifts is always outward. Examples such as these demonstrate the accuracy of the Scripture. The writers of the New Testament realized the accuracy of the Old Testament, and they yielded themselves to the interpretation of the Lord's Spirit. We also must see the accuracy of the New Testament, and we should also give ground to the Lord Spirit's interpretation. We need both the New and the Old Testaments as our basis before we can have a rich ministry of the word. We need to study the Bible, but it is not enough just to study the Bible; we need the interpretation of the Holy Spirit.

A minister of the word does not receive an isolated, unrelated, great, and unprecedented revelation all at once. Rather, he builds his light upon God's past speakings. This was the way with Paul, Peter, and all ministers of the Lord. This is the way with the ministers of the Lord today. There were other men before Paul, and before us there are Paul, the apostles, and the sixty-six books of the Bible, God's written Word. Today's revelation must match that of our predecessors, and today's light and word must match that of our forebearers. Paul needed the Spirit's interpretation before he could be a minister of the word. If we want to be a minister of the word today, we also need the interpretation of the Holy Spirit. God's word is handed down from generation to generation, and His word also begets more of the word from generation to generation. No one can speak anything that is independent. The second person always sees more than the first, the third person always sees more than the second, and the fourth person always sees more than the third. As time moves on, more things are seen. With the first person, God had to intervene directly, but the second person treads on the pathway of the first and sees more. The third person treads on the pathway of the second and sees even more. God's word continues to grow. Word begets word, and as time goes on, more words are released. In order to see more and receive more, we have to see what our predecessors have seen and receive what they have received. If God is merciful and gracious to us and opens our eyes to what He has spoken, we will have a basis upon which to serve as ministers of His word.

The ministers may be many in number, but the word is one. Generation after generation, many men have acted as ministers, but all these ministers came out of the same one word. Those who come after should ask God for the interpretation of the words of those who came before. Only then will they be linked up with God's great "word," and only then will they be able to stand together with all ministers of God. This is a very basic principle: There is one speaking, but many ministers.

CHAPTER SEVEN

THE REVELATION OF THE HOLY SPIRIT

We have seen that a minister of God's word must have God's Word as the basis of his ministry. He must also have the Holy Spirit to interpret God's word for him. Now we have to go on to consider another, even more important, matter. A minister of God's word must know God's past speaking and have the interpretation of this speaking, but he must have another basic qualification: He must be a man of revelation. If he does not have a spirit of revelation, he cannot serve as a minister of the word. He must have revelation concerning God's Word and must possess the anointing of the Spirit concerning this Word. Without revelation and without the anointing of the Spirit, he cannot serve as a minister of God's word.

ONE

The Bible is an amazing book. One outstanding characteristic of this book is that it is made up of words spoken by men, yet it is God's word in every sense. It was written by men, yet it was written by God's own hand in every sense. It contains many expressions, sentences, and words, and God's breath is upon all of these words. The word used in 2 Timothy 3:16, which is translated as *inspiration* by some versions, is *breath* according to the original language. The Bible is God's breath. It is written by holy men of God under the leading of the Holy Spirit (2 Pet. 1:21). When God created the world, He created man out of the dust of the earth, but the created man was not alive. Man became a living soul after God breathed His living breath into him. The Bible is a book written by men. It is composed of words spoken by men, but God's breath is upon it in addition to this. Therefore, it is a

living book. It is the living word of the living God. This is
the meaning of all Scripture being God's inspiration.

This book, the Bible, contains human elements and human
words. When many people read this book, they touch only the
human elements and words; they do not sense God's speaking
in this book. What makes the Bible so unique is its dual
character. On the one hand, there is the outward, physical
dimension of the Bible. As far as man's physical dimension
is concerned, he is made of the dust of the ground. But on
the other hand, there is a spiritual dimension of the Bible.
The Bible is related to the Holy Spirit; it is God's speaking
and God's breath. As far as its outward shell is concerned, it
was written from man's memory and can be retained in man's
memory. It issued from man's mouth and is heard by man's
ears. It is written in human language and understood by
human understanding. Man can preach the truths contained
in this book, and these truths can be retained in man's
memory, understood by man's mind, and passed on from one
man to another. All of these things go on when one deals with
the outward shell of the Bible. This is the physical aspect of
the Word. Doctrines and teachings can be included in this
category, because these are things that man's mind can grasp,
things that can be understood and comprehended by his
intellect. This is the physical dimension of the Bible.

However, there is another dimension to the Bible. The
Lord Jesus said, "The words which I have spoken to you are
spirit and are life" (John 6:63b). The other aspect of the Bible
involves spirit and life. In this dimension, God speaks His
word within man. This is not something that a clever man
can understand or a man with a good memory can grasp. Nor
is it something that an intelligent man can fathom. This
requires another organ for understanding. The ears, the eyes,
and the mind cannot see or understand this dimension of
things.

A minister of God's word serves the church not by touching
the physical dimension of the Bible but by touching the
spiritual dimension of it. Those who serve the church by
touching only the physical dimension are not ministers of
God's word. If the Bible did not have a physical side, a man

would either be a minister of God's word or not; there could be no mistake about it. But the Bible has physical and human elements. In this aspect, it can readily be understood and accepted by man. This is where the danger and problem lie. Man can preach the human elements in the Bible by the power of his own human faculties, and he can presume that he is a minister of the word. He can present all the human elements in the Bible to the church, and he can presume that he is serving the church with God's word. He can presume that the truths he preaches are scriptural truths and that they are teachings that conform to the orthodox and pure faith. He can deceive himself by thinking that his teachings are orthodox teachings. But we have to realize that these teachings have nothing to do with the spiritual aspect of the Bible; they are of another realm.

Some young people think that as long as they can understand Greek, they can understand God's word. Little do they realize that many people who understand Greek know very little of God's word. In fact, they may not know anything at all. A man who understands Hebrew does not necessarily understand the Old Testament. A man who understands Hebrew and Chaldean does not necessarily understand the book of Daniel. A man who understands Chinese does not necessarily understand the Chinese Bible. The Bible contains words which are beyond the Chinese language and the Greek language. It contains words which the Hebrews or Chaldeans may not have understood. The words that a minister of the word has to strive to understand are God's own words. Not everyone who understands Chinese can understand the Bible. Similarly, not everyone who understands Greek can understand God's word. It is one thing to understand a language, and it is another thing to know God's word. In fact, it is an entirely different thing to know His word. We should never have the misconception that the more we study God's word, the more we can be a minister of His word. It is not a matter of whether or not we study the Bible, but how we study it. God has to speak His word into man before it can become God's word to him. Man has to know God's voice. Only God can speak God's word. Man has to know God's voice, and

God has to speak to him before he can become a minister of God's word.

In preaching the gospel, we preach the gospel itself; we do not preach the basis of the gospel. We serve others with the gospel, not with the basis of the gospel. The Bible is the basis of the gospel; it is the basis of God's speaking. However, we cannot say in a general way that this is what God is speaking to us today. God has spoken through this book. Without a doubt, God spoke these words at one time. But God must breathe His breath through this book again today before it will become living to us. God's Spirit has to breathe into His word before it will become living to us. Today we still need God's revelation in His word so that this word can come alive to us. The difference between the word being living and dead is very great. We must see what God's word is. God's word is His speaking today. God's word is not just His speaking in the past. His past speaking was His word, but today He must breathe His breath once again upon this word. God's word is not just His speaking at some point in the past; it is His speaking today. We have to realize that there are two realms to God's word. One is the realm of the written Bible. The written word, including all the biblical doctrines, knowledge, teachings, prophecies, and truths, is in this realm. But this is only the visible realm of the Bible. We may have heard that Abraham believed in God and that God reckoned him to be righteous. God's justification of those who believe may be nothing more than an outward teaching to us. A man with a good memory and strong intellect can preach this; he may think that he is preaching God's word. But actually he is merely preaching the superficial aspect of the word. This is not the ministry of God's word.

We have to pay attention to what the Bible is. The Bible is God's speaking in the past. At one time God spoke, and the Spirit's breath was upon His speaking. When that word was released, some touched "God's word," but some did not. When Paul wrote to the Romans, two things happened. First he wrote his letter utilizing some physical things. He might have written it on a lamb's skin and might have used some kind of tree sap for ink. The words were recorded in some form of written language. This is the physical side of the Epistle, and this is the realm we are in when we read it in an outward way. When Paul delivered this Epistle to the Romans, they might have been impressed with only the letter of the Epistle. If this were the case, it would only be a letter and nothing else; there would not be God's word in it for them. But if while the Romans were reading it, God breathed His breath upon every single word, and every word was filled with God's breath, they would realize that they were sinners and that justification would come by faith. They would believe in God's word and receive it. This is the ministry of the word. While they were reading, studying, and trying to understand God's word, they would touch the "word" that Paul was speaking through the book of Romans. Another person who was clever, intelligent, and born with a good memory might be able to read Paul's Epistle with ease and might even be able to memorize it with little effort. Yet he would not know the meaning of justification by faith. He could understand the doctrine of justification by faith, but he could not touch justification by faith. He could touch the things that belong to the physical dimension of the Bible but not its spiritual dimension. He could only touch the doctrine of the Bible, the content of the Bible, and the surface of God's word; he could not touch the life in His word.

We have to realize what the Bible is. The Bible is God's past speaking. It is the ministry of God's word by His servants in the past. The book of Romans was Paul's past ministry of the word. At one time God spoke these words. But today when we read the book of Romans, we may only touch the surface of the Bible, the physical and outward side of it. Today God has to breathe His breath upon this word once again before we can know God's word and before we can be a minister to Him. It is not enough for God to breathe His breath just once. He has to breathe again before we can touch His word.

TWO

What is inspiration? What is revelation? The meaning of the Bible being God's inspiration is that at one time God breathed His breath upon this book. Without God's inspiration, the Bible could not be called the Bible. Inspiration is the basis of the Bible. God inspired Paul to write the book of Romans. It was through God's inspiration of and His breath upon Paul that he wrote Romans. What then is revelation? It is God's breathing upon the book of Romans once again as we open to it two thousand years later. Through revelation we touch God's word once again. Inspiration is a once-for-all occurrence, but revelation is a repeated occurrence. When God breathes His breath upon His word a second time, when we find light again through the Holy Spirit and the anointing upon His word to see what Paul once saw, we have revelation. Revelation means God is doing something today; He is reviving today what He once gave to man through inspiration. This is a great matter.

Brothers and sisters, this is something exceedingly glorious. What is revelation? It is when God's Spirit revives His word in such a way that it becomes as living and full of life as when Paul wrote it. When God wrote that word through Paul, life was vibrant in both the writer and the writing. Today the same words can be released once again. God can fill His word with the Holy Spirit once again. His anointing can once again act upon His word. When this happens, the word becomes as powerful, enlightening, and life-giving as it was before. This is what revelation is all about. It is useless to merely study the Word. If a man does not have revelation, he can study every word from the first page to the last without hearing a single word from God. The Bible is the word of God. At one time God spoke this word. But if you want this word to be God's word today, you have to ask God to speak this word once again. This speaking will bring in many things—God's word, light, and life. If there is not this kind of speaking, the Bible will remain a closed and dead book to you.

Suppose one hundred brothers and sisters gather in a place, and God is speaking through them. It is possible that not everyone will hear God's word. Everyone hears the sound and the words. But some may hear God's speaking, while others may not. Some may be in touch with things of both realms, while others may be in touch with things of only one realm. Some may hear the doctrine, the truth, conveyed through the sounds and the words. They may understand the thought, and those with a good memory may be able to recite the words over and over, but they may not have heard God's speaking at all. Hearing God's speaking is an altogether different matter. Brothers and sisters, God's word is not just a doctrine or a teaching. We need to hear the doctrine and the teaching, but in addition to hearing these things, we need to hear something else. We need to hear God's personal speaking to us. Only after we have acquired that kind of hearing can we say, "Thank God, I have heard Your word." Only then can we say that we have touched something real.

Suppose one hundred people listen to the gospel. Ninety-nine may hear and understand everything that is said. They may know the doctrine, the teaching, and the truth. They may nod their heads and say, "Yes, yes." All ninety-nine may know these things, but it is possible that only the hundredth one, the one apart from the ninety-nine, receives a teaching beyond the teaching that the others receive, hears a voice beyond the voice that the others hear, and grasps a word beyond the word that the others grasp. He hears God's speaking in addition to hearing the teaching, and he bows his head and confesses, "I am a sinner. O God, save me." Such a man has heard God's word. The other ninety-nine have only touched things related to the human and physical aspect of the word; they have not heard God's word. There is a fundamental difference between the two.

The same thing can be said about reading the Bible. It is true that the Bible is God's word. At one time God spoke to Paul, Peter, and John through this word. But when some read this word, they only find words, expressions, doctrines, truths, and teachings. They have everything except God's speaking. They can read the Bible for ten years without God having spoken to them once. Brothers and sisters, have you ever heard someone testify, saying, "I have been reading the Bible for twenty years, but I still do not understand what it is saying"? Have you ever heard someone stand up and say, "I have been reading the Bible for five or ten years. I thought I knew everything about it. But one day, God was merciful to me. He spoke a word to me. Now I know that I did not know anything before"? Brothers and sisters, an experienced person can readily tell the difference between these two. One must have God's word in addition to man's word. In addition to man's speaking, there must also be God's speaking. If God does not open His mouth, nothing will avail. These are two entirely different realms. One is the realm of doctrines, truths, teachings, words, language, and expressions. In this realm anyone who is diligent and intelligent, who has a good mind and a sharp memory, can get by well. But in the other realm, God has to reiterate His word to men. Brothers and sisters, do you see the difference between the two? God has spoken, and the words He has spoken are recorded verbatim in the Bible. But God also can speak to men a second time through the words of the Bible. This is what we call God's speaking today. God has to speak to us a second time through the words He once used. He has to enlighten us a second time through His revealed light. He has to grant us fresh revelation within His established revelation. This is the basic principle of the ministry of the word. Without this we do not have the ministry of the word.

Lest some among us do not understand the relationship between the Scripture and God's present revelation, I will use another illustration. Suppose you realize that God once used you to speak something for Him. It might not have been anything dramatic, but at least you can say that you had a definite sense that the Lord spoke something through you; there was definitely a special kind of speaking. Suppose two months later you encounter a similar situation. You face the same kind of people, and the same kind of need arises. You may feel that what you said two months ago is the most appropriate word for these people today. You may have great assurance that you can help them in this way. But when you spoke two months ago, the anointing of the Spirit was with the word. When you repeat the same word today, however, you feel that you have failed. The power in the word is gone. What is wrong? Since you are speaking the same words that were so full of anointing, you think that the Holy Spirit will surely continue to anoint your word. But this does not happen. The Holy Spirit may have anointed your word at one time, but this does not mean that He will anoint it whenever you speak the same thing.

We must remember that a man can receive a word of revelation. But this does not mean that it will be a word of revelation whenever he speaks the same word. The words may still be there, but the revelation may be gone. We can repeat the word, but we cannot repeat the revelation and the anointing. Revelation and anointing are in God's hand. We can only repeat and recall the words; we cannot repeat or recall the revelation. We have to see the relationship between the ministry of the word and the Scriptures, or the relationship between the Bible and the word. A sinner may come to us today. If we speak John 3:16, he may readily confess that he is a sinner. A little later another person may come to us. We may be in the same room and quote the same verse, but the Holy Spirit may not speak, and the second person may not be saved. John 3:16 has not changed. The question is whether or not the anointing and the revelation are still present.

THREE

We who serve as ministers of God's word must learn this lesson. It is not how much of the Scriptures we understand, how many biblical truths we have seen, or how many verses we can quote. These will not constitute us as a minister of the word. We need to see the biblical truth, and we need to quote and understand the Bible. But in addition to these things we need one basic ingredient. If we have this basic ingredient, we have the ministry of the word. Without it, we do not have the ministry of the word. This basic ingredient is the revelation of the Holy Spirit. The ministry of the word needs the revelation of the Holy Spirit. One must not only speak the same word but have the same revelation. Without the same revelation, the ministry of the word ceases to exist. We must be thoroughly and unmistakably clear about this.

God has spoken. He has to speak the same thing again today before the word will produce the same effect. God used His word once. He has to use the same word again today; His anointing has to be upon the same word before it will become effective to us. We must see the balance here. On the one hand, God has to use the word that He once released. When we preach God's word, we do not have to look for new words. Rather, we should base our speaking on what has already been spoken. Yet on the other hand, what we preach should not be just the old words. It should be the same word and yet not the same word. It is the same word, because without that word as the basis, God cannot speak; there is no disagreement in His speaking. Yet in another sense there is the fresh anointing and revelation of the Holy Spirit with this word. Without the fresh anointing and revelation of the Spirit, the same word will not produce the same result. A man has to maintain a proper balance between these two aspects.

One great temptation today is that man seeks and hopes merely to repeat the same words. He thinks that by speaking the same thing, he will repeat the same power, light, and revelation. We must remember that these are things that belong to two different realms. You can repeat the same words, the same doctrines, the same testimonies, the same parables, and the same expressions. These things can be repeated, and man can repeat them with his own power. But while the words may be repeated, God may not repeat His use of these words. You can repeat the outward things, but you cannot repeat the inward things. God's realm remains God's realm, and our realm remains our realm.

Another illustration may make things even clearer. God's speaking is in the principle of resurrection. What is resurrection? Resurrection does not give life; it merely calls to life what is dead. This is resurrection. The birth of a baby is not resurrection. But when a dead man comes out of the tomb, that is resurrection. The daughter of Jairus was resurrected, the only son of the widow of Nain was resurrected, and Lazarus was resurrected. They were dead and then became alive. This is resurrection. God's ministers of the word serve according to the principle of resurrection today. God put His life in His word. The word is still here, but God has to breathe His life into His word once more. Do you see this? This is the principle of resurrection. The principle of resurrection is different from the principle of creation. The first time a word was released, it was released according to the principle of creation. When the word was spoken, something was created. A "son" was born; there was a new birth. But the ministry of the word does not function this way today. God's word is already here, and He is merely repeating what He has already spoken. God is putting His life into His word once more, and when this word becomes living in man, it is revelation to man.

Aaron's rod was a type of resurrection, because at one time the rod was living. In fact, all the rods were living at one time. They were not made of iron. They were wood and had life in them at one time. But when life left, the wood became a dead rod. Aaron's rod was the only exception. It was placed before the ark, and it sprouted, blossomed, and bore fruit. This is resurrection. God's word is based on the principle of resurrection. There was no need to get another piece of wood. The original rod sprouted, blossomed, and bore fruit. God's word is one. There is only one word. We cannot set aside the Bible to preach God's word. The rod remains the same, but when life visits it again, we have resurrection. It must be the same rod, and life must enter the rod a second time. It must be the same word, but life must enter the word again and again. Life has to enter the word again and again, revelation has to come upon it again and again, and light has to shine upon it again and again. Only then is the word living to us. Anyone who tries to reject the Bible is rejected by God because he is rejecting the words that God has written down. Every word of the Scriptures is God's inspiration, and we have to honor it. Without it as the foundation, there is no orthodox faith, and there is no revelation from God. Yet with the words of the Scriptures, there is still the need for man to go to God to receive revelation and light. It is the same word of God. But upon this same word there is the need for the same revelation to be revealed once again. The rod remains the same, but fresh life has to enter it once more before it will sprout, blossom, and bear fruit. This is what God's word is all about. This is the meaning of the revelation of God's word.

There is one inspiration, but there must be repeated revelations. God's one word has to be spoken by Him again and again. We have one Bible, but we need a continual anointing of the Holy Spirit. Only then will there be the ministry of the word. Whenever a man tries to explain the Bible without the anointing, revelation, or light, the ministry of the word stops in him. We must pay attention to this fact. Man's diligence, memory, understanding, and intelligence are all useful. But they are not enough. God must grant mercy to a man and must speak to him again.

In reality, if a man does not hear God's speaking, he can do nothing about it. God must be willing to speak to man again. If God does not want to speak, man can do nothing. If the Lord will not speak, the ministers will not accomplish anything even if they all speak. It is a great thing for the Lord to speak. If He does not speak, nothing will happen. Even if man tries his best to speak, no result will come. The more one tries to speak in the physical realm, the more he will fail. The more one speaks in the spiritual realm, the more the speaking will work. The more you learn to speak according to your spirit, the more you will realize that this is something that is beyond anyone's control. The words can be the same, the sounds can be the same, and even the inward feelings can be the same, but what is released will not be the same. There can be a word-for-word, sentence-by-sentence correspondence. The whole message can be repeated verbatim, and everything can be the same. But what is released will not be the same. We must remember that only God can speak God's word. The Bible is God's word, and we need God to speak this word to us. The work of the ministers is to allow God to speak this word once again. As oracles of God, when we allow God the liberty to speak His word, there is the ministry of the word. We can only serve within this realm.

The difference between theology and God's speaking is intrinsically very great. Whenever we listen to a sermon, we should never just consider whether or not the doctrine is right, the teaching is scriptural, and the truth is correct. This is not to put down these factors. However, everyone who has been taught by God and whose eyes are opened should know what kind of sermon is being spoken as soon as he sits down to listen. A person may have a good mind, yet he may not have God's word. Another person may not have a quick mind, yet God's word is with him. There is a fundamental difference between God speaking through a person and not speaking through a person.

If all the brothers could learn this lesson, the church would not pay that much attention to gifts. Instead, it would pay more attention to ministry. The problem today is that many young brothers and sisters cannot tell the difference between gifts and ministry. This is the reason that gifts are more welcome and popular in the church, while ministry is neglected. The words may be the same in both cases, but the reality is different. The two may be the same in letters, in outward appearance, but those who have the discernment can tell the difference between them. A brother once said, "I have preached everything that Brother So-and-so preached." This brother had a good mind and thought that he could preach just as well as others. He did not realize that his preaching was in an entirely different realm. Some people preach according to their mind, while others preach according to their spirit. These are two entirely different realms. We should never think that just by repeating the same words we will produce the same results. Some can speak the same words, but God may not speak through them. Others have the ministry of the word because God speaks through them.

FOUR

In looking back at church history, we find that God has been taking the way of recovery from the time of Martin Luther. God raised up Luther and his contemporaries to usher in the work of recovery. Since 1828 many truths have been gradually recovered. There is one thought in the mind of many lovers of the Lord: How far will the Lord go in the way of recovery? But we need to ask what recovery is. Recovery does not mean that we preach what the apostles preached and speak every truth that is in the Bible. This is not recovery. It does not mean that we have the revelation of the New

Testament once we preach the truth of the New Testament. Nor does it mean that we have the apostles' word once we preach the apostles' teaching. Many people can preach baptism today without knowing what baptism is. They can preach the laying on of hands without knowing what the laying on of hands is. Some can preach the church without seeing the church at all. Others can preach submission without knowing anything about God's authority. Do not think that the content will be the same as long as the subject is the same. Do not think that the message will be the same as long as the doctrine and terminology are the same. Many people preach in the realm of outward letters. Such ones do not have the ministry of the word.

If you want to be a minister of the New Testament, you must have the revelation of the New Testament. Only as we receive the same anointing that the apostles received do we have the ministry of the word. Only by receiving the same revelation do we receive the ministry of the word. We do not receive the divine speaking that they received simply by repeating the words they spoke. We can reiterate the words they used without receiving the divine words they received. God's word is totally different. Suppose a church is deceived like the Galatians were deceived. What should we do? Can we take the book of Galatians as it is, copy it, and send it to this church? The Epistle to the Galatians was written by Paul, but the Galatians received God's speaking. When the Galatians received Paul's letter, they touched God's speaking. Today we can copy the words of the Epistle to the Galatians and send it to the problem church. The recipients may only touch the transcribed words without touching God's word. These words are in two different realms. It is not uncommon for a man to touch the Bible without touching life. He only touches the Scripture, not life. He only touches the words that God once used, not God's present speaking. A man can touch the inspired Bible without touching the revelation of the Holy Spirit. Brothers and sisters, why is it that so many people read the Bible today yet so few receive anything from it? Why is it that so many people preach the Bible yet so little of God's word is sensed? The only explanation is that men only touch the outward shell of God's Word. They have touched what God once said, but they have not touched what God is saying again today. God has not spoken to them through the word which He once used.

We must realize that the responsibility of the ministers of the word is to allow God to speak through the Scripture once again. God's ministers of the word are those through whom God can speak His word once again. God is willing to speak through them. It should be His speaking that is released, not just the Bible that is released. Who are the ministers of God's word? They are those who open the Bible and convey to their audience the words of God's present speaking, not just the words from the book itself. This is what it means to be a minister of the word. If the hearers have a problem in themselves, or if they choose to shut up their spirits, hearts, or minds, that is their own concern. But as long as a man will open his spirit, heart, and mind, he will hear God's speaking. If others hear nothing of God's speaking while we are interpreting the Bible and expounding its teachings, we are a complete failure in God's eyes. A minister of the word is one through whom God speaks. Others should have the feeling that God has spoken to them, and they should fall on their faces. The reason the church is so poor is that the ministers are poor. We complain that so few people have received revelation. Why do we not give them the revelation? It is our business to give them the revelation, yet we blame the church for being poor. Why do we not make it rich? It is our business to make the church rich. The function of the ministers of the word is to release God's word, not just the Bible, out of their mouth. The words of the Bible become the word of God in their mouth. They become life and light, not mere outward letters.

Do not be deceived to think that as long as a man preaches from the Bible and interprets prophecies from the Bible, he is a minister of the word. Such a person merely teaches others the outward shell of the Bible; he is not a minister of the word. Some people complain that the church is short of revelation. We agree that the church needs revelation, but we must ask who will give the church revelation. We cannot put all the blame on the brothers and sisters. If God's ministers are in poverty, the whole church is in poverty. If the church does not have prophets, if it is short in vision, God's people will be void of light. Today God is dispensing light to the church through the ministers. How great is the responsibility of the church! We should never think that we can call ourselves successors to the apostles just as long as we preach the same Scripture that they preached. We must remember that we can consider ourselves the apostles' successors only to the extent that we have received the same revelation they received and have experienced the same anointing they experienced. It is not a matter of having the same doctrine but a matter of having the same anointing. This is the basic test of all things.

In the church nothing is more serious than the absence of men who supply others with God's word, revelation, and light. If we do not supply others with these things, can we expect others to receive them simply through prayer? By asking them to pray for these things by themselves, we are shirking our responsibility and casting the burden on their shoulders. The responsibility is not on their shoulders. We should not pass it on to them. The ministers of the word have a responsibility to minister to the church. With the ministers of the word, there should be much revelation, light, and anointing of the Spirit. When they stand up to speak from the Scripture, God should speak through the same Scripture. God should be willing to release His own speaking through the same passage. This is what it means to be a minister of the word. This is what it means to minister to the church with God's word. To minister is to serve. It is like preparing a meal and serving it to others. This service satisfies others' hunger. A minister of the word should prepare God's word in such a way that he can minister and feed others with the word.

Many people can expound the Bible today. But the problem is that God will not speak. We have to know the difference between understanding the Bible and having God's word. We may study the Bible for many days, yet God may not speak a single word to us. When God decides to speak to us, all problems are settled and everything is changed. We will say, "For years, I had read the Bible foolishly. I did not understand anything, but that day I knew." It is a matter of whether or not God has spoken. Some people do not have spiritual insight on anything. They may not have experienced any speaking other than the time when they were saved. Such ones will not touch anything in the spiritual realm. Some people have been listening and listening for a long time. Some words have been repeated over ten times in their ears, yet they still do not sense anything. But when some brothers speak, they suddenly hear something and are struck by it. During the previous times, they only heard the letters of the Bible. But this time they hear God's speaking. There is a fundamental difference here. What is God's word? God's word is God's release. We have to see what God's word really is. Only as the word is released and as God speaks are we able to function as ministers. This is a most fundamental issue. God must speak to us, and He must speak through us. If He does not speak to us, we cannot speak His word. Many people desire to be God's oracles and ministers. In order to be one, they must be men of revelation.

Today the building up of the church, the reaching of the measure of the stature of the fullness of Christ, and the arriving at the oneness of the church's faith depend on the functioning of the ministers of the word. God is raising up His ministers to do the work of the ministry. Ephesians 4 shows us that only as the work of the ministry is realized is there the growth of the stature of Christ and the arriving at the oneness of faith (vv. 12-13). The problem today is that few can be ministers. There is preaching every day, but it is hard to say how much of this preaching releases God's word. God's people are short of light and revelation, and the responsibility is on us. Do not put all the blame on the brothers and sisters. Souls are not saved and believers are not edified today because there is no release of the word. The ministers have failed. If the ministers have failed, how can we expect the church to prevail? The whole problem lies in the fact that we are closed to God; we have refused to allow God's light to shine on us. This is why we cannot bring our brothers and sisters to God's light. The problem is with us, not with them. This is a serious thing, a very sobering thing. One reason the church is in ruin today is that the Lord cannot have a breakthrough in us. He is looking for ministers of the word everywhere. God's word is never short; His light and His revelation are never lacking. The problem today is that He has not gained the right men. He is bound by us. The light cannot shine out through us.

Many workers claim to be God's oracles. Yet while they are expounding the Bible, they do not have the faintest hope or thought that God would speak through them. Their sole interest lies in their desire to present their own doctrines. They think that as long as they have the doctrines, they have everything. They are interested only in their own truth, their own pet ideas, and they think that as long as these can be propagated, all will be well. They do not have the faintest expectation of God being released through their speaking. We must remember that we have God's word only when He is released. If God is not released, all that men hear will be man's word. Only when God is released is there revelation. If He is not released, the same teaching will only pass from one person to another, from one mouth to another mouth, and from one mind to another mind. If, by the grace of God, He is released from us, how great a difference it will make!

Brothers, we have to realize how different the exposition of the Scripture is from the impartation of God's revelation to man. We must realize that even though we may say many words that sound reasonable, wonderful, nice, and precious, God is not in our speaking. Once we can tell this difference, we will prostrate ourselves before God and say, "Lord, from now on, I abhor works that are void of revelation, works that impart no revelation to man." We should never be professional preachers. Once we become professional preachers, we will speak because it is our job to speak, and we will preach because it is our job to preach. We will not speak or preach as a result of receiving something from God. We must live in the presence of God. Without His presence we will not have the ministry of the word. God has to gain this among us. By the mercy of God we have to receive revelation from

His word and then convey this revelation to others. For this we can do nothing except ask for His mercy. If the Lord does not speak through us, we cannot convey His word to others. If what we have is nothing more than a book—the Bible, we have nothing that is living. It is true that the basis of the ministry of the word is the Bible, but the Bible alone is not enough; there is the need of the revelation of the Holy Spirit.

Brothers, we need the anointing of the Spirit upon us. We need to learn to expect the anointing. Many times we have to say to the Lord, "Lord, anoint Your word once more today so that I can take it and use it." When we stand in front of others, we have to say to the Lord, "Anoint the words that I am about to speak and release them with Your anointing." Now is the time to plead for mercy. All of the problems are with the ministers. Without God's word, the ministers are poor and the church is poor. It seems that too many people are setting their hopes on truth and knowledge. Few have set their hopes on revelation. In the end the gospel is preached, but few souls are saved. Messages are delivered, but few receive any blessing. If God's life does not follow His word, everything is in vain and is worthless. Our failure lies in the fact that we only see men praising God's word and God's preachers. Yet the words themselves do not convey burning light; the revelation is not strong enough to knock men to the ground. What is needed today is not more admiration of God's word, but more men falling on their faces at God's light. If as ministers we cannot accomplish this, we can only blame ourselves for the failure. May the Lord be merciful to us.

CHAPTER EIGHT

CHRIST AS GOD'S WORD

ONE

John 1:1-2 says, "In the beginning was the Word, and the Word was with God, and the Word was God. He was in the beginning with God." Here we are told that the Son of God is the Word. Christ is God's Word. Hence, the ministry of the word is the ministry of God's Son. To serve the church with God's word means to serve the church with God's Son. A minister of God's word dispenses God's word. Just like the seven deacons in Acts 6 who served by dispensing food to the saints, a minister of the word is one who serves by dispensing the word to others. Yet this word is not merely words per se; this word is a person. This word is Christ Himself. For this reason, serving others with the word means to serve them with the Son of God. A minister serves the church by ministering God's Son.

Some people can only serve others with biblical teachings. They cannot serve others with the Lord Jesus. They live in the realm of letters. They can only serve others with truths, doctrines, and teachings. Their service only goes this far. They cannot serve others with the Christ who is contained in the word. They cannot minister Christ to others. This is the problem with many people. God's word is Christ. The Bible is not merely a book; it is not merely pages of writings from which men receive doctrines and teachings. If the book, the Bible, is separated from the person, Christ, the book is a dead thing. In one realm the Bible is a book; in another realm it is Christ Himself. If a person remains in the first realm, all he has is the book, and he cannot serve as a minister of God's word. He can only minister doctrines, truths, and teachings to others; he cannot minister Christ to them. Only those who are in another realm can minister Christ to others.

TWO

Paul's word is clear. He said, "So then we, from now on, know no one according to the flesh; even though we have known Christ according to the flesh, yet now we know Him so no longer" (2 Cor. 5:16). Today we do not know Christ according to the flesh; rather, we have to know Him according to the Spirit. In other words, we do not know Him as the Jesus of Nazareth who walked on the earth, that is, the historical Jesus. Today we know Him as the Christ in the Spirit. We have to remember that those who know Him as the historical man do not necessarily know Him at all. Many Jews thought that they knew the Lord. They said, "Is not this the carpenter's son? Is not His mother called Mary, and His brothers James and Joseph and Simon and Judas? And His sisters, are they not all with us?" (Matt. 13:55-56). They thought that they knew Him because they knew these things. But we know that they did not know Him.

John the Baptist was a man from God. Yet he confessed, saying, "He who is stronger than I comes after me, the thong of whose sandals I am not worthy to stoop down and untie. I have baptized you in water, but He Himself will baptize you in the Holy Spirit" (Mark 1:7-8). To stoop down and untie someone's sandal was a work of slaves at the time of the Romans. When the master came to the door, the slave would stoop down and untie his sandals. This was a very humiliating work. John knew that the One who was to come after him was far greater than he. Did he understand it? Yes, he did. Was he clear about it? Yes, he was. Yet he did not know that the Lord Jesus was this very One who was to come after him. He was not clear about this. As far as their fleshly relationship went, John was Jesus' cousin. They had known each other since their youth. But he did not know that the Lord Jesus was the One who was to come after him. He said, "And I did not know Him, but He who sent me to baptize in water, He said to me, He upon whom you see the Spirit descending and abiding upon Him, this is He who baptizes in the Holy

Spirit. And I have seen and have testified that this is the Son of God" (John 1:33-34). On the day when the Lord Jesus was baptized, the Holy Spirit descended upon Him, and John recognized this Jesus, who had been his cousin for thirty years, as the Son of God. Prior to this time he was close to the Lord and very intimate with Him. Yet he did not know Him. It was the Spirit who opened his eyes to recognize such a One. A man could be with the Lord Jesus for thirty years on earth and yet still fail to know Him. During those thirty years, John the Baptist kept up his acquaintance with the Lord. Yet he only knew Him as his own cousin. He knew the historical Jesus, the Jesus from Nazareth, but he did not realize that this Jesus of Nazareth was God.

The Lord Jesus is God. At the time He walked on earth in disguise, men did not know Him. God was disguised among men, and men did not recognize Him as God. It takes God's Spirit to open men's eyes before they can recognize this Jesus as the Son of God and the Christ. The Bible, in a way, is like Jesus of Nazareth. Humanly speaking, it is a book. Perhaps it is a little more special than other books. But when God's Spirit opens a man's eyes, he will see that this is no ordinary book; it is God's revelation. It reveals God's Son. Just as Jesus of Nazareth is the living Son of God, this book is a revelation of the living Son of God. If we only see this book as a book, we do not know God's Bible. Those who do not know God's Son do not know Jesus. In the same way, those who do not know God's Son do not know the Bible. Those who know Jesus know God's Son. In the same way, those who know the Bible should know that the Lord Jesus is God's Son. They should know the very Son of God spoken of in the Bible. This book—the Bible—reveals God's Son; it reveals Christ. This is not an ordinary book.

When the Lord Jesus was walking on earth, His contemporaries had many things to say about Him. They criticized Him in many ways. Some said that He was Jeremiah; others said that He was one of the prophets. Some said this and some said that. But the Lord Jesus asked the disciples, "But you, who do you say that I am?" Peter answered, "You are the Christ, the Son of the living God." What did the Lord say? He said, "Flesh and blood has not revealed this to you, but My Father who is in the heavens." Knowledge of the Lord Jesus does not come from flesh and blood, but from the revelation of the heavens. Following this, the Lord said, "Upon this rock I will build My church" (Matt. 16:15-18). Without such a revelation there is no church. This is the foundation of the church. The whole church is built upon this foundation. When a man recognizes that the historical Jesus is God's Christ and Son, this seeing becomes the foundation upon which the church is built.

Some people lament, saying, "I was born two thousand years too late. If I had been born two thousand years earlier, I could have gone to Jerusalem and could have seen the Lord Jesus face to face. The Jews did not believe Jesus was the Son of God, but I would have believed." But even if these ones had been able to live, walk, and work together with the Lord Jesus every day, they still would not have known Him. They would have known the man Jesus only; they would not have known who He is. When the Lord was on earth, men conjectured much about Him. They realized that He was quite special, that He was different from other men. But they did not know Him. Peter, however, was a man who did not have to guess about Him. He saw Him and he knew Him. How did he know Him? First God shone His light on him and showed him that Jesus of Nazareth is the Christ, the Son of God. Without God's revelation, a man can follow the Lord everywhere and still not see. Even if a man followed the Lord to Caesarea Philippi, he still would not know who He is. A man can be with the Lord every day and still not know Him. He is not known through outward acquaintance but through revelation. The knowledge of the Lord Jesus is something that comes from revelation, not from acquaintance. If you do not have revelation, you may live with Him for ten years without knowing who He is. You will only know Him as the Christ and the Son of God when you have God's revelation, when He speaks within you, and when He unveils your inner eyes. Your outward acquaintance of Him is not a true knowledge of Him.

The same thing can be said of the Bible. God's Word is a person, and God's word is also a book. God's Word is Jesus of Nazareth, and His word is also the Bible. We need God to open our eyes before we can recognize Jesus of Nazareth as being the Word of God and the Son of God. In the same way, God has to open our eyes before we will recognize the Bible as being the word of God and a revelation of His Son. Those who were acquainted with the Lord Jesus and who lived with Him for many years did not know Him. In the same way, those who are acquainted with the Bible and who have read and studied it for many years do not necessarily know the Bible. There is the need of God's revelation. Only that which God reveals to us through revelation is living.

The story of the healing of the woman with a flow of blood in Mark 5 shows us that many people were pressing upon the Lord Jesus, but no one touched Him. Among them all, only the woman with the flow of blood touched the garment of the Lord. She thought that if she could only touch the Lord's garment, she would be healed. She had faith, and she was sensitive. She came to touch the Lord. As soon as she touched Him, she was healed. The Lord immediately asked, "Who touched My garments?" When the disciples heard this, they said, "You see the crowd pressing upon You and You say, Who touched Me?" (vv. 30-31). The disciples complained about the crowd that was pressing upon Him all around and wondered how the Lord could even ask who was touching Him. Yet as soon as someone touched the Lord, He knew it, and He could feel it. Many people pressed upon Him, but nothing happened to them. But the one who touched Him experienced an immediate change. Today, even if the Lord were to stand right next to you, He would do you no good if you were only pressing upon Him. Jesus of Nazareth is not known by pressing. Those who pressed against Him did not know Him. Only the one who had faith and discernment touched His garment and knew who He was. This man was Jesus of Nazareth, yet He was also the Son of God. Jesus of Nazareth was the Son of God. Many people pressed upon Jesus of Nazareth, but they did not touch the Son of God. Many people touch the outward Jesus, but they do not touch the Son of God.

The same principle can be applied to our reading of the Bible. Many people are pressing upon the Bible, but few touch the Son of God. You can touch God's Son through Jesus of Nazareth. You can also touch God's Son through the Bible. The problem with many people is that they only see the Bible; they have not touched the Son of God. When the Lord Jesus was on earth, men knew Him according to two different realms. In one realm men heard His voice and observed His movements but did not know Him at all. In another realm one person touched His garment and was healed. Many people saw Him, but only one knew that God was with this Jesus of Nazareth. I am afraid that when we introduce Jesus of Nazareth to others, we are merely introducing them to the Jesus of Nazareth who was in the flesh. In the same way, I am afraid that when we introduce the Bible to others, we are merely presenting a book to them. We should remember that those who pressed upon Jesus of Nazareth did not receive any benefit from Him. Many sick ones were not healed even though they pressed upon Him. Likewise, those who are pressing upon the Bible do not receive anything from this book. They receive nothing, just as the pressing crowd received nothing from Jesus of Nazareth. But some receive the light within, and they touch the Son of God within the book. The word that the Lord speaks to us is spirit and life. As soon as we touch this, we touch the ministry of the word. What we present to men should not be just a simple book. In presenting the book, we should also present the Son of God to them. A minister of the word is one who, while serving others with the word of God, also serves them with the Son of God. We serve men with Christ. Only as we present men with Christ can we serve as a minister of the word.

Some people only know the historical Jesus. They do not know the Son of God at all. When many people read the Bible, they only see the historical Jesus; they have never touched the Son of God within the Bible. The Bible is not merely a book, inasmuch as Jesus was not merely a man. Within the Bible we find Christ. If a man only touches the book without touching the Son of God, he does not have the ministry of the word.

In Luke 24:13-31 the Lord Jesus met two disciples on the way to Emmaus, and He walked with them. While they journeyed, the Lord asked them questions and they answered, or they asked and the Lord answered. The conversation was not short, and the Lord expounded the Scripture to them. When they were near Emmaus, they constrained Him, saying, "Stay with us, because it is near evening and the day is already gone by" (v. 29). The Lord went in and stayed with them. They even invited the Lord to their meal. During this long conversation, they did not recognize the Lord Jesus. Only when the Lord took the bread, blessed it, broke it, and gave it to them were their eyes opened. Then they recognized the Lord. This shows us that even when a man walks with the Lord side by side, he still may not know who He is. Even when he talks with the Lord, he can still be ignorant of who He is.

Brothers and sisters, even if the Lord were to speak to us, we still might not know who He is. Even if He were to stay with us, we still might not know who He is. We should know something about the Lord that is far deeper than the knowledge we can gain from staying with Him, walking with Him, or talking to Him. We will only know who He is when He opens our eyes. Walking with Him, talking with Him, and having Him expound the Scripture to us are not enough to guarantee that we will know Him. We must realize that genuine knowledge of the Lord is deeper than these things. We may lament in our heart that we were not with Him when He walked on the earth, but we should realize that even if we had been with Him, we would not have known Him any more than we would today. Today, one of the least or weakest of brothers knows the Lord Jesus as much as Peter. When the Lord Jesus was on earth, the twelve disciples knew Him but not in a way that was greater than the weakest among us can know Him today. We should not think that we will know Him just by staying with Him for a few years. We have to realize that the Lord the disciples knew in their spirit is no different from the Lord we know in our spirit today.

The fundamental question is what constitutes real knowledge of the Lord. Real knowledge of Him does not come from the outside. We need God's revelation before we can know the Lord. The Lord has to open our eyes and show us something before we can know Him. The Lord has to open our eyes. This is what being a minister of the word is all about. A man may spend much time studying. He may recite all the verses in the Bible and may be clear about all the doctrines in the Scripture. He may answer every question quickly, but it is possible that he does not know God's Son at all. One day when God opens his eyes, he will see the Son of God. When God opens our eyes, we see Jesus of Nazareth and we see Christ. In the same way, when God opens our eyes, we see the Bible and the Son of God revealed in the Bible.

This is not to say that the work of the Lord Jesus on earth was not important. We are saying that a man has to believe that Jesus is the Christ before he can be begotten of God. If a man believes that He is the Son of God, he is begotten of God. We not only must see that Jesus is the Christ, the Son of God, but we must see the Bible. One cannot take away Jesus of Nazareth and still have the Son of God or Christ. Jesus of Nazareth is the Son of God; He is the Christ. In the same way, one cannot take away the Old Testament or the New Testament and say that he knows Christ. He cannot take away the Bible and say that he knows the Son of God. Through the Bible, God gives us the knowledge of the Son of God. If we do not have revelation, we may read the book but only have knowledge of doctrines; we will not know the Christ contained in the book. This is a very fundamental issue. We can understand everything about this book and yet have not seen Christ at all. It is possible for us to touch this book without ever touching Christ.

What makes Christianity so complicated is the fact that there are two different realms. If all the outward things were taken away and only inward things were left, the situation would be much simpler: Those who have it would clearly have it, and those who do not have it would clearly not have it. But the problem is that there is a realm of "pressing" and there is also a realm of "touching." Some are pressing, while others are touching. The two are completely different. Pressing upon Jesus is absolutely different from touching Him.

Can we see the difference between these two? There are two different realms. The pressing ones are in one realm, and the touching ones are in another realm. Those who are in the pressing realm experience nothing, while those in the touching realm are healed of all their sicknesses and relieved of all their problems. In one realm there are intellectual ones who can understand the Bible, the doctrines, and the truth. But in the other realm, one encounters light, revelation, and the anointing of the Holy Spirit. Brothers, do we see this? There are two different realms. In one realm there are the teachers of letters. In the other realm there are the ministers of God's word. We can only preach what we know. God has to bring us to a point where we touch the inner realm. We cannot know the Lord Jesus in the realm of "pressing"; we cannot know the Bible in that realm either. We must get into the realm of "touching" before we can be useful. Only in that realm do we find God's speaking. Only that realm will issue in any results, and only that kind of "touching" will yield any results. The amazing thing is that the Lord did not feel anyone pressing upon Him, but He was very conscious of someone touching Him.

A simple brother who has nothing and who knows nothing may come to the Bible and contact the word in fear and trembling, and in the Lord's presence, he may see light. Another brother may be well acquainted with the Greek and Hebrew languages. He may be very good at Chinese and English and may have read the Bible from cover to cover many times. He may even have memorized the Bible. But if he has never received any light from God, he cannot be a minister of God's word. The most he can do is pass on Bible knowledge to others. He cannot minister Christ to the church. The Bible is living; it is a person. In fact, it is the Son of God Himself. If we do not touch this living word when we read the Bible, whatever we know will not yield any fruit.

THREE

Our Lord taught many things when He was on the earth, and many heard Him. In John 8 the Lord Jesus said many things. He spoke of an adulterous woman being forgiven.

Later He told the Jews that the truth would set them free and that they did not have to remain slaves but could be free instead. The Jews responded by saying that they were the descendants of Abraham and were not slaves. But the Lord replied that everyone who sins is a slave of sin (vv. 32-34). The Jews might or might not have understood this word. Yet they certainly could not say that they had not heard it. Their ears were not heavy, and they were not deaf. Yet the Lord Jesus said something very peculiar: "He who is of God hears the words of God; for this reason you do not hear them, because you are not of God" (v. 47). Hearing something involves more than just hearing the voice. Some people hear the voice and have God's speaking. Others hear the voice but do not have God's speaking. These are two different realms. If we were to ask the Jews whether or not they had heard the Lord's words, they would have said yes. Yet the Lord said that they had not heard anything, because they were not of God.

This is a very sobering matter. One does not hear God's speaking simply by being at the place where He is speaking. A man may be present at the site of the speaking and yet hear nothing at all. He may hear all the sounds and all the words, but the Lord Jesus may say that he has not heard anything. The hearing referred to by the Lord Jesus is something totally different. There are two kinds of hearing, and they belong to two different realms. One can hear things of one realm but may not hear things of the other realm. This is a basic problem with many people. They hear the words of the Scripture, but they do not hear God's speaking. The Lord was speaking to these people. We cannot say that they were all fools. We cannot say that they were all sick in their mind or heavy in their ears. They all knew what the Lord was saying. Otherwise, how could they have rebuffed the Lord Jesus? They rebuffed Him because they had all heard His word. Nevertheless, the Lord Jesus said that those who are of God hear God's words but that the others did not hear because they were not of God. This is where the fundamental problem lies. Many people only hear voices from one realm; they do not hear any voice from the other realm.

They only understand words from one realm; they do not understand any word from the other realm. They do not hear because they are not of God. The Lord Jesus was saying that some do not understand His word because they are wrong in their person. In verse 43 the Lord Jesus said, "Why do you not understand My speaking? It is because you cannot hear My word." Fleshly ears can only hear words of flesh; they can only hear words from one realm. Words from the other realm can only be heard with a different kind of ear. Only those who are of God can hear; those who are not of God cannot hear.

When many people come to the Bible, they only hear the outward shell of the Lord's word. They only grasp the appearance of His word. But God's word is in an entirely different realm. We must deal with this matter. If we cannot hear His word, we cannot be ministers of His word. What do we mean when we say that a man does not hear God's word? It is possible for the Lord Jesus to stand in front of you and speak for two hours, yet you hear nothing. This means that you have not heard God's word. You may hear everything that the Lord says and write it all down. When you go home, you may memorize it all, yet you still have not heard anything. In other words, you have heard nothing of God's speaking; you have only touched the outward shell of the word. You have heard it, yet you still do not understand it, and it has not entered into you. Some people are all the time touching the outward shell of the Bible; they think that they are ministers of God's word. But we must emphasize that this is not what is required at all. Today inspiration must be complemented by revelation before it can become God's speaking; inspiration alone is not enough. The Bible is God's inspiration, but it must be complemented by revelation before it can be called God's speaking. If all we have is inspiration, we do not have God's speaking; instead, we only have the outward shell of the word. We may boast that we have read the Bible a great deal, but I do not know if we have heard God's speaking. We cannot deny that those in John 8 heard the Lord's word. Yet the Lord said that they had not heard it.

We must understand what God's word is. God's word is the word behind the word, the voice behind the voice, and the language behind the language. What makes God's word so special is that the natural ear, the ear of flesh, can hear His word and yet this hearing does not count. A man may be very intelligent in his natural makeup. He may be very capable, possessing very quick thoughts and a very good mind. Do you think that such a person can hear the Lord's word? Please remember that his hearing may only touch the outward shell of the Lord's word; it may only touch the things related to the physical side of the Bible. This hearing only brings a person into contact with the physical realm; it does not bring him into contact with the spiritual realm of God's word. God's word belongs to another realm. It is wrong to presume that anyone can hear God's word. No, only those who belong to God can hear this word. Whether or not there is the capacity to hear depends on the very person himself. If my physical ears have a problem, I cannot hear the Lord Jesus' word in one realm. If my spiritual ears have a problem, I cannot hear the Lord Jesus' word in another realm. I can be in two realms, and His word can be in two realms as well. One of these realms is physical, and the other is spiritual. If I remain in the physical realm, the most I can hear is the physical side of the Lord's word. I can hear and understand it, but the Lord will still say that I have not heard it. He does not want me to hear those kinds of words. He wants me to hear words of another realm. There may be thousands and millions of men who have heard one kind of words, but there may be only eight or ten people who have heard the other kind of words. This is the problem with many people when they come to the Bible. They only touch the outward façade of the Bible without touching the Christ who is within the Bible. This is like a man touching Jesus without touching the Son of God. It is useless to just see the Bible, the book, without touching God's word or His Christ.

Let us read 1 John 4:6: "We are of God; he who knows God hears us; he who is not of God does not hear us. From this we know the Spirit of truth and the spirit of deception." John was not at all apologetic. He said that we should have the confidence that we are of God and of the truth. Those who know God will hear us, and those who do not know God will not hear us. This is what John meant. This shows us that the apostles felt that it was not just a matter of whether or not one heard the sound, the physical voice. At that time John was very old. Those who listened to him might have been very familiar with his voice. They could not have missed the voice of John. Yet the strange thing is that John said only those who knew God would hear him; those who were not of God could not hear him. This shows us clearly that it is not a matter of having or not having a voice or having or not having ears. There is no problem with the ears; they can hear very well. Yet John said that those who are not of God could not hear. God's word is in another realm, another world. Not everyone who knows the Bible knows God's word. Not everyone who can speak about the Bible can speak God's word. Not everyone who receives the Bible can receive God's word. A man has to build up a certain relationship with God before he can hear God's word.

Three verses in the Gospel of John can be put together and considered in parallel. John 4:24 says, "God is Spirit, and those who worship Him must worship in spirit and truthfulness." John 3:6 says, "That which is born of the flesh is flesh, and that which is born of the Spirit is spirit." John 6:63 says, "The words which I have spoken to you are spirit and are life." These three references to the word *spirit* are very significant. God is Spirit, the Lord's word is spirit, and the Spirit begets spirit. The Lord's word is spirit. Therefore, only a man of spirit can understand it. Only things of the same nature can understand each other. The word which is outside is merely a voice. A man can read the words of the Bible, study them, hear them, and know what they say. But within this word is something called spirit. It is something that the ears cannot hear and the mind cannot understand. The word of the Lord is spirit. Hence, it is impossible for the mind, the intellect, or any amount of human wisdom to understand this word. It is likewise impossible for the mind, the intellect, or any amount of human wisdom to convey this word. The Lord's word is spirit. Therefore, only those who are born of the Spirit will hear it. Those who are born of the Spirit are men of spirit. They have something within them. With regard to God's word, a man must be retrained and reconditioned before he can hear God's speaking. This is something that belongs to another realm. It is not something that belongs to the ordinary realm.

By now, brothers, do we see this? Why must the outer man be broken? Because without such breaking, a man can never be a minister of God's word. The outer man has nothing to do with God's word. Our wisdom, emotions, feelings, thoughts, and understanding are useless. (Shortly, we will see that they do have some use. What we are saying here is that they are useless as fundamental organs for receiving spiritual things.) God's word is spirit, and only those who exercise their spirit will hear it. We must be very clear about this principle: God is Spirit and those who worship Him must do so with their spirit. God is Spirit, and those who receive His word must receive it with their spirit. We cannot receive spirit with the mind. Only things of like nature can receive each other. Nothing else will work.

Matthew 13:10-15 says, "And the disciples came and said to Him, Why do You speak in parables to them? And He answered and said to them, Because to you it has been given to know the mysteries of the kingdom of the heavens, but to them it has not been given. For whoever has, it shall be given to him, and he will abound; but whoever does not have, even that which he has shall be taken away from him. For this reason I speak to them in parables, because seeing they do not see, and hearing they do not hear, nor do they understand. And in them the prophecy of Isaiah is being fulfilled, which says, 'In hearing you shall hear and by no means understand, and seeing you shall see and by no means perceive. For the heart of this people has become fat, and with their ears they have heard heavily, and their eyes they have closed, lest they perceive with their eyes and hear with their ears and understand with their heart, and they turn around, and I will heal them.'" The disciples asked why the Lord would speak in parables. He answered, "Because to you it has been given to know the mysteries of the kingdom of the heavens, but to them it has not been given" (v. 11). What is the reason for this? Something happened in Matthew 12. Certain ones blasphemed the Holy Spirit. The Lord Jesus cast out demons by the power of the Holy Spirit, yet these ones hated the Lord so much that they insisted the Lord's casting out of demons was by Beelzebul (vv. 28, 24). They knew very well that it was a work of the Holy Spirit, but they insisted that it was a work of Beelzebul. They knew that the Holy Spirit was the One who had done this, but they insisted that Satan, "the lord of the dunghill," was the one who had done this. To call the Holy Spirit Beelzebul, "the lord of the dunghill," was a blasphemy to Him. Therefore, in chapter thirteen, the Lord spoke in parables. In other words, from that time forward, these people would see but not understand what they saw. They would hear that a man went out to sow, but they would not know what this meant. They would hear that an enemy came in to sow tares while the man slept, but they would not know what the tares meant. They would hear that a net was cast into the sea but would not know what the casting of the net meant. They would hear that a woman took leaven and hid it in three measures of flour but would not know what the leaven meant. They would hear everything but not understand it.

From the time the Jews blasphemed the Holy Spirit, they no longer heard anything but parables. Today we speak in parables in order to make people understand. But when the Lord Jesus spoke to these people in parables, His intention was that they would not understand. The Lord intentionally used the parables to keep them in the outward realm without understanding what the words really meant. They only heard the outward letter of things, such as the sowing, the wheat, the tares, the net, and the leaven; they did not know what they meant. Many people today read the Bible in the same way that the Jews listened to the parables; they only know that the sower went out to sow. They only know about the good ground, the thorny ground, the shallow and stony ground, and the thirtyfold, sixtyfold, and hundredfold return. They do not know anything more than this. They hear the words, yet they know nothing. This is the way many people read their Bible. They only see the outward things, not the inward things. It is interesting that the Lord Jesus purposely spoke in parables to keep them from understanding anything. The Jews thought that they knew everything. Actually, they knew nothing.

FOUR

What is the ministry of the word? The ministry of the word is related to the things behind the parables. It is related to the things behind the outward words. A man can only see these things when his condition before God is proper. The Jews' hearts had become fat. Of course, they could not hear this word. Their ears had become heavy, and their eyes had become closed. The problem today is not the lack of God's word but the ignorance among God's children concerning His word. What men today consider as God's word is nothing but parables and outward words. Brothers, a man can touch the Bible, but that does not mean he is touching God's word. In order to touch God's word, one has to touch the Bible. This is a fact, and this is necessary. However, it is not enough to just touch the Bible. We have to say to the Lord, "I want to see the word within Your word. I want to see the light within Your light, and I want to see the revelation within Your revelation." If we do not touch the very thing behind the word, we can say all we want to others, but we will have nothing to minister to them. If we do not see the thing behind the word, we cannot communicate Christ to others. We have to see the Lord behind the word. We should not see the Bible only but the Lord Himself. Once we know the Lord, we know the Bible. One does not know the Lord simply by understanding doctrines. It is possible many of those who understand doctrines do not know the Lord. One does not know the Lord simply by knowing the truth contained in the word. Only as a person sees the light of glory on His face is he clear about everything. When we see the light of glory on His face, many of the problems with God's word go away. When we know the Lord, we know the Bible. When we know Christ, we know God's word. Unless we have this kind of experience, we have no way to minister Christ to the church.

Once a man lives before God and finds out what the Lord is like, he will spontaneously find the same thing in the Bible. He will readily be able to relate a passage to something he sees in the Lord or to something the Lord has expressed through him. This is the reason someone has said that every part of the Bible is about Christ. Brothers, once we know Christ, the Bible becomes living. The crucial matter is whether or not we have the revelation of Christ. If we have the revelation of Christ, the knowledge of the Bible will confirm our knowledge of Him. Otherwise, the Bible will remain the Bible, and the Lord will remain the Lord. We will only be able to minister the Bible to the church; we will not be able to minister Christ to the church. But if in presenting a portion of the Scripture, we present Christ, we are ministering Christ to people. As we present a portion of the Word, we present Christ to men. As we present another portion of the Word, we present Christ again to men. We are not just quoting biblical terms and biblical words, we are ministering Christ to the church. If a man does not learn to know Christ, he cannot know the Bible. It is useless to engage in mere exposition, exegesis, or some superficial understanding of the Scripture. We must remember that leading people to a knowledge of the Bible and leading them to a knowledge of Christ are two entirely different things.

The ministry of God's word is a very subjective thing in man. It is not a matter of finding out what the Bible says and then telling others about it. This kind of telling is altogether objective; it cannot be considered as the ministry of the word. Every minister of the word has to be a man of revelation, one who has seen something subjectively. A man must have revelation, and he must see something subjectively. Then he can claim the Bible as his basis. Only then will he be able to minister Christ to others through the Scripture. One person may expound the Bible according to the Bible. Another person may expound the Bible according to Christ. These are two entirely different matters. Today we can find many people expounding the Bible. Their inward condition may be altogether different however. Some expositions may focus on the Bible, while others may focus on Christ. The latter is based on first receiving a revelation, a vision, or some kind of knowledge before God and then learning what the Bible says. The message that is delivered is based on a comparison of the two. This is to minister the Christ of revelation. It is not a mere presentation of the Scripture according to what is objectively understood. We admit that many exegeses are useful, and that these exegeses can save a young, inexperienced person from many errors and frustrations. But any serious ministry or service is not built merely upon exegesis. When a man lives before God, knows the Lord, and knows Christ, he can pick up a passage here and a passage there. He serves as a minister, and he has God's word. He picks up various passages of the Scripture and puts them together. This is how he ministers Christ to the church.

In order to be a minister of God's word, one must have a fundamental knowledge of Christ. Many times, as a person's knowledge of Christ before God increases, he finds that what he knows of Christ has gone beyond what he knows from the Bible. Eventually, he may find the very same thing in the Bible. Then he will know that he has a message to deliver, because Christ has become the word to him. This is a very basic factor in ministry. At the beginning the Lord reveals Himself to you and shows you what He is; you see something which you have not seen in the Bible. After a few days, perhaps a year or two, you see the same thing in the Bible, and you exclaim, "This was what I learned from the Lord on that day!" Perhaps one, two, three, or four passages of the Scripture will stand out, and gradually, the Christ you know in your revelation becomes the word, and you know that the Lord is preparing you to be a minister of the word. Perhaps after a few days, the Lord will arrange a situation for you to release this word. In this way, the words you release will become the embodiment of Christ to others. If God is merciful to them, these words will become Christ to them, and they will know Christ. This is the ministry of the word. The Christ we know by revelation gradually becomes the word in us. We search the Scripture, and gradually find this word in one, two, nine, or ten different places in the Bible. When this happens, we minister this word, which is the embodiment of Christ, to others. If God grants mercy and grace to the listeners, the Holy Spirit will operate in them when they hear such a word, and the word will become the Christ who ministers to their need. This is what it means to minister Christ. We minister Christ through the words of the Scripture. When others receive the word, they receive Christ. This is the basis of all ministry of the word.

Brothers, we have to see and differentiate between the outward way and the inward way. In order to be a minister of the word, we must have the word. But this word is what we see before the Lord. This word is what we touch in Christ. Once we touch Christ, the Son of God, this book will spontaneously become the living word to us. If before the Lord we only see this book, the Bible, we will not have many words to minister to others. At the most we will only have exegesis. This may provide others some understanding of the Bible, but it is not enough to lead men to the Lord. It may render others some help in the truth, but it is not enough to lead them to Christ.

We must realize what God's word is. What does it mean to touch His word, and what is a minister of the word? We need to pay the price. Our heart must not become fat, our eyes must not be closed, and our ears must not become heavy. We need to see God. May our ears hear God and our eyes see Him. We should never be those who see, yet do not see, and who hear, yet do not hear. What is before us are two realms. We need to possess the things of both realms. We need the word that belongs to the outer realm, and we need to touch the word that belongs to the inner realm. If we do, we will gradually become a useful vessel in the hand of the Lord.

May the Lord be merciful to us, and may we see that God's word is Christ, just as Jesus of Nazareth was Christ. The man of flesh and blood who walked on the earth was Christ, and the Bible is also Christ. Jesus, the man who walked on the earth in flesh and blood, is God's Word. In the same way the Bible, the written and printed Scripture, is also God's Word. We must touch not only the outward things but also the inward things. Only then will we have the ministry of the word. Those who do not know Christ can memorize all the Scripture, but they still cannot be a minister of the word. We should prostrate ourselves before God. We need revelation. When our words go forth, God's children should fall on their faces. It is not a matter of degree but a matter of one's basic nature. The very nature of many ministers is wrong. If God is merciful to us, we will prostrate before Him, and we will have a new beginning. We have to touch the Bible through the Lord, and our service in the ministry of the word must be based on this. If we do this, we will have a way to go on.

CHAPTER NINE

KNOWING GOD'S WORD THROUGH CHRIST

ONE

A minister of God's word is one who has received the revelation of Christ. This means that it has pleased God to reveal His Son in him. One must not only be able to speak the word with his mouth but must know in an inward way that Jesus is indeed the Christ, the Son of the living God. Jesus of Nazareth is the Christ, the Son of the living God. This statement only takes a few minutes to memorize, but the Lord said, "Flesh and blood has not revealed this to you, but My Father who is in the heavens" (Matt. 16:17). The knowledge of Christ is a matter not of words but of revelation. A minister of the word is one who receives mercy from God to have a revelation concerning God's Son. He is a man to whom God has chosen to reveal His Son; he has a basic revelation that enables him to know who Jesus of Nazareth is. When a man has seen the Son of God, all holiness, righteousness, light, and life pass away under such a vision, and only Christ remains.

Nothing in this universe can compare with Christ. No spiritual thing can compare with Christ. Christ is all and in all. Apart from Christ, one cannot find life, light, holiness, or righteousness. Apart from Christ one cannot find anything. Once God brings a man into the revelation of Christ, he will realize that there is nothing outside of Christ. Christ is everything. He is God. He is the Son of God and the Word of God. He is love, holiness, righteousness, salvation, redemption, freedom, grace, light, and work. Christ fills all. All that we have seen in the past cannot stand up to the light of the Lord today. All things will pass away. Nothing can stand up to this great revelation. Moses is gone. Elijah is gone. Peter,

James, and John are all gone. Only Jesus remains. He fills all and is all. Christ is both the centrality and the universality. God's center is Christ, and God's universality is also Christ. He is the center and the universality.

When a man is brought to Christ and has a knowledge of Him, this basic experience will enable him to know God's word and to minister Christ to others. In order to serve, to minister Christ to others, and to supply others with Christ, a man must have the revelation of Christ. Every minister of Christ must have the revelation of Christ. He cannot supply others with what he has not seen himself. He cannot minister to others a Christ that he does not know. He cannot supply others with a fragmented knowledge of Christ. Such a "fragmented" Christ cannot constitute the basis of ministry. A ministry is not built on the basis of a fragmented knowledge of Christ. Since the day of Paul and Peter, everyone who has a ministry of the word before God has had a fundamental revelation of Christ. A man must be brought on by God to the point where he knows God's Son face to face in the deepest part of his being. To him, Christ must be the One who transcends all, is all, and fills all. Only then can he minister such a Christ to others. From that day forward, he can minister Christ to others. From that day forward, the Bible becomes a living book to him.

Do you see what I am saying? God's revelation enables us to know Christ. A man can say with his mouth that Jesus of Nazareth is the Christ, the Son of the living God, and the Anointed One through reading the Bible. But this does not mean that he has touched Christ. A man can understand something about Christ through studying the Bible, but this does not mean that he has the revelation. Many are "pressing" Christ along the way, but they do not necessarily touch Christ. Today what we need is God's mercy. We need His light and His grace. God has to grant us mercy and grace and reveal His Son in us. It is not a matter of studying and researching but a matter of mercy and revelation. It is a matter of inward enlightening, inward discerning, and inward knowledge. This is what it is all about. From the day we receive mercy and revelation, the Bible becomes a new book, a living book. The words which were once unintelligible are now transparent. Before, the more we talked about things related to the Bible, the more we did not seem to understand them. They seemed logical, and yet we could not comprehend them. But once we see Christ, they become very clear to us. God's written word becomes obvious and transparent. We are inwardly clear; we are inwardly enlightened. We know Christ in an inward way, and we begin to understand the Bible. This fundamental revelation of Christ enables us to know who Christ is.

TWO

What does it mean for God to reveal His Son in us? We cannot describe this; no one can describe it. Even Paul could not describe it. How can we tell whether or not a person has God's revelation in him? Some people can say that they have seen the revelation, whereas others are unable to say this. Some are clear, but others remain unclear. We struggle, labor, think, and pursue, yet we still do not see anything. But when God grants us mercy one day, our eyes are opened immediately.

Today we may pray to the Lord, "May You be my all. May You fill all and be all." We pray this way, yet we do not know what this means. We say what we do not understand. When God grants us mercy and reveals His Son in us, we will say spontaneously and effortlessly, "Thank God, He is everything. Christ is everything. All my past spiritual experiences are behind me. All my past works and pursuits are behind me. Even my love, faith, righteousness, holiness, and victory are behind me. Everything but Christ is behind me. Christ is everything." Only then can we say that He is over all and fills all. This is a fundamental revelation. It is on the basis of this revelation that we seek to understand God's word. This is the starting point from which we seek to understand the Bible. We begin by knowing God's Son. After this we proceed to know the Bible. As we go on in this way, everything will become transparent to us, and we will say, "I did not understand many things, but today I am beginning to understand them."

This is where a man must learn to turn and become like an infant. He must learn to be like a child. How does a child learn about a cow? There are two ways. First, he can have a book with the picture of a cow on the page and the word *cow* beside it. Second, he can be taken to see a cow. Which of these ways gives the child a more genuine understanding of the cow, a picture or a real-life cow? The cow in the picture is only a few inches tall. The child may think that a cow is only that tall. If you put him in front of the cow, however, his understanding will be different. Suppose a child has seen a living cow. Within him there is an impression of something—a cow. But he does not know what it is called. Now if you point out a cow to him in the book and tell him that it is called a cow, he will readily understand. His questions will be answered. We should be like a little child. May God cause us to know Christ at least once, to touch Him in a fundamental way at least once. When we read the Bible again, everything will be clear and obvious to us; we will see everything through the light of this book. Once the foundational experience is right, everything else will be right. Once this is established, everything else will be in place. Everything will be related and linked together.

If you merely give a person a Bible and tell him the things contained in it, you will not get very far. One brother studied many books on botany. He read about a certain plant with a certain kind of leaf and flower. He went up to the mountain in search of this plant but could not find it. It is relatively easy to learn a word by looking at a picture. But it is not that easy to identify an object by comparing it to a picture. This brother tried to find the plant by the description in a book, but he could not find it. The same is true when it comes to identifying a man. It is easier to look at a man first and then look at his picture. It may not be easy for us to identify a person from his picture. This is a very simple illustration. We find this experience among many children of God. We find this in Paul and Peter. One day God granted mercy to them, and they knew Christ. The Lord Himself said, "Flesh and blood has not revealed this to you, but My Father who is in the heavens" (Matt. 16:17). This is entirely a matter of

God's mercy and grace. We know His Son because He has chosen to reveal Him to us. From the day we begin to know Him, we begin to know the Bible. In order to know the Bible, we have to know Christ first.

THREE

The basic issue is: Are you simply ministering to others from this book, the Bible, or are you one who has met Christ and who has a revelation of Christ? Are you one who has met and encountered the Lord fundamentally? Do you have a fundamental understanding of the Lord? If you do, you will spontaneously say, "Thank God, many things in the Bible are clear to me now." From that time forward, day by day as you read the Bible, you will find passage after passage making sense to you. An inward knowledge of the Lord comes first, while a knowledge of Him through the Bible comes later. Once you have the subjective knowledge, you will find God's word understandable and self-harmonizing when you study it again. What were problems to you now become meaningful revelations, and what was once insignificant now becomes very significant. Everything fits together; all the parts are linked up and nothing is insignificant any longer. From that point on, your days on earth will become days of knowing the Bible. Day by day what you see will match what the Bible says; the two will testify to the same things. You may not see everything all at once, but it will appear to you little by little, and you will see more as the days go by. We do not understand the Bible through the Bible. Rather, we know the Bible through inward light and inward revelation.

The misguided mind always wants to take the way of the intellectual man. Man thinks that he can study the Bible by himself. He thinks he can make the effort to understand it. He thinks that he can read it with or without prayer. He thinks he can study it, and he trusts in his study. But this is a wrong way. When the Lord Jesus was born, many Jews were very familiar with the Bible. Herod asked where Christ would be born, and the chief priests and scribes answered without looking it up that Christ would be born in Bethlehem of the land of Judah. They even quoted the Scripture which

says, "And you, Bethlehem, land of Judah, by no means are
you the least among the princes of Judah; for out of you shall
come forth a Ruler, One who will shepherd My people Israel"
(Matt. 2:6). They could recite the Scripture. But did they
know Christ? Although they were so familiar with the Bible,
they did not use it to find Christ. Instead, they used it to
try to kill Christ. They used it to help Herod try to kill God's
Anointed. How wrong one can become in reading the Bible!
How wrong a man can become by being familiar with the
Scripture! What kind of things a man can do by the so-called
understanding of the Bible!

When the Lord Jesus was on earth, the Scripture was
fulfilled point by point. While a person who knows nothing
about the Bible can be excused for not recognizing this, those
who knew the Scripture should have recognized immediately
that Jesus of Nazareth was the Son of God from the many
fulfillments of the Word. But did the Pharisees know this?
They did not know Christ nor could they accept Him. They
sewed the Scripture to the hem of their garments and their
girdles. They had a knowledge of the Scripture and could
expound biblical prophecies. They could tell others about the
teachings and doctrines of the Scripture, but they kept Christ
outside the door. A man can touch the Scripture without
touching Christ. The Pharisees made the Scripture mere
reading material, study curriculum, an object of doctrinal
research. They could understand the doctrines, but they
rejected the Savior.

At the same time that this was going on, there was
another group of people. They did not have any Bible
knowledge. Matthew was a tax collector. Peter was a fisherman. Even in Acts, they were considered "uneducated men
and laymen" (4:13). Yet they had met the Lord. They had
met Christ. God revealed His Son in them, and they knew
the Lord. Peter received from God the revelation of His Son
at Caesarea Philippi. He knew inwardly that Jesus was God's
Anointed, the very Son of God. As far as Christ's ministry
is concerned, He is the Christ of God. As far as His person is
concerned, He is the Son of God. As far as His work is concerned, He is the Christ of God. As far as His person is

concerned, He is the Son of God. This is the greatest revelation. The entire church is built upon this revelation. These
uneducated laymen knew the Son of God, and they knew the
Bible. Matthew was a tax collector; he had not previously
known the Bible. But because he knew the Lord, he could
tell us so much about the Old Testament in the New Testament. Once he knew the Lord, everything became clear. This
is not learning a word by seeing the picture, but rather,
identifying a picture by seeing the object. He first knew the
Lord, and then he found out about Him from the books of
the Old Testament. Suppose you know a brother personally.
When another person brings you a picture of this brother,
you can identify him in the picture immediately. You must
first know Christ before you can know His book.

The trouble with some people is that they turn the order
of Christ and the Bible around. They want to know the Bible
first and then know Christ. But it is possible for a man to
know the Bible yet at the same time to not know Christ.
Matthew and Peter received mercy from God to have Christ
first revealed in them. When they read the Scripture afterwards, every sentence was clear to them. We are not Jews
and may not realize the significance of this. Suppose we were
Jews and lived as Old Testament men in the land of Judea.
When we studied the Old Testament according to the outward
letter, the whole book would be a mystery to us. Today, the
Old Testament is still a mystery to many unbelievers and
so-called theologians. But Peter, Matthew, John, and James
met Jesus of Nazareth, and God revealed His Son in them.
The more they read the Old Testament, the more it was opened
to them. When they came to a passage, they could say, "This
is a fulfillment of what was written." Throughout this book,
from Genesis 1 to Malachi 4, they found that this Jesus of
Nazareth was the Son of God, the very Christ. They did not
know the Scripture through the Scripture itself, but through
Christ. Those who know Christ know the Bible spontaneously.
Many so-called Christians, nominal Christians, have read the
Bible for years but know nothing about it. However, once they
see that Jesus is the Savior, they have a different feeling
altogether when they read the Bible. It is a new book to them.

Hence, when one knows the Lord, he knows the Bible. Revelation comes from Christ. Once a person has a revelation of Christ, he has a revelation of the Bible. Those who think that they know the Lord just from the book do not necessarily have revelation. The experiences of many who know the Lord tell us that it is useless to study the Bible by itself. We must remember that a man must first know Christ before he can know the Bible. This was the case with the twelve disciples. It was the same with Paul. He was a Pharisee, that is, one who knew the Scripture very well. The Pharisees were very familiar with the Scripture, yet they did not know the Lord. Although Paul was a good and pious Pharisee, and although he knew the Scripture very well, he persecuted those who were of the Way (Acts 9:2; 22:4). It is possible for a man to know and be familiar with the Bible and yet still persecute the Lord Jesus. Paul was such a man. Paul did not study the Scripture and then suddenly realize one day through his study that Jesus is the Son of God. Rather, God shone on him one day, which brought him the realization that this One was the Lord. Here was a man who hated and persecuted the Lord. He sought out believers, both male and female, in order to bring them bound to Jerusalem. He was a stern persecutor of the church. What a wicked person he was! Yet as soon as God flashed His light on him, he fell to the ground and heard a voice saying to him, "Saul, Saul, why are you persecuting Me?" Immediately he answered, "Who are You, Lord?" and went on to inquire of the Lord what he should do (Acts 9:1-6; 22:10). The prostration was genuine. The fall was real. Paul's body fell, his self fell, and his whole being fell. Paul was humbled in his outward man, and he was humbled in his inward man. After he received this revelation, what do we learn of Paul in the rest of the book of Acts and in the Epistles? He was able to interpret the Old Testament. He was able to tell us that Jesus of Nazareth is the Christ, the Son of the living God. The Old Testament became an open book, a living book, to him.

You can read the Bible. But if you set aside the knowledge of Christ, your Bible becomes a closed book to you. This is why many educated and intelligent people find the Bible confusing and mysterious. You can tell them about all the merits of this book, but they will only shake their heads. To you this book is very clear, but to them it is very confusing. They do not know Christ. If a man knows Christ, he will know God's word. This does not mean that no one can find God by reading the Bible. Some do find God from reading the Bible. But this is a case of God's mercy; He chooses to enlighten such a person this way. While he is reading the Bible, God takes pleasure in revealing His Son to him and saving him. The way to know the Bible is by knowing Christ. Paul was led by God to the point where he could explain to others in his many Epistles who this Jesus was. When we read Romans, Galatians, and Ephesians, we find a man who was crystal clear about the Old Testament. Where did Paul's knowledge come from? He first knew Christ, and through that knowledge, he knew the Scripture.

FOUR

In order to be a minister of the word, we must begin by having a knowledge of Christ. Only after we have known Christ will we know the Bible, and only then will we be able to serve as a minister of the word. Anything short of that will not qualify us to be a minister of the word. Paul saw a great light and knew Christ. After he was saved, he went immediately to the synagogue to tell others that Jesus is the Christ. Acts 9:19-20 says, "And he was with the disciples in Damascus for some days. And immediately he proclaimed Jesus in the synagogues, that this One is the Son of God." However, the Jews would not believe his word. What did he do? "But Saul was all the more empowered, and he confounded the Jews dwelling in Damascus by proving that this One is the Christ" (v. 22). The Jews believed in the Old Testament. In order to confound them, Paul quoted from the Old Testament to prove that Jesus is the Christ. What a surprise that only a few days earlier this man had been persecuting those who called on this name and had brought them bound to the high priest! How could he be so empowered to prove that Jesus is the Christ from the Old Testament Scripture? This shows us that ministry of the word is based on the knowledge of Christ.

Let me repeat this: We do not lightly esteem the Bible. The foundation of God's word is based on the Bible. What we are saying is that those who depend on the Bible alone cannot be a minister of the word. Those who do not read the Bible do not have God's word. But those who are familiar with the Bible are not necessarily ministers of the word. Only those who know Christ can be ministers of the word. If you want to be an oracle of the Lord's word, you need a thorough and powerful shining to realize that Jesus is the Christ, the Son of God. Such a realization will humble you; it will cause you to forget about everything and to have a one-hundred-eighty-degree turn. Once you know the Lord this way, the Bible will become a new and open book to you, and you will understand this book.

This revelation of the knowledge of Christ was common to all the apostles. Matthew had this revelation. So did Peter, John, and Paul. The Lord Jesus said to Peter, "Upon this rock I will build My church" (Matt. 16:18). This meant He would build the church upon this knowledge. *Rock* does not refer just to Christ but also to the revelation of Christ. The Lord said that Peter's knowledge was not revealed to him by flesh and blood but by the Father who is in the heavens. This is revelation. This rock is Christ; this rock is also the Son of God. Our knowledge of this rock today comes from such a revelation. The Lord said, "Upon this rock I will build My church." This means the church is built upon Jesus as the Christ and as the Son of God. This is the foundation of the church. The gates of Hades will not prevail against the church because the foundation of the church is Christ; this foundation is the Son of God. But this is not all. We should pay attention to how we can know this Christ, this Son of God. Jesus of Nazareth is known to us by revelation, not by Bible expositions in the hands of flesh and blood. Today many people—men of flesh and blood—are expounding the Bible. Yet we do not know Him by such expositions. Our knowledge of Him comes from a revelation that is beyond flesh and blood; it comes from the Father who is in the heavens. It is God's speaking that ushers in a knowledge of who Jesus of Nazareth is. Today the church is built upon this rock. The church is built upon the rock of the knowledge of Christ that comes from revelation. Today the whole church should be built upon this rock.

A revelation concerning Christ was not only crucial to Peter, to Paul, to John, and to Matthew, but to the whole church today as well. If we want to serve God in the ministry of the word, we have to have this fundamental revelation. Otherwise, a man can teach the Bible, but he cannot minister Christ. A minister of the word serves men with Christ; he dispenses Christ to men. This work is based on our revelation of Jesus. We need revelation to see who Jesus is. The church must be built upon this foundation. Without this revelation, the church has no foundation. It must have the revelation and knowledge that Jesus of Nazareth is the Christ, the Son of God. Everyone who has received this revelation is begotten of God. Everyone who believes that Jesus is the Christ is begotten of God (1 John 5:1). Everyone who believes that Jesus is the Son of God is begotten of God. Such a one comes from God. God's life and power enable such a one to recognize Jesus as the Christ, the Son of God. When God gives a man a fundamental recognition and when he sees this matter clearly and accurately, his understanding of the Bible is drastically changed. He no longer supplies others with just the Bible but with Christ.

Anyone who wants to be a minister of the word needs to experience what Peter, Matthew, John, and Paul experienced at the beginning. Some brothers do not have a great deal of knowledge of the Bible. However, there is something special about them: They were all humbled by the Lord at one time, and they now know something. They know that Jesus of Nazareth, who is God's Christ, transcends all works. This Jesus of Nazareth, who is God's Son, transcends everything. Once this realization comes to a man, he begins to know how to teach the Bible. He knows Christ, and his exposition of the Bible is an excellent ministry of the word. Please remember that the basis of the ministry of the word is the knowledge of Christ, not a good knowledge of the Bible. This is not to say that Bible exposition is worthless or that Bible knowledge is harmful in any way. We are merely saying that a man who does not know Christ and who is just touching the Bible outwardly does not have the ministry of the word. Ministry of the word is based on inward revelation—not just the isolated revelations of different portions of the Scripture, but one basic revelation concerning Christ. Without this, one cannot minister anything even if he has memorized the Bible. If he has this inward revelation, an outward knowledge proves to be useful, and his exposition of the Bible is not only right but living as well. Then everything works together for good to the ministry. But if inward revelation is missing, outward things are worth little. Once a man is clear inwardly, the outward things fall into place.

Ministry of the word involves a knowledge of the One behind God's word. It is a question of who that person is. Once a man sees this, he has a basis upon which he can minister Christ through the Scripture to others. Ministry of God's word means to know Christ and then to supply others with Christ through the Bible. There is a difference between knowing Christ and knowing the Bible. A man does not have to be prostrate on the floor to know the Bible. As long as he has a good mind and applies some diligence to look in reference books, he will know the Bible. But being a minister of the word is a different story. A man has to be broken by God before he can be used as a minster of the word. If a man is honestly seeking God and then meets God one day, everything will become clear to him in the light. This revelation demands the sacrifice of our entire person. When a man begs for mercy, rejects his own thoughts and decisions, and prays for God's conquering light, which will cast him at the feet of Jesus of Nazareth and enable him to proclaim Him as Lord and confess, "Lord Jesus, from now on, I acknowledge that You are all, that You transcend all and fill all," this light will spontaneously produce a message in him, and he will become a minister of the word.

FIVE

What does a minister of the word do? We can say that a minister of the word translates Christ into the Bible, that is, he takes the word of the Bible and uses it to tell others about

Christ. In the end the Holy Spirit translates the words of the Bible back into Christ within those who have received the word. This is what it means to be a minister of the word. You must know Christ, and you must have a basic revelation and fundamental knowledge. A minister of the word translates Christ into the words of the Bible. This may sound peculiar to you, but it is a fact. He knows Christ as a living person, and the Bible is full of Christ. He receives mercy from God to see Christ, and he sees Christ in the Bible. Having familiarized himself with the Bible, he can speak with assurance concerning a certain passage, a certain story, or a certain teaching. We should note that there is a world of difference between having and not having this translation process going on behind the word. Some people proceed from the Bible when they talk about Christ; the Bible is their starting point. Others have Christ as their starting point. For them the living Christ is transformed into the word of the Bible. They put the Christ they know into the words of the Bible and present these words to others. When these words are presented before men, the Holy Spirit opens up the words and conveys Christ to them. If you do not know Christ and you merely present to others the words of the Bible, your work ends when your words end; nothing more will happen. You have merely passed the Bible on to others. The Bible is your starting point.

A man needs to know Christ. Those who have a fundamental knowledge of Christ put this Christ into the words of the Bible and release them to others. The Holy Spirit acknowledges these words. On the one hand, the ministers are speaking the words, and on the other hand, the Holy Spirit does the work. The Holy Spirit releases the speaking through the ministers, and the audience sees Christ. This is what it means to minister Christ. This is the ministry of the word. We are responsible for putting the Christ we know, gain, and see into words and presenting these words to others. This is the only way for the Holy Spirit to convey God's word to others. If our starting point is the Bible, doctrines, or teachings, then, when we are finished speaking, the Holy Spirit will not take up the words and will not be responsible for supplying others with Christ. We should not think that an exposition of the Bible alone ministers Christ. We can only minister Christ after we have known Christ. We must be thoroughly broken by the Lord. Only then do we have a way to go on. We must ask the Lord to give us a basic understanding, a knowledge of the basic revelation. We must know what Christ is like and what the Lord is like. Only then will our speaking of the Scripture be living.

What is a minister of the word? A minister of the word is one who ministers Christ by the words he speaks. When the word is released from his mouth, the Holy Spirit works, Christ is realized and known, and the church receives the benefit. We should not put all the blame on the listener. We should realize that we are the ones who should bear the full responsibility. The audience is used to teachings and expositions. For them a messages begins with the Scripture and ends with the Scripture, and it stops where the Scripture stops. They do not see the revelation or the Lord behind the Bible. This is why the church is poor and desolate. When we translate the Christ we know into the words of the Bible and allow the Holy Spirit to translate these words back into Christ, we have the word of God. We should translate the personified Word into spoken words. The Holy Spirit will then translate these spoken words back into the personified Word. Without such a translation work, there is no speaking. A minister of the word blends the personified Word together with audible words. When a minister of the word stands up to speak, one finds God's Christ and God's Son through the words he utters. A minister of the word puts Christ's very person into the Bible and then delivers Him to others. When he supplies others with the book, he supplies others with the person as well. This is what it means to be a minister of the word. Such a man is chosen by God to be a minister of the word. When his word goes out, God's word goes out. When the Bible is released, Christ is released. The two become one.

Today the church is poor because the ministers are poor. We have to ask God for mercy and light so that we will realize the meagerness of our revelation. Today many works are conducted in an outward way; many exegeses touch only superficial things. We do not know Christ deeply enough. We are not dealt with seriously enough. This is why the supply of Christ is meager along our pathway. We can tell others about the words of the Bible, but we cannot tell them about God's Word, which is Christ Himself. When God grants mercy and light, we see that in the beginning was the Word and this Word was with God. This Word was God; the Son of God is the Word. This Word became flesh. In other words, Jesus of Nazareth is the Word. This Bible is God's Word. This man is God's Word. When God chooses us to be a minister of the word, we find out that as we are speaking from this book, we are speaking about this man. When we convey the words of this book to others, we are conveying His person as well; we are conveying Christ to others. Our preaching should be for the ministering and dispensing of Christ to others. The ministry of God's word is the ministry of this very person.

One day when we find out what a minister of the word really is, we will realize that there is nothing we can do except to prostrate ourselves before God and say, "Lord, I cannot make it." Whether or not a person can be a minister of the word depends on his attitude before the Lord. What a hard word this is! Who can take this? We speak Christ by speaking Him through the word. We are not speaking about Him but speaking Him forth. We are not giving a message but speaking a person; this person is conveyed through us. When others receive our word, they receive Christ. When others hear our word, the Holy Spirit conveys Christ to them. This is what it means to be a minister of the word.

This is a grave matter. It is something beyond our capacity, something absolutely beyond our capabilities. Every servant of God should be conscious of his own worthlessness. All ministers of God's word have to prostrate themselves before Him. They should know that even though they can expound the Bible, preach the word, and teach others, they are powerless when it comes to supplying and ministering Christ to others through the ministry of the word. They can only prostrate themselves before the Lord. Today we have to look to God for mercy. We should make a fresh evaluation of everything we do. We have to see our worthlessness, our utter hopelessness. Unless the Lord grants us mercy, we can do nothing. It is a very solemn thing to be a minister of the word. It is not easy to be a preacher of the word. It is not a matter of how many times we have read the Bible. What we need is to minister Christ as a minister of the word before God so that others touch Christ when they touch the words we speak.

SECTION THREE

THE MINISTRY

CHAPTER TEN

THE BASIS OF MINISTRY

We have considered the subject of the person—the minister, and we have considered the word of the Lord. Now we turn our attention to the ministry itself.

We have seen that God's speaking, both through the Old Testament ministry of the word as well as through the New Testament ministry, contains human elements. But there is a danger: If a man does not have an ear and tongue of "an instructed one" (Isa. 50:4), he will project himself into God's word. If a man has not been dealt with and has not gone through the molding work of the Holy Spirit, it will be very easy to inject his own thoughts and feelings into God's word. When this happens, God's word is contaminated and defiled by man. What a danger this poses! Therefore, in order to secure a pure ministry of the word, God has to work on man; the outward man must be broken. A minister of God's word must come under severe restriction and divine discipline. Unless he comes under God's control, he will damage God's word.

There is a need not only for the breaking work of the Holy Spirit but also for the constituting work of the Spirit in us. Not only must the Holy Spirit deal with us through the cross to remove undesirable elements, but God must constitute the life of the Lord Jesus into us. In the case of Paul, the Holy Spirit constituted Christ into him so that he became different from his unregenerated condition. Paul's change was not due to a change in the flesh, but to a reconstitution of the Holy Spirit. When he spoke, the Spirit of God spoke. He stood on a high plane. He was so high that his speaking was the Lord's speaking. He said, "I charge, not I but the Lord..." (1 Cor. 7:10). This is what it means to have the ministry. Here was a man who was a minister of God's word. His human elements had been so thoroughly dealt with by the Lord that their addition to God's word did not contaminate it. God's word remained God's word. Not only was it not damaged, but it was perfected through the addition. The Holy Spirit can work in a man to such an extent that when he stands up to speak, others realize that the Lord is speaking. Here was a man who was given complete freedom to speak his own words. Because the Holy Spirit had done such a deep constituting work in him, however, his speaking became God's speaking, his judgment became God's judgment, and his approval and disapproval became God's approval and disapproval. This is the result of the deep work of the Holy Spirit in man.

Previously, we covered the subject of God's word. We saw that two crucial matters are involved. First, all subsequent revelations are based on preceding revelations. All of the New Testament ministries of the word were based upon the Old Testament ministries of the word. All of the ministries of the word today are based upon the ministries of the word in the past. All of God's revelations today are based upon His revelations in the Old and New Testaments. Hence, the Bible is the basis of all speaking. God does not speak additional words or independent words anymore; He speaks through what He has already spoken. He releases His light through His existing light. Today God does not shed independent light; He does not give men independent revelations. Rather, His revelations to men come through existing revelations. Second, in order for a man to be a minister of the word, he cannot base his speaking on God's Word alone, that is, on the Bible alone. He must touch Christ in a fundamental way at least once. He must have a fundamental revelation before he can build up his ministry of the word upon the Bible. These two things do not contradict one another. Ministries of the word today are based upon ministries of the word in the past. The New Testament is based upon the Old Testament. That which is latter is built upon that which is former. This is a fact. However, we have another fact before us: All ministers of the word must first meet the Lord apart from the Scripture and receive His revelation, the revelation of Christ, before they can use the Scripture as the basis of their ministry of the word. We must not neglect this point. One should not presume that he can speak as long as he has a Bible and is speaking from it. He must have a fundamental revelation from God before he can serve as a minister of the word through the existing written words of the Bible. He must have a basic revelation; he must meet Christ in a fundamental way before he can quote the Scripture.

EACH REVELATION RESULTING IN ONE OCCASION OF MINISTRY

In speaking of ministry, we have to realize that there are two kinds of revelations. The first is a basic revelation that is once for all. The other is a fine, gradual revelation. If we have received the revelation of Christ, this revelation is a basic revelation. Paul received this revelation. After receiving such a revelation, we will find what we have already seen of the Lord whenever we open up the Bible. This kind of finding is based on the initial vision and knowledge of the Lord. We must first prostrate ourselves before the Lord and acknowledge that none of what we knew before could stand before Him. Even our zealous service to God, like Saul's endeavors, must be ruled out. We should remember that Saul fell to the ground. He did not fall because of his sins. His fall was a fall with respect to the work. It was not a fall related to backsliding, but a fall related to zeal. Here was a man who knew the law, knew the Old Testament, and was more zealous than all the other Pharisees. He was so zealous that he was able to focus on only one thing at a time. When his mind was set on persecuting the church, he did his best to persecute the church. Because he thought that this was the way to serve God, he gave himself to it absolutely. Even though he was deceived, his zeal was real. When he was enlightened and smitten to the ground, he realized that what he had done was a persecution of the Lord, not a service to Him.

Although many people are saved, they are as blind as Saul was in their work and service. They think that they are on the way of serving God. But one day the Lord shines His

light on them, and they cry out from within, "What shall I
do, Lord?" I am afraid many people have never asked this
question once in their life. They have never once been moved
by the Holy Spirit to call the Lord, "Lord." The way many
people say "Lord" is like those in Matthew 7:21. They do not
call Jesus Lord in the way of 1 Corinthians 12:3. Here we
see a man who for the first time confessed Jesus of Nazareth
as Lord. For the first time, he said, "What shall I do, Lord?"
(Acts 22:10). He had done many things in the past. But here
he said, "What shall I do, Lord?" This was a falling down.
He fell from his work, from his zeal, and from his own
righteousness. Once this man received such a basic revelation,
the Bible became to him a new book, an open book.

Many people can only read the Bible with teachers by
their side. They can only understand the Bible according to
reference books. They do not have an understanding of the
Bible that comes from meeting the Lord. The amazing thing
is that once a person meets the Lord and is enlightened, the
Bible immediately becomes a new book to him. From that
day on, he touches a new book whenever he reads the Bible.
A brother once said, "When the Lord puts me under the light,
what I receive in an instant will be enough for me to preach
for a whole month." This is a word of experience. We must
have this basic revelation, a revelation that involves a touch
with the Lord. Such a revelation will lead us to many other
revelations, revelations that open us up to God's word. Once
we have this basic revelation, our reading of the Bible will
be a discovery. We will find God speaking in this and that
passage. We will know the Lord through one passage and be
clear about things concerning Him through another passage.
Day by day and passage by passage, we will accumulate many
revelations. When we serve others with this kind of revelation, we have a ministry.

Ministry is based on words that one receives from God.
When we meet Christ, we serve the church with the Christ
we know. Every time we serve, we need a fresh revelation.
Ministry involves seeing something before God. God presents
something in a new and fresh way to us. When we present
this to the church, we have revelation. Earlier, we said that

there are two kinds of revelation. The first is basic, while the second is detailed or supplementary. One kind occurs once for all, while the other kind occurs repeatedly. If we do not have the once-for-all revelation, we will not have repeated revelations. We must have the basic revelation first, before our person, our spirit, and our knowledge of the Lord and of the Bible can be useful. However, this does not mean that we can be ministers of the word immediately. The basic revelation qualifies us to be a minister. But the actual beginning of our service must be accompanied by the repeated addition of revelations.

Ministry is based on some basic knowledge and revelation. However, when God wants us to speak something, we have to learn to receive a fresh revelation that pertains to that particular speaking. A minister of God's word cannot presume that he can speak just because he has received a revelation once. Every time there is the ministry of the word, every time someone renders a supply from the word, there is the need for a fresh revelation for that particular purpose. With every service there is the need of a new revelation. For every supply there is the need of a new revelation. One must have a revelation before he can have a ministry. One does not receive a revelation and then live by it for the rest of his life. The basic revelation enhances one's ability to receive gradual and progressive revelations. The first revelation brings in many more revelations. The basic revelation brings in many subsequent revelations. Without the basic revelation, there can be no subsequent revelations. But even when there is the basic revelation, there is still the need for more revelations. A man may receive one basic revelation from God, but it does not mean that he can use this basic revelation year after year, continuously for the rest of his life and serve as a minister of God's word this way. Just as we depend on the Lord moment by moment for our life, our work follows a similar principle. Every revelation produces one occasion of ministry. One must have multiple revelations before he can have a multiple occurrence of ministry.

We must remember that every revelation only affords us the opportunity to fulfill our ministry once. It is impossible to have one revelation for two occurrences of ministry. A revelation is good only for the ministry of the word once. All subsequent revelations are built upon that first basic revelation. Without the basic revelation, it is impossible to have subsequent revelations.

These basic issues must first be settled before one can be a minister of God's word. Revelations have to be progressive, one being built upon the other. A single revelation cannot support a ministry forever. One revelation can support the ministry once. One revelation can only render service once. It is useless for a person to prepare a number of sermons and then try to use them when occasions call for them. It is not a matter of being familiar with a sermon and then preaching it everywhere. We have to remember that God's word is *God's word;* it is not our word. You may be very familiar with a message and may even be able to memorize it. However, in order to minister God's word, you must receive a word from Him whenever you are about to speak. You need repeated revelations before you can fulfill a ministry repeatedly. Each revelation will equip you for the fulfillment of your ministry just once.

SPIRITUAL THINGS BEING NURTURED
IN REVELATION

When you receive your basic revelation for the first time, you realize that the Bible is living. For example, you may see that Christ is your holiness, with emphasis on the word *is.* Christ *is* your holiness; it is not a matter of Christ making you holy. It is not Christ giving you His holiness but Christ becoming your holiness. Your eyes are opened to see that your holiness is not a work but Christ Himself. Your holiness is a person, just as your righteousness is a person. Your righteousness is not the sum of fifty or more things that you do. Christ is your righteousness. God has made Christ your righteousness. Your righteousness is a person. This is a basic revelation: Christ is your righteousness. He is your holiness. Your righteousness is a person, and your holiness is also a person. This is a glorious vision. After two months an occasion may arise for you to take up the ministry of the word. You have to tell the brothers and sisters that Christ is your holiness, and you have to show them the difference between holiness as a thing and holiness as a person. However, you must remember that you cannot count on the revelation you received two months ago. You need to ask the Lord again, "Lord, what should I say?" Only after the Lord has shown you the need to speak such a word will you have the ministry of the word. Every time God wants you to speak such a word, He has to shine once again upon the revelation you received. You have to see the same thing all over again, and you have to see it like you have never seen it before. It has to become something new in you. You are enlightened within, and you see the meaning of Christ as your holiness. When this happens, you can go to the brothers and sisters and preach to them about Christ as holiness.

What is a revelation? A revelation is a seeing of what is in Christ. The Bible is full of Christ, and revelation enables us to see all the things that are in Christ. Christ is our holiness; this is a fact. It is recorded in the Bible. But the first time we see it, it is new to us. When a man sees something by revelation, it is brand new; nothing in the world seems as new as it. It becomes vibrant with the power of life; it is fresh. Revelation is always new; it makes old things new.

We wish to point this out: Revelation not only makes the letters living, turning old things into new things and converting what is objective into something subjective; it actually makes the subjective things altogether new once more. A basic revelation turns all the objective things in Christ into subjective things in man. Before a man receives such a basic revelation, everything in Christ is objective to him. Once he receives such a revelation, all the objective things become subjective to him. But this does not mean that once this word is opened up, the job is finished. It does not mean that this one opening will supply a man with what he needs for the rest of his life. Even if we have received a revelation, we need a fresh revelation from God every time we minister the word and serve others with Christ so that the old things can once again be new.

We must remember that spiritual things have to be nurtured in the environment of revelation. God intends that all the things of Christ and concerning Christ be living in us. He intends that all these things be nurtured through revelation. His revelation can make the old things continually living in us. All the things of Christ have to be kept alive continually by revelation. Once revelation is removed, spiritual things no longer are living. You may think that you saw something in the past and that this vision qualifies you to say something today. But you will find out that you cannot give anything to others. The same is true with preaching the gospel. It is easy to remember that the Lord is the Savior and that your sins are forgiven. Sometimes you touch something when you preach the gospel. At other times, the more you speak, the less boldness you have; you feel like a dried-up bottle of glue. Clearly one speaking is with revelation, whereas the other is without revelation. Only things that are kept in the realm of revelation are living, fresh, powerful, and full of life. We must bear in mind that all spiritual things become dead the minute they are separated from revelation.

Today when we minister the word to men, we should not depend on our memory. We should not think that we are free to speak the same things again just because our past experiences and past speakings are still intact in our mind. Even though it worked for us the first time, it will not work for us this time. We may speak the same thing again, but afterward, we feel that something is wrong, that what we said was not the right thing. We feel that we are, in fact, quite far from the thing that we were speaking about; we do not touch that thing at all. Revelation is distinctly different from teaching. Man always has a wrong concept that he wants to be a teacher. We must see that doctrine and teaching are useless by themselves. We should never think that the ability to speak is all that matters. We may be able to speak, and others may appreciate our speaking, but we can be our own judge; within we know that something is wrong. We should bear in mind that many people receive help ignorantly. We should not congratulate ourselves just because others say that they have received help from us. Some may say that they have received help, but in actuality they have not received anything. We know within whether our speaking was on the mark or off the mark, old or new, dead or living. As we are speaking, if the Lord's revelation is with us and God's mercy is upon us, we will touch reality; there will not be a feeling of estrangement. We will be in touch, and the things we say will be living to us. As long as we have the assurance that the things in us are living, we are all right. We must forever remember that we need a fresh revelation from God every time we fulfill the ministry. This is what it means to have the ministry of the word.

First Corinthians 14 covers the subject of prophesying. All the prophets can prophesy and speak. But "if something is revealed to another sitting by, the first should be silent" (v. 30). Suppose there are some prophets, and one of them has a word to say to the brothers. While he is speaking, another also receives a revelation. He may say, "Brother, let me speak." The one who is currently speaking should let him speak, because the one who has received the revelation is the freshest; he has the most life and power. This is why he should be allowed to speak. Although all are prophets, the one who has received the latest revelation is the living one. It is possible that on this particular day, no one else has that word; only this brother knows this word because he has the revelation. Therefore, the rest should allow the one with revelation to stand up to speak. Our service in the ministry of the word is based on the revelations we continually receive. If we do not have continual revelations, we cannot serve properly as a minister of the word.

We should never presume that a message that once contained God's speaking will always contain His speaking. We should never presume that a message that once brought about repentance will always bring about repentance. This is impossible. The same message delivered in the same manner does not guarantee the same result. Only the same anointing will produce the same result. Only the same revelation will produce the same light. The same word may not produce the same light. How easy it is for a spiritual thing to become dead in us! It can easily become as dead as stagnant water in us. The ability to deliver the same message that was delivered three years ago does not mean that we have the same light that we had three years ago. Today we need to have the same revelation we had three years ago. Only then can we preach the same message we preached three years ago. Ministry of the word does not depend on the words we have spoken in the past, but on the new revelation we have acquired in the present.

The biggest problem with the church today is that many people think that they have many messages to give. They think that if they repeat the same message again and again, they will have the same result again and again. But this is impossible. It is a fundamental error to pay attention to doctrines rather than revelations. Even if a person spoke Paul's or John's very own messages, it would not work, to say nothing of repeating his own message. Only the same revelation will produce the same result; the same words will not produce the same result. Hence, the ministry of God's word is not a matter of word but of revelation. We do not serve on the basis of word but on the basis of revelation. We must remember that the ministry of God's word is the ministry of God's *revealed* word. We must differentiate between doctrine and revelation. What God said yesterday and the day before is doctrine; what He says today is revelation. What we remember is doctrine; what we see is revelation.

We know that the ministry of the prophets involves things for today and the future; it does not involve things of the past. The ministry of the prophets unveils God's desire today and in the future. This is why the Bible calls such men seers or prophets. A prophet is a seer; he is one who sees. In the Old Testament many prophets spoke prophecies. But some prophets did not really speak prophetically; rather, they proclaimed God's will for men in their times. When Nathan went to David, he foretold a little concerning the latter's wife and children. But Nathan primarily expressed God's thought; he was expressing God's heart concerning certain things that were happening then (cf. 2 Sam. 12:7-15). In the Old Testament the highest expression of the ministry of God's word was the prophesying and preaching of the prophets. If anyone wants to be a minister of God's word, if he wants to have the highest degree of ministry, he has to know what God wants today and what He wants for the future. He must have God's present-day revelation. He cannot remain in the old words or even words of the recent past. Many people can only hold on to what they saw in past years or past days. They do not have the present-day revelation. These ones cannot be ministers of the word.

TWO DIFFERENT REALMS

We must realize that there are two different realms. One realm is the realm of doctrine. In this realm a man only needs to convey to others what he has learned from school, books, and Bible expositors. All it takes is some work, cleverness, and eloquence. The other realm is the realm of revelation. In this realm a man can do nothing unless he has God's revelation. We must see that in the ministry of God's word, man is powerless and helpless apart from God's revelation. If God does not speak, we cannot force any word out of our mouth. If God does not give us His revelation, we do not know what to do. When God gives us revelation, we have the ministry. If God does not give us revelation, we have no ministry. The exercise of our ministry is based upon corresponding revelations. We have to be linked up to God in this realm. We must come to the Lord. If we do not come to the Lord, we cannot stand before men and speak. In the other realm we can use what we have memorized, learned, or spoken from the previous month or week. In that realm, man can do something; he can resort to his own ways. All he needs is memory, cleverness, and eloquence. But in the realm of revelation, no one can be a minister of the word unless God does the work. All who have learned this lesson before the Lord can discern this. Everywhere they go, they can tell which realm a person is in when he speaks.

Some brothers commit the fundamental blunder of regarding eloquence and intelligence as qualifications for a good message. They think that preaching is one hundred percent a matter of eloquence. But the Bible shows us that preaching does not depend on eloquence but on receiving revelation from the Lord. Preaching that contains no revelation merely nourishes man's mind. It can stimulate man's thoughts, but it cannot provide revelation.

This should be our concern: Unless we first have the basic revelation, we cannot have many subsequent revelations. Those who do not have the basic revelation do not have subsequent revelations. Even if they teach many doctrines, they cannot convey revelation to others. Those who are in one realm can only produce fruits from that realm. A listener with a good memory may retain a message for a few days, but after that time, the message goes away and nothing remains. A man can listen to our messages, but our word does not result in any condemnation of evil, the flesh, or the carnal man in him. Words from one realm can only produce fruits from that realm; they do not produce fruits from a different realm. Fruits of the outward realm consist of nothing but a collection of words, doctrines, and expositions. Sermons that are propagated in this realm consist of nothing but the fruits of this realm. But the other realm is different. If a person has received revelation once and is continually receiving revelations, he imparts revelation to others as he speaks. Only revelation produces revelation. Only light produces light. Only God's word results in the work of the Holy Spirit in man. Knowledge begets only knowledge. Doctrine begets only doctrine. In the same way revelation begets only revelation.

It is not enough for us to give doctrines to others. Neither is it enough for us to give old revelations to others. What are doctrines? Doctrines are past revelations. The words in the Bible were once living, but they are not necessarily living for everyone today. Only the words that the Holy Spirit has reiterated are living to man. When many people read the Bible, they only touch the words of the Bible; they do not touch the word of God. This is not enough. We need the Holy Spirit to speak a second time. We need the Lord to speak a second time apart from His established speaking. God has to speak directly to a person before he can hear God's word. A hundred people may listen to a sermon, but only two among them may receive any help. God may only speak to these two among the hundred; the other ninety-eight will not hear anything. Unless the Holy Spirit speaks, the words of the Bible are doctrine to us. We have to remember that all past revelations are but doctrines to us. Although God might have spoken to us and revealed Himself to us once through these words, the same words and revelation will be but doctrines to us without the anointing of the Holy Spirit today. They can only produce fruits of doctrine; they cannot produce fruits of revelation.

The problem today is that doctrines are passed on from generation to generation, yet there is no revelation. A believing father does not necessarily produce a believing son. The Holy Spirit may regenerate the first generation. He may regenerate the second generation. The third and fourth generations may turn out to be unbelievers. God's Spirit may work on the fifth generation again and regenerate it. Every regeneration is the result of the operation of the Holy Spirit. When a man begets a son in the flesh, his physical attributes pass on from his generation to the next generation, but there is no work of the Holy Spirit involved in this transfer. Regeneration involves the work of the Holy Spirit. Once the work of the Holy Spirit is withheld, there is no regeneration. These are two different things. One way conveys the doctrines. It is not hard to preserve doctrines for hundreds or even thousands of years. Doctrines produce doctrine, and the cycle continues. A man may know nothing except doctrines. While he preaches doctrines, two or three thousand people may be listening to him. What is in him are doctrines, and what goes out of him are also doctrines. These doctrines are passed on from generation to generation. This is like begetting children in the physical realm; one does not need the operation of the Holy Spirit to beget a son. But the same is not true with revelation and the ministry of God's word. The ministry of God's word requires the anointing of the Holy Spirit each time. The Holy Spirit has to operate in man in order for him to experience salvation. Similarly, there must be the revelation of the Holy Spirit before there can be the ministry of the word. As soon as the Holy Spirit stops His revelation, the word becomes nothing but doctrines. The Holy Spirit must operate before there can be the ministry of the word. Whenever the anointing ceases, there is no vision, no revelation, and no ministry of the word.

Hence, we have to say to the Lord, "I can do nothing. Lord, I cannot do anything with Your word unless I first prostrate myself before You and move beyond the pressing of the ordinary crowd." Today many people do not realize how helpless they are as far as God's word is concerned. Many people are like professional preachers. They can say anything; they can preach doctrines, teachings, truths, and the Scripture. They can speak whenever they feel to speak. This is too easy, far too easy!

The ministry of God's word is totally beyond our power. We must remember that the only way to regenerate others is to do it through the operation of the Holy Spirit. We can pass on doctrines to others, but in order to be a minister of the word, we have to have the revelation of the Holy Spirit. We must realize that this task is beyond our power. This is the Lord's task; it is not our business. In this realm a man is not free to speak whenever he pleases. It is not that simple. God wants to have ministers of the word on earth; He wants to see men speaking. Hence, today is the time for us to seek His face. We have to say to the Lord, "I can do nothing. I cannot speak." Man is totally helpless in this regard. Only a foolish person is proud. A foolish man does not realize that spiritual things have nothing to do with man; he does not know that man cannot handle spiritual things by himself. No eloquence, natural talent, or method can help a man touch the ministry of God's word. The ministry of the word is something that belongs to a different realm, a realm that has nothing to do with ourselves.

Brothers, God must bring us on to the point where we see the uselessness of man. We cannot beget or regenerate anyone by our own resolve. Parents can beget children in the flesh, but they cannot beget anything in the way of regeneration. In the same principle, we can pass on doctrines to others. We can tell others what the Bible says, but this does not make us ministers of God's word. A minister of God's word is produced through God's speaking. If God does not speak, it is useless for us to present the Bible to others. God must first speak to us before we can convey this word to others. If God does not give His word to us, we can never convey any word to others. This is not our business. Many people can tell stories, and they can preach doctrines, but they may not be able to tell you what God's word is. If God grants us mercy, we can tell others what God's word is. If God does not grant us mercy, we cannot do anything. We have the word only as God gives us the word. This is something totally beyond our control; we can do nothing about it. Yet this is something that God wants to do. God wants to have the ministry of the word. He has chosen us to be ministers of the word. Yet we cannot do it. In fact, we cannot do anything. It is God's mercy and revelation that give us the word to speak to others. Hence, we have to receive a basic revelation from God. At the same time, our spirit has to be disciplined by the Lord and come under His control. It must be so disciplined that it can open to Him all the time for fresh revelations. The Lord has to deal with us and with our work to such an extent that we bow down and say, "Lord, do Your own work. If You do not have mercy on me, I can do nothing."

We must see that ministry is based on the revelation of the word, and the revelation of the word is based on the revelation of Christ. When it comes to spiritual things, things related to God's word and His ministry of the word, we must remember that there is no such thing as a long-term deposit. No one can boast about what he has, and no one should imagine that he can keep on working with what he has in his hands. Every time we come to God we should be emptied so that we can be filled and pour out once more. Whoever is self-satisfied is not qualified to be a minister of the word. Ministry of the word results in a state in which a man becomes as empty as a newborn babe as soon as the word is released. He knows nothing before God, and he looks to God for another filling and another infusion of the word and revelation. Then he pours out God's word and revelation once again upon others and becomes empty once again. We must be continually emptied. Only by being continually emptied will we have the ministry. In the spiritual realm, God is the One who accomplishes everything; man can do nothing. We should never think that anyone can open his mouth and speak God's word. To take up God's word and to serve as a minister of this word is a task that is beyond any human power to achieve. This work belongs to another realm. The Holy Spirit has to work on us specifically every time. Human beings can do nothing about this. May the Lord be merciful to us, and may we see before the Lord how useless man is. May we not be foolish. Once a man becomes proud, he becomes foolish. When he does not see the basic spiritual things, he becomes foolish.

CHAPTER ELEVEN

REVELATION AND THOUGHTS

The starting point of the ministry of the word is revelation. Once revelation comes, God shines in us, and we feel that we have a little light within. However, even though we seem to see something within, this light does not seem to remain for long. It seems as if we have seen something, and yet we cannot say what we have seen. To deny that we have seen anything is wrong because we clearly have seen something. A vision will appear to be with us for a time and then disappear. This is an actual description of the enlightening process. When we are enlightened, our inner being seems to be clear about everything. Yet we cannot explain anything. It seems as if we are more than clear, and yet we cannot explain what we are clear about. On the one hand, we are very clear within, but on the other hand, we do not have the assurance that we are clear at all. Inwardly we are clear, but outwardly we are confused. It is as if there are two persons in us. One is very clear, and the other is confused. After some time, we seem to forget everything except the fact that God's light has shined on us at one time. Perhaps after some time, God will shine on us a second time. The light comes again, and we seem to see something again. The second encounter may be exactly the same as the first, or there may be some differences. In fact, the two may actually be totally different. Because of our first experience, we may react differently the second time by trying to grasp hold of the light for fear that it will disappear again.

THE NATURE OF LIGHT

We should pay attention to a characteristic of light—it easily fades. It seems to run or fly away every time. It comes to us in a flash and does not stay for long. It does not remain. All ministers of the word have such an experience. They all wish that the light would make itself clear before it goes away again. They wish that the light would remain long enough to clear them up completely. But the strange thing is this: Many of those who are familiar with the ministry of the word have the experience that they cannot hold on to the light; they cannot grasp it. A man can remember many things, but it is hard to remember light, and what he remembers may not be what he has seen. God's light is so great and so strong, yet it flies away quickly, and we have no way to remember it. The more light we have, the harder it is to remember it. Many brothers have remarked, "The more we read the writings of those with revelation, the more we tend to forget them." We must admit that it is not an easy thing to remember light. In fact, light is the most difficult thing to remember. We see with our eyes, not with our memory. The more light we see, the harder it is for us to remember the light. Our memory cannot grasp hold of light. The nature of light is to provide only revelation; it does not provide anything for our memory.

We have to pay attention to the nature of light. Even while the light is shining on us, it seems to be moving away at the same time. In fact, it often does fly away. It often appears that it is passing away and, in fact, does pass away. Our memory cannot retain light. Therefore, we do not know how many times a person has to be enlightened before this shining becomes a revelation to him. When light comes to him the first time, it may pass away. He may not remember anything of the content of what he has seen, other than the fact that he has seen something. The only thing he retains in his memory is the registration that he has seen something. When light comes the second time, he may see something more but still may have no way to grasp its content. He may only remember that he has seen something again. Light comes quickly, yet it is hard to retain it. When light comes the third time, he may see what he saw the previous two times. He may see something more clearly, or the light may stay longer than the previous two times. But he faces the same problem of not being able to remember the light. He knows that he has seen the light, and he knows that he has had an encounter with light. Light comes again and again. Each time the light comes, it is different. Yet each time he is enlightened, he has the sensation that the light passes by too quickly. It flies away. It escapes easily. It is too transient. He remembers nothing of what he saw and how he saw it; all he remembers is that he saw something. Sometimes this light shines into a person's spirit directly without passing through any other means, and its shining goes on in a dynamic way. Sometimes a person experiences this shining in his spirit as he is reading the Bible. Most of the time he receives the shining directly in his spirit, but occasionally he receives some shining when he is reading the Bible. Whether he sees the light directly in his spirit or through reading the Bible, there is one characteristic of light—it is fleeting and hard to retain.

TRANSLATING LIGHT INTO THOUGHTS

This brings us to our second subject—translating light into thoughts. At the time of revelation, God shines His light into man. The starting point of the ministry of the word is God's shining and enlightening within us. The shining disappears in a moment; then we forget about it after a while. It is hard to grasp light. No one can make this fleeting light the basis of his ministry of the word. It is impossible to take this flash of light as the source of the ministry of the word. Something more is needed in order to have the ministry of the word. One needs something more in addition to light: Thoughts are needed. If a man has been dealt with by the Lord and his outward man is broken and torn down, he will spontaneously be enriched in his thoughts. Only those who are rich in thoughts are able to translate light into thoughts. Only those who are rich in thoughts are able to understand the light. A brother once said, "I must understand Greek before I can understand clearly the meaning of the word and before I can translate its meaning more clearly to myself." In the same principle, light is God's word. It conveys God's will. Yet if we do not have thoughts, we do not know the meaning of the light, and we do not know the content of the light. Our thoughts must be powerful and rich enough in order to understand the meaning and content of the light. When our thoughts are strong, we capture the light, and we are able to translate it into intelligible thoughts for ourselves. We only remember the light after we have translated it into thoughts that are understandable to us. We can only remember our thoughts; we cannot remember light. Only after we have translated the light we have seen into our thoughts are we able to retain the light. Before light is transformed into thoughts, we cannot remember what the light was all about, nor can we retain the content of the light. After the light becomes thoughts which, in turn, unveil the significance of the light, we can remember the light and retain it.

Here we see the crucial significance of our thoughts, our mind, and our understanding in the ministry of the word. In learning to serve as a minister of the word, we have to realize the significance of the word *mind* in 1 Corinthians 14. That chapter directs our attention to the matter of prophesying. We have to pay attention to the matter of prophesying because it makes the mind fruitful. This chapter does not emphasize speaking in tongues because it makes the mind unfruitful. Verse 14 says, "For if I pray in a tongue, my spirit prays, but my mind is unfruitful." Verse 15 says, "What then? I will pray with the spirit, and I will pray also with the mind; I will sing with the spirit, and I will sing also with the mind." Verse 19 says, "But in the church I would rather speak five words with my mind, that I might instruct others also, than ten thousand words in a tongue." Man's mind occupies a crucial part in the ministry of God's word. It is God's intention that light reach the mind of every minister of the word.

When light shines, it first shines in man's spirit. But God does not want this light to remain in the spirit; He wants this light to reach man's understanding. Once light reaches man's understanding, it will never fly away; it will be retained in us. Revelation is instantaneous; it flashes and goes away like lightning. But when this light shines and man's mind is enlightened, the latter begins to interpret the former. Thus the light is *retained,* and we discover the content of the light.

When light is in the spirit, it can come and go as it pleases. But once it reaches our mind and our understanding, it is retained. From that point onward, we can utilize this light. We should remember that light is unusable when it is only in our spirit; it has not become utilizable light. Before God we are a "living soul" (Gen. 2:7). If something has not reached our soul, our personality cannot make any use of it, and our will cannot control it. We are not just spiritual entities. We have a spirit, a soul, and a body. When the light of revelation is in our spirit, we cannot say that this light is ours. The light of revelation should not remain in the spirit; it must reach our outward man. The outward man cannot receive any revelation; revelation comes into our spirit. But revelation cannot remain in our spirit; it must reach our mind.

The translation of light into thoughts varies in different people. If a man is rich in thoughts, he will make a great difference in this respect. If a man's thoughts cannot match God's light, God's light will suffer loss. If a vessel cannot match God's light because of either its limitation or lack of capacity, God's light will suffer loss. If God's light comes to a man and his thoughts are sharp and in focus, they will retain the light. A wandering mind cannot retain God's light, nor will distracting thoughts understand the light. You may know that light is present, yet because of distractions and unrelated burdens, you cannot translate the light you see into thoughts. Some thoughts are not wandering or unduly burdened, but they are dull. When God's light shines on them, they do not know what it is all about. God has one basic requirement for those who serve as ministers of His word—their minds must be renewed.

The problem with many people is that their minds are active yet confused. They cannot translate God's light; they have no way to know what the light means. Many people's thoughts are too shallow; they are constantly paying attention to low things. They cannot retain the light or find out what God's light means to them. God is light; light is God's nature. Hence, God's light is as great, as rich, and as transcendent as God Himself. When God's light is unveiled and our thoughts are low, narrow, or confused, we will surely miss much of its shining. God has no intention of giving us small revelations. If God gives a man any revelation, that revelation is always great, and its scope and content are always rich. Anything that comes from the God of glory has to be glorious. Everyone has to admit that God's measure to man is always an overflowing cup. God is always rich, great, and all-inclusive. The problem today is that many minds do not have the capacity to contain this light. Many people are too petty and low to contain God's profound light. Brothers, if our thoughts are undisciplined and out of focus all day long, how can we expect to retain God's light? If God gives us light, yet our thoughts are so low and base, how can this light be retained, and how can we translate this light into intelligible thoughts?

We must remember that the first thing the ministry of the word needs is revelation from God. Yet in order for the human element to be present in God's word and in order for man to be a minister to God, the light of revelation has to pass through man. It has to enter man's spirit and be translated into man's thoughts. If our spirit is not in the right condition, we will not receive any revelation or light. On the other hand, if something is wrong with our mind, light will not reach our outward man and cannot be translated into thoughts. After light shines into our spirit, there is still a need for a strong and rich mind to translate this light into understanding and then into words. If we are pressed all day long by our own worries over such things as food, clothing, and family, and if our thoughts wallow in these things all the time, our mind does not have the capacity to meet the need. A man's mental capacity is like his physical capacity. If a man's arm has a capacity to lift fifty pounds of weight, he can only lift fifty pounds of weight; one more pound will become too heavy for him. Our mind has similar limitations. If our mind is occupied by other things, we cannot use it in the things of God; we will not be able to translate God's light into thoughts. Brothers, the sooner we acknowledge our limitations, the more blessing we will receive. A vain struggle is a great loss.

Some brothers set their minds on food, clothing, family, and affairs of this world all the time. How much room is in their minds for God? Their minds are full of things already; their thoughts are pressed by too many things. Their spirits cannot receive any light. Even if their spirits can receive light, the shining will only be a vain exercise. They will still not be able to serve as an outlet of the ministry. When light shines in their spirit, they do not have a stable mind to receive the light. When light comes, only a free, powerful, and rich mind can retain this light. If our thoughts are revolving around other things, we will be in a maze, and we will not be able to come out of it. Our thoughts will never understand the light. Light has indeed entered our spirit, but it may stop there. Light must follow a definite pathway. God's word also has its pathway; it has to go through some definite steps before it can be released as the ministry of the word. If a man wants to serve others with the word, he has to allow God's word to come out of him step by step. If something is wrong with his mind, God's word will remain in his spirit as light; he will not be able to translate it into thoughts.

The interesting thing is that every time light comes to our spirit, we do not know what it means or what it is saying. By the time we try to understand it and retain it, it is gone. Our minds and thoughts are not sufficient enough to understand the light. We see something, yet we do not know what we see. Many times, light has to come to us two, three, or even more times before we can capture it. If our thoughts are rich enough, we can retain the light more easily. If our mind is not burdened or occupied by other things and if our thoughts are sufficient and inclusive enough, we easily see what the light is and what it all means. All experienced ones agree that while our minds try to translate the light, this light seems to run away. Our minds have to be very quick. The quicker our mind is, the easier it is for us to translate the light. Once our mind misses, the light runs away. If God is merciful to us, the light will come back the second time. But if He does not have mercy on us, it will not come back. Sometimes we feel as if we have lost something; we feel as if something is gone. This means that our mind has not been able to function properly. Many times we feel that our mind is not quick enough. Many times we see something, and like a rescue team rushing to a burning house, we quickly try to translate the light into thoughts. If our minds are quick enough, we may catch a few things, but the rest is gone. Light does not wait patiently for us to ponder and understand. It flies away quickly. We have to snatch it quickly before it runs away.

Brothers, once you find that you cannot retain the light, you realize how useless your mind is. Before you try to engage your mind in the pursuit of God's light, you may think that you are a very clever man. You may boast that your mind is sharp, but when God's light needs to be translated into intelligible thoughts, you find out how poor your thoughts are. This is like the experience of interpreting for a speaker on the podium: You need to interpret for him, yet you cannot do it because the words do not come to you fast enough. When you interpret for a human speaker, he is able to wait for you to find the right words. However, light is different; it does not wait for you. If you cannot catch up with it, it flies away. I cannot tell you why this is so, yet it is a fact. You can only retain as much light as your capacity allows; what cannot be retained is lost. If light comes back a second or third time, you can thank the Lord and capture it again. But if the light does not come back, you suffer a loss, and the church suffers a loss as well. If you lose the light, the church loses the ministry.

Who decides who the ministers are? God decides. Yet if our thoughts cannot match the light, we miss our opportunity to serve as a minister. This shows how crucial our thoughts are in relation to the word of God. Many people have a foolish idea: They think that a minister of God's word does not need to exercise his mind at all. There is no such thing. First Corinthians 14 clearly tells us that a minister of the word needs to exercise his mind. Without exercising his thoughts and mind, he cannot serve properly as a minister of God's word.

THE BREAKING OF THE OUTWARD MAN

Some may ask, "Does not 1 Corinthians 2:13 teach us that spiritual things require no human wisdom?" What should we say? We have to realize that this verse refers to the breaking of the outward man. If our mind can be like a servant standing at the door of God's light, waiting for its shining and looking for the interpretation of its meaning, it is the best servant of all. Without it, there is no ministry of the word. But if the mind is not employed in the interpretation of light and instead is being used to devise one's own thoughts, it is the worst master of all. There is a big difference between the mind acting as a servant and the mind acting as a master. When the mind is the master, it tries to find God's light by itself; it tries to figure out God's will or understand God's word. This is human wisdom. When man tries to come up with something by himself, he is exercising human wisdom, and this should be condemned and destroyed. Our mind should be a servant standing at the door, waiting and preparing itself for God's use. We do not create light; God is the One who shines the light on us, while the mind only prepares itself to retain the light, to understand it, and to translate it. We can say that the mind is an important servant in the ministry of the word. There is a fundamental difference between the mind creating light and retaining light. All those who have learned their lesson before the Lord know when they listen to a message if a speaker's mind is acting as his master or if it is translating the light it has received. When man's mind intrudes into God's affairs and tries to be the master, it becomes a frustration to God. This is why the outward man has to be broken. Once a man's mind is broken, it is no longer confused or independent.

We should bear in mind that when the outward man is broken, the power of the mind is not damaged; rather, it is enhanced. The breaking of the mind refers to the breaking of the self-centered mind, the self-motivated and self-propelled mind. Once such a mind is broken, its usefulness is greatly increased. Suppose a man's mind is always occupied with a certain matter. He thinks about it day and night to the point that he is obsessed with it. If a man's mind is in such a state, is it reasonable to think that he will be able to read the Bible well? Surely not! We should realize that in God's eyes our mind is already disoriented. Sometimes our mind can be obsessed with one matter all day long; it can be totally occupied with it. Or our mind may be occupied with thoughts about what we want; it can be totally centered upon ourselves. Then when God wants to use our mind, it has no more capacity for anything else. As a consequence, God cannot use our mind. Brothers, we have to realize the seriousness of this matter.

One basic qualification of the ministry of the word is an uncluttered mind, a mind that is reserved for God. This is a basic requirement for anyone to participate in the ministry of the word. When we say that the outward man needs to be broken, we do not mean that our mind should be so torn down that it can no longer function. Rather, we mean that it should no longer be full of thoughts for the self; it should not think in an undisciplined way. It should not be taken hostage by outward things. The wisdom of the wise has to be broken, and the cleverness of the clever has to be removed. Then our mind will become a useful organ; it will no longer be our life or our master. Some people simply love to think; they love to be clever. Their thoughts become their life, and they live by their thoughts. If you tell them not to exercise their mind, you are asking them to give up their life. Their minds are turning all day long. They are so active that we are not sure whether or not God's Spirit can shine into their spirits at all. But even if He can, their minds cannot receive such light. We should know that in order for one to see anything, he must not be subjective. If he is subjective, he cannot see anything. If a person's mind is his very life, it is impossible for him to see and understand God's light. This is because he is too subjective. In order for the mind to become a useful organ, it must be dealt with by God. It must be totally smitten. This is the breaking of the outward man. If our mind remains the center of our being and our whole being is centered around ourselves, thinking about our own things, with everything revolving around ourselves, our minds are unavailable even if God's light shines into our spirit. We do not know what God is saying, and we do not understand the meaning of God's word. As a result, the ministry of the word stops in us; it terminates in us. If the word cannot get through our mind, there is no ministry of the word. The ministry of the word needs a channel, and that channel has to be through us. We are the channel through which God's water flows. He uses living men to be His channel, and the water flows out in stages. Once there are obstacles along the way or a section of the channel is blocked, water cannot flow through. Many people are blocked from having a ministry of the word through a blockage in the mind; the mind is blocked, and the ministry of the word cannot flow out.

Brothers, do not think that squandering our mental energy is a small thing. Many people often waste their mental power on unrelated things. All day long they dwell on unimportant things. This waste of mental energy becomes a frustration to God's way. This is not to say that the mind is useless. Revelation requires the cooperation of the human mind. Everything that God has given us is useful. The mind is created by God, and we should not think that it is useless. But a mind that is self-centered and self-propelling is useless. The mind should be God's servant. If it remains a servant, it is useful. But if it tries to be the master, it becomes God's enemy and an arch-opposer of God. This is why 2 Corinthians 10:5 says that every thought has to be taken captive unto the obedience of Christ. God does not want to annul our mind. He wants to take every thought captive unto the obedience of Christ. The issue is whether or not man's mind is under control. If we are so assured of our own wisdom and mental ability, God has to break us. We have to be utterly and totally destroyed. But we should not misunderstand this breaking work; this work does not break down the organ itself or the function of the organ. The breaking merely breaks down the life, the center. God still uses the organ. The soul being one's life and the soul being one's organ are two entirely different things. God does not want our mind to be our life; He does not want it to control us. He wants our mind to be His servant. The soul that acts as one's life has to be broken. But the soul that acts as the servant of the spirit is necessary.

Romans 8:2 says that God has freed us in Christ Jesus. How has God freed us? He has freed us by the law of the Spirit of life. How then can we have the law of the Spirit of life? We have to walk according to the Spirit. If we walk according to the Spirit, the law of the Spirit operates in us. If we do not walk according to the Spirit but according to the flesh, the law of sin and of death is manifested in us. Romans 8 tells us that those who walk according to the Spirit overcome the law of sin and of death. Who are the ones who walk according to the Spirit? They are the ones who set their mind on the spirit (v. 6). Those whose minds are set on the spirit walk according to the Spirit, and those who walk according to the Spirit have the law of the Spirit of life in them, and they overcome the law of sin and of death. What does it means to set the mind on the spirit? To set the mind on the spirit is to set the mind on the things of the Spirit. If a man spends all of his time thinking about wild and strange things, he is surely of the flesh. If his mind is set on bizarre things, he is surely of the flesh. But if a man is led by the Lord to the point that he can think about the Spirit, he becomes spiritual and understands the spiritual things. Some people's minds are constantly occupied with human affairs; it is impossible for them to live by the law of the Spirit. Likewise, it is impossible to ask those whose minds are set constantly on fleshly things to live by the Spirit. We should always remember that our mind cannot be the center of our being. It should be the servant, and it should listen carefully to the voice of the Master. If we do not exercise care to listen to the Spirit, we will follow our own will, set our mind on many different things, and fall into the very things that our minds have been set on. If our outward man is broken, our self is no longer the center, and our mind is no longer the focus. We no longer act according to our mind but instead learn to listen to God's voice. We wait on God like a servant. When His light flashes within us and our spirit perceives this light, our mind immediately knows its meaning.

Contrary to what some would like to think, a minister of the word cannot serve merely by memorizing a message. If this were the case, Christianity would be a religion based on the flesh; it would not be based on revelation in the spirit. Christianity is based not upon a religion of the flesh but upon a revelation in spirit. We know the things of God in our spirit, and we study, translate, and realize these things in our spirit through our mind. Therefore, we cannot allow our mind to wander. Once our mind wanders, we cannot retain the light. If our mind is not lofty enough, we cannot capture the light. Different levels of understanding result in different perceptions of light. Some may see the meaning of justification before the Lord; this is a common and elementary truth. They do see the matter of justification, but when they stand up to speak about justification, there is a great shortage in them. The basis of the ministry of the word is God's light in man's spirit. However, the interpretation of this light varies according to the condition of the minds of different people. The light that a lofty mind captures is very different from the light that a lowly mind touches. What a man touches is affected by what his mind can grasp. The richer his mind is, the more thorough his understanding of justification will be. When God's word is released through him, his utterance is richer and higher. If a man's thoughts are always low, he may see the matter of justification, but he understands it according to his low thoughts and speaks about it according to his low thoughts. God's word is the same in both cases. But among those with low thoughts, His word is being discounted. There are human factors in the ministry, and the first human factor is the mind. If our mind is not under strict control and does not soar high, we will lose God's word. One problem with the ministry of the word is that there is a danger of adding improper words to God's word and mixing improper thoughts with God's light. When this happens, the word is ineffective when it is released, and there is much loss.

Brothers, do we see this? Our responsibility is great. If our mind is dealt with, God's word will be served properly by our thoughts, and the addition of our human element will be a glory to God's word. We can see this in Paul, Peter, and John. Paul was a man with his own characteristics and personality. He had distinctive features. When God's light fell upon him and the word was released through him, God as well as Paul himself could be found in the word. This is precious. God's word can be perfected in man without hindrance. In fact, God's word can be glorified. We also see this in Peter. When God's word was released through him, the outflow of God's word contained the flavor of the man Peter. God's word was perfected through Peter. His word did not suffer loss. Today the ministers of God's word must be the same as the first ministers of the word. God still needs ministers of the word. But there is a question of how much of God's light is lost when it passes through our spirit and mind. How much of it is perfected? May the Lord have mercy upon us. If our mind has not been dealt with and is unable to read and interpret God's light, the light is released in a weak way. The word is weak because our mind is weak; the ministry is weak because our mind is weak. We are the channels for God's word. As channels, we control the word just as a water pipe controls the flow of water. A pipe can leak, or it can be contaminated. Similarly, we can convey God's word to the brothers and sisters in a strong way, or we can convey it in a contaminated, weak way. Our responsibility is indeed great. Those who only pay attention to doctrines are on an altogether different track. Those who are on this track must be dealt with. If they are not dealt with, they will be useless.

We have emphasized the matter of the mark of the cross and the breaking of the outward man. Without breaking, there is no ministry. This is not something optional; it is fundamental. If we want to be ministers of God's word, supplying others with Christ and God's word, our outward man must be broken. This is the reason that we have to continually return to the matter of our very person. We cannot avoid this. If our person is useful, we will be useful. If our person is not useful, we will not be useful. The condition of our person is the crucial issue.

TRAINING OUR MIND

We must not waste our thoughts. We have to treasure and conserve every bit and every drop of our mental energy. The more powerful and enriched our thoughts are, the higher we will climb. We should never waste our thoughts on useless things. We can tell how useful people are with respect to the ministry of God's word by the way they use their mind. If a man wastes and squanders his thoughts on vain things, how can he have any capacity for thoughts pertaining to God? A subjective person is useless because he constantly thinks about his own things, looks at his own surroundings, and is fettered by his own thoughts. The more his thoughts revolve around himself, the less he can put his thoughts to good use. We cannot allow our thoughts to constantly be wild, confused, unchecked, and untamed before God. We must not allow our thoughts to remain low by constantly walking according to the flesh, setting the mind on the flesh, and minding the things of the flesh. If we do, we will have little room in our mind for God. The ministry of the word needs the mind. If our thoughts have been dealt with, we will catch and retain the light when the word appears in our spirit. Light tends to run away. We often lament how hopeless our mind is in catching God's light. As long as our mind is occupied with other things, God's light runs away. Our thoughts must be like a servant waiting at the doorstep of the master. This is the pathway of the ministry of the word. We have to know this pathway. Bear in mind that light comes quickly. Many things are contained in its speedy flash. Only those whose thoughts are perfect, lofty, rich, and clear have the ability to retain the contents of that flash. Even then we should realize that there are still many things God wants us to see which we cannot retain. The perplexing thing is that we know that there is a speaking in our spirit and that this speaking has a certain significance. But we do not know what the significance is. We know that we have lost something, but we do not know what has been lost. Our mind is short in its useful capacity.

We should realize that even the sharpest mind in the world is short of capacity for God's light. If we waste it on useless things, it will be even less productive. We should never allow our thoughts to freely roam; this is not wise. Light can only be retained by minds, and it is only useful in accordance with its retention in our minds. Light is spiritual and runs away easily. If we want to retain the light, our minds have to be powerful, rich, and strong. God is great, and our ability to discover the extent of His shining and speaking is limited. Therefore, when He shines, our thoughts must be rich. Even when we come to the Lord, we often feel that we are short and that our minds do not match the need. Many times we are conscious of the poverty of our mind. We lose many things and miss much shining. How much worse will our situation become if we waste our thoughts on distracting things!

We have to discipline our mind before the Lord every day. The way we use our thoughts is very much related to the way we function as ministers of the word. The ministry of the word has dried up in many people because they have wasted their thoughts. This is like a man who wastes his energy making wrong turns; he does not have any energy to take the right pathway. Many people waste their thoughts away; they have no energy left for the shining of the Spirit. Brothers, do not think that our mind is unrelated to the shining of the Spirit. We must realize that our mind is related very much to the shining of the Spirit. While it is certainly true that thoughts cannot replace the shining of the Spirit, they are necessary in order to understand the shining of the Spirit. Hence, we must not waste our thoughts at ordinary times. Many people engage their thoughts in unnecessary things. As a result, they cannot capture the light. A man is poor in his thoughts because he has too many desires. We have to learn to conserve our thoughts; we must not waste them. I am not saying that we should not use our minds. I am saying that we should not waste them on distracting things. Much mental energy can be wasted. If we waste our God-given mental capacity on unnecessary things, we will find that there is no capacity for the understanding of God's word. There are many minor issues in the Bible, the discernment of which is not critical. We should not waste our thoughts on these things. Moreover, we should realize that we cannot solve every spiritual problem with our mind. We may be able to think of solutions, but we cannot solve them. Spiritual problems can only be solved by God's light. Many people use up all their energy in trying to solve biblical riddles or spiritual problems. They waste their thoughts on doctrines and reasonings. Even if they think that they have solved these problems, others only come into contact with their thoughts when they touch them. The greatest loss comes with the inability to retain God's light. The mind's usefulness lies in its ability to capture the shining of God's light as it breaks forth. A minister of the word must learn the important lesson of employing his thoughts in useful matters. He must put his thoughts in a suitable place where God's light can shine. He should not put his thoughts in a place where God's light cannot shine. We cannot see anything just by using our thoughts alone. God must first shine on us before we can exercise our mind. Do we see this way? We should not come to the Bible with our mind alone. Before we can exercise our mind to translate the light and before we see anything, God must first shine. But if our mind is open to Him, we will see God's light, and we will take the first step in receiving God's word.

May the Lord create ministers of the word among us. Without the ministers of the word, the church will always be poor. A man must receive the supply of God's word before he can minister to the church. The problem today lies in man, in the channel. When God's light shines on us, it first has to get through our mind. Light is in our spirit, but it first must pass through the mind. Since the light is in our spirit, how can we expect to have a powerful ministry if it is discounted as soon as it reaches our mind? This is a very basic issue. May the Lord grant us to know the way of the ministry of the word.

CHAPTER TWELVE

BURDEN AND WORD

A minister of God's word not only needs the light of God's revelation and the power to retain this light, but he also needs a burden. *Burden* in Hebrew is *massa,* which is used in two ways. One way is found in the Pentateuch, which means "a bearable load" (cf. Exo. 23:5; Num. 4:15, 19, 24, 27, 31-32, 49; 11:11, 17; Deut. 1:12). The other way is found in the books of the prophets (cf. Isa. 13:1; 14:28; 17:1; 19:1; 21:1, 11, 13; 22:1; 23:1; 30:6; Jer. 23:33-34, 36, 38; Nahum 1:1; Hab. 1:1; Zech. 9:1; 12:1; Mal. 1:1). The revelations the prophets received were the burdens they received. There is such a thing as a "burden," which is intimately related to the ministry of the word. When the prophets served as ministers of the word, their service issued from their *massa,* that is, from their burdens. Without burden, there is no ministry of the word. Hence, a minister of the word must have a burden.

THE FORMATION OF BURDEN

We have seen that the starting point of the ministry of the word is light. When light shines on us, it comes as a sudden flash of revelation that goes away quickly. If our thoughts have been dealt with by the Lord, this light from God will be retained in our mind. Our mind can then translate this light in our spirit into comprehensible thoughts. Such a shining and fixation becomes our burden. A minister of the word needs to have a burden. But without light, he cannot have a burden. Neither can he have a burden if the light is not translated into thoughts. Furthermore, if the light goes away and only thoughts remain, there is again no burden. Burden only comes when there is light plus thoughts. We must see before the Lord that without light there is no burden.

Light alone, however, does not make up a burden. Even after light has been translated into thoughts, there will be no burden if the light goes away and only thoughts remain. A minister can have a burden before the Lord only insofar as light is complemented and retained by translated thoughts.

Why do we call this a burden? When light is successfully translated into thoughts, but subsequently goes away, leaving behind only thoughts, there is not the feeling of any weight. We feel weight only when we touch the thoughts and at the same time come under the shining. At such times we feel pressed, discomforted, or even pained within. This is the burden of God's word. The burdens the prophets received could only be released through the word. If we do not have the word, our burdens will not be released.

In order to learn to be a minister of the word, we have to find out from God what is the relationship between the word, the thoughts, and His light. First we receive light, then we receive thoughts, and lastly we receive the word. The function of the word is to release God's light. From God's point of view, light becomes thoughts, and then it becomes the word. Today I am transferring my burden to others when I impart God's light to them. When I have light and thoughts, I have a burden upon me. Under this burden I am not free; I feel pressed, weighted down, suppressed, and at times even pained. But as I pass on this burden to others and communicate it to other children of God, my spirit is relieved and my mind is once again free, as if a burden has been lifted off my shoulders.

THE SHEDDING OF BURDEN DEPENDING ON
THE PRESENCE OF THE WORD

How can we relieve ourselves of our burden? In order to unload our burden, we must have the word. Physical burdens are unloaded with our hands. The spiritual burdens are unloaded with the word. If we cannot find the proper word to release the burden, the latter will remain heavy on us. Our burden is released and we are relieved when we come up with the proper words. All ministers of the word have the common experience that thoughts alone are not enough to constitute a message in them; they must have the word before they can release a message. Thoughts alone cannot lead men to God. If a man only has thoughts and nothing else, his speaking will be confused, go around in circles, and get nowhere, as if he were in a maze. But if he has the utterance, the more he speaks, the more he will be released. Many times a minister of God's word has a heavy burden on him. When he comes to the meeting, God shines on him and burdens him to speak. But after an hour of speaking, he returns home with a heavy burden still on his shoulder. He comes with a burden, and he leaves with a burden. Other than the possible excuse of the audience, the only reason for this failure is a shortage of words. When there is a shortage of words, the more one speaks, the more uneasy he becomes, and the less he is released. He is not silent. In fact, he can be quite wordy, yet the very utterance within cannot be released. This means that there is a shortage of words. It is not a matter of a shortage of thoughts but a matter of a shortage of words. If he has the right words, the result will be different. Even though he comes with a heavy burden, he will feel relieved as he speaks. As the words are released sentence by sentence, his burden will be released little by little. The more he speaks, the more released he will be. He will come with a burden, and after the speaking, he will feel that the burden is discharged. This is similar to the way the prophets discharged their burdens. The prophecies of the prophets were their burdens. Their work was to discharge their burdens. They discharged their burdens by the release of the word. A worker relieves himself of his burden by the release of the word. Without words, he cannot discharge his burden. The burden will remain on him. Others may praise him for his wonderful speaking; they may tell him that they have received much help. But he will realize that nothing has gone out from within him. Others have only heard his words; they have not heard God's word.

In relating his ministry of the word to the Corinthians, Paul said, "Which things also we speak, not in words taught by human wisdom but in words taught by the Spirit, interpreting spiritual things with spiritual words" (1 Cor. 2:13). If we have not received a word from the Lord, we cannot be a minister of the word. We have to have a word that the

Lord has commissioned us with and placed in our mouth. When that word is released, the burden is released. Every worker of the Lord has to learn to discharge this burden. Those who work according to their mentality or their knowledge do not understand this fact. Whether or not a man can discharge his burden depends not so much on his utterance and thoughts as on whether or not he has God's word. When he has God's word and releases this word, the discharge of this word equals the discharge of his burden. Therefore, we have to learn to receive God's word from Him. When God's light comes to our outer man through our thoughts, these thoughts can be translated into words. When the words are released, they become God's word. This is the ministry of the word. We have to be clear before the Lord how our thoughts are turned into words and how the inner words are turned into outer words. In the very act of discharging our burden, we have to realize the difference between the inner words and the outer words. We need to have words, both the inner words and the outer words. The inner words are the word we have received within us, while the outer words enunciate the inner words.

THE RELATIONSHIP BETWEEN
BURDEN AND THE INNER WORD

Let us first consider the inner word. After we receive light from God and after we have the thoughts, we only have enough material to have a burden, but this is not enough to discharge it. Light and thoughts can only become our burden; they cannot serve to discharge our burden. Light and thoughts must first become words to us; the thoughts must first become words before we can release these words through our voice to the outside world. We cannot utter our thoughts; we can only utter our words. We cannot turn our thoughts into words extemporaneously. We must first translate these thoughts into words before we can announce them to the outside world. The ministry of the word is different from ordinary speaking. With ordinary speaking, one can speak as long as he has thoughts; his speaking is based on his thoughts. The same, however, is not true with the ministers of the word. Their thoughts must first be converted into words. Their inner being must be filled not only with thoughts but with words as well. They will be able to release their inner word to the outside world only after they have both.

The Lord Jesus served as the highest example of the minister of the word when He was on earth. He was not God's thoughts becoming flesh; He was God's Word becoming flesh. A minister of the word must be supplied with words before he can serve as a minister of the word. One does not become a minister of the word simply by having thoughts. Thoughts must be converted into words before he can have a ministry before God. If we only have thoughts and no words except our own, we still are short of one thing, and we are not able to be a minister of the word. These are basic principles. We need light, we need thoughts, and we need the inner words. After we have light from God and after this light is retained in our thoughts, we have to learn to pray for words before God. We have to be watchful. We have to pray and beseech Him before we will have the words.

When God's light shines into our spirit, it is a revelation; we have to translate this revelation into our thoughts. Without revelation, there is no shining. Shining is God's work. But the retaining of light by the thoughts is man's work, a work that belongs to those who have learned the proper lessons from God. After light is translated into thoughts, there is still the need to translate the thoughts into words. We translate light into thoughts for ourselves, and we translate thoughts into words for others. If we only intend to have light for ourselves, thoughts are good enough. But in order for the light to be dispensed to others, these thoughts have to be translated into words. Without thoughts, the light is too abstract. Without the light, thoughts are useless. But the light must be translated into thoughts before it becomes tangible to us. Furthermore, the thoughts must be translated into words before light becomes tangible to others. We need thoughts to translate the light, and we need words to translate the thoughts. Only then will we have the ministry of the word. Light alone is not enough to qualify a person to be a minister of the word, and thoughts alone are not enough to qualify a person to be a minister of the word. Even the combination of light and thoughts is not enough to qualify a person to be a minister of the word. There must be light, thoughts, and words before one can serve as a minister of the word. We need words to translate the thoughts. This does not refer to ordinary thoughts but to the thoughts that pertain to revelation. Our thoughts are the very light that we see. Yet we cannot share these thoughts with others; they have to be converted into words. Hence, another great step in the ministry of the word is to receive words from God to anchor and then to translate our thoughts. We need the words. Light from God can only be retained with disciplined thoughts. Moreover, we have to anchor these thoughts with words that also come from God. The words that anchor our thoughts must be from God. Sometimes revelation is in the spirit, and sometimes it is in the word. Let us consider these two things.

Revelation in the Spirit
and Revelation in the Word

When God gives us a revelation in our spirit, we have the shining. However, the shining does not stop with God's revelation in our spirit. We have to retain the light with our thoughts. Yet our natural thoughts are not suitable for this task. We cannot turn our thoughts immediately into words. What then should we do? We have to ask God for further shining, not for a shining in our spirit which communicates its meaning to us, but for a shining that conveys words which translate the meaning of the light into words. Here we see two revelations, one in the spirit and one in the word. The revelation in the word is a sentence or two that God gives to us. When we pray to God, we receive a clear light, and we are able to retain and hold on to this light; light is translated into thoughts in us. Yet when we try to speak to others about this revelation, we cannot do it. We understand this revelation ourselves, but we cannot communicate it to others. We can understand it a little, but we do not have the words to make it known to others. At this point we should begin to pray to God for a word. We should pray watchfully and comprehensively, opening our heart to Him and dropping all prejudice.

Our spirit has to be open to Him as well. As we do this, we
will begin to see something before God; He will give us a
word or two that aptly expresses the sense within. Just these
few words become a revelation. The words of this revelation
hold God's light in place.

Light is translated into cognizance and thoughts, and then
the thoughts are translated into words. It is right to say this,
and I believe that there is no question about this. Light
becomes thoughts, and thoughts are then released through
us as words. Light comes to us and is retained by the
thoughts. Today these thoughts are expressed through us
with words. This is absolutely right. It is not very accurate
to say that the relationship between revelation and thoughts
is limited merely to a relationship between revelation in the
word and thoughts. We receive words from God in the second
revelation, but the words of revelation which we receive from
God the second time are for the purpose of capturing the
light which we see in the first place. We can say that there
are two capturings in us. First, thoughts capture God's light,
and second, the words which we receive from God also capture
His light. Just as we capture the light we receive in our spirit
with our thoughts, we capture light through the words which
God gives to us today. In this way, the revelation we receive
through the words becomes one with the revelation we have
received in our spirit. What we see in our spirit goes away
in an instant; but the content of this vision is not measured
by time. It does not mean that if a revelation lasts for a
second that the speaking will also last for just a second. What
we see in our spirit in an instant can involve many things.
This is the reason our mind must be strong and rich in order
to capture the light. The more we put our mind to use, the
more light we will capture from God. The words we receive
from God follow the same principle. In contrast to the vast
amount that is revealed to us in an instant in our spirit,
God's word comes to us only in one or two sentences. When
God gives us a sentence or two to capture the light, these
sentences contain not merely words but the whole revelation
behind them.

In ordinary speech, one only needs to speak eight words if there are eight words to say, or ten words if there are ten words to say. If a speech needs to last for ten minutes, it can be finished in ten minutes. The speaking of this world can be counted by words, minutes, and seconds. But this is not revelation. A word of revelation may consist only of one or two sentences, yet this word of revelation is as impregnated with riches as God's revelation is. A revelation encompasses a great amount of riches; the instantaneous shining contains many riches. God may give us one sentence only, but that one sentence is packed with God's rich utterance and over-flowing revelation. If we can receive a great amount of riches in an instant of revelation, we can also receive a great amount of riches in a single sentence. If God can pack His riches within a moment of revelation, He can pack His riches within one sentence. What one sees in an instant may require a few months to explain. In the same way, what one receives in one sentence may require a few months to paraphrase. Here we have to differentiate between the inner words and the outer words. The inner words are not long, yet they contain many riches. The riches they contain are as rich as the riches one sees in a split second. We are not given long speeches to deliver to others. What we receive may only be one or two sentences. Yet these sentences contain many spiritual things. These one or two sentences carry one outstanding charac-teristic—they are words that release life.

What is a word that releases life? When God grants us revelation, He grants us life. He dispenses life to us through His revelation. This revelation becomes a burden to a worker or a minister. When this burden is discharged, life is released. If this burden is not discharged, life is not released. The heavier the burden is, the more powerful its release will be when it is discharged. If the burden cannot be discharged, it remains in us, and it will become heavier and heavier as time goes on. Suppose we have a large bag full of water that is very heavy in our hands. If we puncture the bag, the water will be discharged, and our hands will not feel the weight after a while. The release of the word works in this same way. If we have a burden within us, we should also have suitable words within us. One sentence will be enough; our burden will be discharged like water being discharged from the bag. But if we do not have this one word, we will feel like a water-tight bag. What then is a word of revelation? A word of revelation is a word that releases life. Previously, life was locked up, but through the discharge of our burden, it is released to others. We must have suitable words to release the pressure within. If we do not have such a word, we cannot release life.

Every time we have a burden, no matter how heavy it is, we will receive a word related to it if we wait long enough before God. Sometimes we may have to pray for days before we have a word to match the burden. In capturing the light, our mind may understand what is involved, but we may not have the words to express our understanding. There are times, however, when we receive the words at the same time that our mind captures the light. As the weight of the burden is felt, the words come instantaneously. We cannot dictate when the words will come. Sometimes God gives us the words immediately upon seeing something. Sometimes we have to wait, and the words come only after the burden has become heavier and heavier. No matter when the words come, they are always suited for the occasion. These words become our light. It seems as if the entire revelation that we have received can be summed up in one word. The one or two words that we have received are as rich in content as the entire revelation we received earlier. These words are like the cork of a bottle; when the cork is removed, the content bursts out. God has to give us one or two words. We call these words the *inner words*. These words come from God, and they are given to capture the revelation and to hold the revelation together. It is God's intention for the revelation that we received from Him to be contained in these one or two words. When we release these words, the revelation is released. Once we utter these words of revelation from God, His light is released.

We should be clear about this before the Lord: Without light, there is no ministry of the word. Without the mind retaining the light and transforming it into thoughts, there is no ministry of the word. But even after the light is retained and translated into thoughts, there is still the need of the word, the word of revelation. This word is what Paul referred to as "words taught by the Spirit" (1 Cor. 2:13). The Spirit has to give us a word. He must not only give us revelation, but He must also give us the revelation in words. Such words of revelation may be only one or two sentences, but they are concise and to the point. As soon as these one or two sentences are uttered, life ushers forth. We may say many things, but if we do not utter these one or two sentences, life will not flow. As soon as these sentences are uttered, however, life flows out.

God's life is released through revelation and nothing else. Take, for example, the crucifixion of the Lord Jesus. As far as the fact is concerned, the Lord has died for everyone in the whole world already. But has everyone received His life? As far as the fact is concerned, He has died for every person in this world, but not everyone has received this life. This is because not everyone has received the revelation. Even if a person can recite the truth of the Lord's death, it will not do him any good if he has not received the revelation. Others, who have received the revelation, can utter thanksgiving and praise from their inner being. Seeing brings life. The Holy Spirit enlivens man through His word. As soon as we see such a word, we are enlivened.

Today God is supplying the church through the word. His intention is to dispense Christ and the life of Christ to the church. But it seems that this life can only be released through the burden we bear. When a burden comes to us, there must be a corresponding word to release the life in the word. Some words do not release life even when they are spoken for two hours. Other words release life immediately. Some words can be spoken repeatedly without carrying any life in them. Other words usher in life as soon as they are uttered. A minister of the word must have the word. Without the word, he will not accomplish anything. Every time a person receives a revelation, he has to receive one or two words as well. When such words are released, life flows. These puncturing and life-gushing words release life as soon as they are uttered. Before they are uttered, no life is released. But as soon as a person speaks these words, others touch life. Without such words, one cannot touch life no matter how hard he tries.

Revelation and light come first. This is the starting point. We must receive revelation and light from God. Yet revelation and light alone do not constitute the ministry of the word. One must be renewed in his mind and understanding. When God shines again, he will then be clear about the content of the revelation. We cannot convey a hazy and foggy revelation. At a minimum the revelation has to be clear in our mind before we can tell others about it. If we are not clear ourselves, we cannot speak of it to others. If the revelation we have received is not clear to us, we cannot release it. Even when we have received revelation, we cannot release it unless our mind is first clear about it. What we say may not be wrong, but we will not have the ministry of the word, and the Lord will not be released through us. After we receive light, our mind must first be clear. If our mind is muddled, the light we see will not remain. Consequently, we need a renewed mind. The old mind cannot be used; it has to be broken. If our mind is not clear, we cannot be a minister of God's word. Yet even if our mind is clear, we still may not be a minister of the word because we still do not have the proper words. Others can only hear our words; they cannot hear our mind. If we do not have the appropriate words, we may speak for hours on the platform without conveying what we know. This is why we have to have words from God. Words come to some people as soon as their mind captures the light. With others, it may take a few days or even a few months. Whether the words come sooner or later, there must be a clear word. We must receive a clear word from the Lord before we can speak. Without such a word we cannot speak. There is not a need for many words; all we need is one or two sentences. Once we receive these one, two, three, or five sentences from the Lord, we can release all the revelation we have received. Unless we have perfect assurance within ourselves, we cannot stand up to speak. If we have not received any light, our ministry will go nowhere. Without light, there is no ministry of the word. But after we have received light and then have thoughts concerning it, we still need some life-releasing words. We are not talking about clever or wise words but life-releasing words. As soon as these words pierce into others, life gushes forth. As soon as these words are released, life is released. Life *has* to be released. Sometimes, one or two phrases are enough to release life. We have to pay attention before the Lord concerning these words. We call these words of revelation. Without such words of revelation, we cannot speak God's word.

We should remember that when God gives us a burden, He also gives us a word to discharge the burden. Both are from God. He gives us light within, and He also gives us thoughts within. When both light and thoughts are present, we have a burden. This burden will make us uneasy; we will be pressed and constrained. Yet the God who gives us the burden will also give us the words to discharge the burden. It is God who gives us the burden, and it is God who enables us to discharge the burden. He will give us the words that will discharge life. One or two phrases are enough to release this life. We should not walk away with a burden on our shoulder. We have to find a way to release this life. Unless we can do this, we do not know how to work for God. When we go to the brothers and sisters, we should not go with an empty water bottle in our hand; we should be prepared to give them water. We must find the way to discharge the water before we open our mouth to speak. I often see a brother speaking at length without releasing what he wants to release. He tries very hard to release it, but he cannot discharge anything. If we have learned some lessons from the Lord, we will notice that this brother is going around in circles. He may reach a certain point where the water is about to flow, yet he circles around again and the water is still held back. When he reaches a certain point, he only needs to speak a certain word and the burden will be released. Yet he lacks that inner word. He has not learned to acquire the crucial words before he begins to minister the word. It is no wonder that the longer he speaks, the more he misses the point.

We must wait before God for the proper word. It is best to have the proper word as soon as our mind captures the light. If we do not receive the word when we capture the light, we should pray for such a word. One day we will find that our own eloquence is useless. The strange thing is that before a man learns to be a minister of God's word, he may think that he has eloquence. But man's natural eloquence can speak of many things except the things of God. Human eloquence is useless in relating the things of God. Life can never be released through human eloquence. Words of life can only be found through revelation. No matter how eloquent we are, we will never succeed in releasing life.

We have to admit that Paul was a good speaker. Yet in Ephesians 6:19 he said, "And for me, that utterance may be given to me in the opening of my mouth, to make known in boldness the mystery of the gospel." In the original language *utterance* is "word." Paul asked the Ephesians to pray for him that he might receive the word to make known the mystery of the gospel. Fleshly eloquence is useless in spiritual things. There must be God-given words. Ministry of the word is something inward, not outward. If we do not have the inward word, we have nothing worth speaking. The trouble with many people is that they keep on speaking, even though they are unable to release what they have within them. We should not search for these words when we are standing on the platform; we should have these words within us ahead of time. We must first find these words before God before we can speak them to others. A minister of God's word must learn to know the inner word. He must learn to first touch the revelation and then release the words. May the Lord make us those who are rich in words. We must not only have a burden; the burden must be supplemented with words so that it can be discharged. The only thing that can discharge our burden is the phrases that we have within us. These phrases are actually a part of the burden.

What then is a burden? First, a burden is the light we receive in the spirit, the thoughts that capture the light, and finally the inner words that supplement the light and thoughts. The last step of the burden is the release of the inner word. The combination of these three things makes up the burden of the prophets. Burden is light plus thoughts plus the inner words. Our burden is to release God's revelation to

man, and God's revelation is released through the words of
revelation that we have received. May God show us the
relationship between burden and the inner words.

How to Receive the Inner Words

Since the discharge of a burden is related closely to the
inner words, how can we receive the inner words? Most of
the time, we receive the inner words through reading the
Bible and in our moments of waiting upon God. Suppose we
receive some intense light, and the Lord mercifully grants us
an active, creative, and energetic mind to capture the light.
God's shining then becomes our thoughts. This is sufficient
for ourselves. The light of revelation and the translated
thoughts are sufficient for our own use. God's revelation has
already generated some benefit in us; it has become perma-
nent, specific, and tangible thoughts in us. Yet as we have
pointed out earlier, this is not sufficient to supply others. We
cannot supply others with our thoughts. We are ministers of
God's word. We cannot dispense our thoughts to others; we
can only dispense words. Yet these words cannot be merely
the product of our mind. An inner word requires a fresh
revelation from God. We must have a word that comes directly
from the Holy Spirit. This word is not just for ourselves but
also for others. It is a word that qualifies us to be a minister.
One thing is clear: We are all members of the Body of Christ,
and God's light must not stop in us. God's shining is altogether
for the ministry; it is not just for ourselves. We have mentioned previously that sometimes light is accompanied by
God's word when it is translated into thoughts, and that it
is this word which enables us to be a minister of the word.
Yet many times, even most of the time, we do not receive a
word when light and thoughts come. In order to receive such
a word, we have to wait on God and study the Scripture. I
am not saying that this is always the case. Each situation is
different. Sometimes the experience is quite special. At other
times the experience is quite ordinary. Under ordinary circumstances, God gives us such words while we are waiting
on Him and reading His Word. We may receive a word from
God today in our study of the Scripture. We may receive a

word tomorrow when we study the Scripture again. In our study of the Scripture, we may receive one or two phrases that aptly express what we have seen in our spirit. These life-releasing words release what we already understand in our mind. When these phrases are released, what is contained in the spirit is also released. These words discharge the light that has been captured by the mind. This is the basis of the ministry of the word. This is what a minister of the word needs.

Let us pay attention to this fact: We need light in the spirit and the retention of the light in the mind, yet we must also wait on God and read the Scripture to receive the proper words from Him. At such times we may receive a word. This word will make us clear within, open our inner eyes, and give us an inner assurance that we can now release this word. We must know how to utter these words before we can release the light and the thoughts that are within us. As soon as we have these sentences in our hand, we have the inner words. Before we have these words, we cannot release the revelation within us no matter how hard we try. A word that is void of revelation will never release any light of revelation. The release of the light of revelation is based on the release of words of revelation. Those who only have the light of revelation without a word of revelation cannot expect to release the light of revelation. The more a person is short of the word of revelation, the more he has to wait on God. He should pray, fellowship, and wait on God with the Scripture open before Him. He should not wait on Him in an ordinary way. He should not pray in an ordinary way or fellowship in an ordinary way. Instead, he should wait on God, pray to Him, and fellowship with Him by opening his Bible before Him. It is easier for God to speak through the Scripture, and it is easier for us to receive His word of revelation through the Scripture. Once we receive a word from the Scripture, something is formed within us. We have one or two words that will bring salvation to a sinner or render help to a believer. These words become God's word. Although they are not God's written word, they are God's up-to-date word. As we mature in age, these words will be useful to us all the time, and as long as our spirit is pure and proper, the Holy Spirit will honor these words whenever we apply them. If a word is God's word, the Holy Spirit will always use it to save men or edify believers. This is not just any kind of word. It is an extraordinary word, a powerful word.

THE RELATIONSHIP BETWEEN
BURDEN AND THE OUTER WORDS

Three necessary steps constitute the ministry of the word: light, thoughts, and word. There are two aspects of the word: the inner words and the outer words. In order to simplify things, we should say that there are four steps: light, thoughts, the inner words, and the outer words.

What are the outer words? What is the relationship between the inner words and the outer words? Their relationship is like the relationship between thoughts and light. These are all spiritual facts and can never be shaken. We have mentioned previously that the light will fly away once it shines within us if there is no thought to capture the light. It will run from our grasp and not be useful to us. Similarly, once we receive one or two inner words, we have to release them through outer words. The inner words consist of one or two sentences. These one or two sentences of God's speaking cannot be understood or accepted if they are released in isolation. They have to be complemented with many other words. In addition to one or two words from God, we must have many other words before we can serve as a minister. God grants us the light of His word, and God also transforms this light into inner words. But this is not enough; we also must have many outer words. An inner word that is without complement is in a form that cannot be accepted readily; it is too condensed. If we release this word in its primitive form, others will not be able to understand it. It will be too strong, too condensed, and too compact to be accepted by others. When the inner word is released, it must be accompanied by many other words. Only then will we be able to effectively express the inner word. Perhaps two thousand words are needed to convey one word from God. Perhaps five thousand or ten thousand words are needed to convey that one word.

We have to employ our own words to convey God's word. This is the meaning of the ministry of the word.

Here we see the need of human elements. In capturing the light with our mind, the human element is involved. Some minds are not capable of this work, while other minds are sufficient. This is the first point at which the human element becomes involved. It is again involved later in the search for outer words. Some people are able to furnish suitable outer words to convey God's word. Others cannot find suitable words to properly convey God's word. Human elements account for a tremendous difference here.

Inner Words Must Be Released by Means of Outer Words

The inner words are in a very condensed form; no one can receive them into him. The outer words are more diluted and can be accepted more readily. Our responsibility is to take care of the outer words. The responsibility for the outer words lies with man, that is, with the minister. A minister's responsibility is to "dilute" God's condensed word and make it easier for others to accept. The inner words are cryptic and condensed, whereas the outer words are lengthy and diluted. Others cannot receive the inner words; they can only receive the outer words. We receive the one or two sentences from God when we receive the second revelation. But after we receive these sentences, we still need many other words to help us release them. Hence, a minister of the word must first receive a divine word from God and then release this word with his own words. Only as we understand this process can we understand the meaning of the inspiration of the Holy Spirit. The pure word that men receive from God does not vary much. Yet when this word was spoken through Peter, it carried Peter's flavor. When it was released through John, it carried John's flavor. When it was released through Paul, it carried Paul's flavor. If one can read the Greek New Testament, he can easily tell which books were written by Peter, which ones by John, and which ones by Paul, because, even though they all contain God's word, they were all written differently. Peter was one kind of person, John was another kind of person, and Paul was yet a third kind of

person. When God's word was spoken through Peter, the
teaching was God's, but the flavor was Peter's. When God's
word was spoken through John, the teaching was God's, but
the flavor was John's. When God's word was spoken through
Paul, the teaching was God's, but the flavor was Paul's. Human
elements are present in the ministry of God's word. God lays
His hand upon men chosen by the Spirit and releases His word
through them. He indeed is the One who gives the word, yet
He wants men to release it in their own words. Those who
have learned many lessons before the Lord will speak as those
who have learned many lessons. Those who have learned few
lessons before the Lord will speak as those who have learned
few lessons. God's word is entrusted to man, and man is
commissioned to release God's word.

Let us turn back once again to the matter of speaking in
tongues. Why should we pay attention to this matter? In his
discussion concerning the ministry of the word, Paul made a
comparison between tongues and the prophetic ministry. We
must not forbid the speaking in tongues because it serves a
purpose for those who are speaking. But it useless as far as
the ministry of the word is concerned because no human understanding is involved. There is a lack of human elements
in tongue speaking; it is something entirely from the Holy
Spirit. The Holy Spirit conveys a word to man, and man
releases it verbatim with his spirit. God's word is released,
yet there is no trace of human understanding or human
element in this word. According to our concept, speaking in
tongues is better than the prophetic ministry. Is it not better
for God to speak directly? Is it not better for the Holy Spirit
to use His own words? Yet the Bible considers speaking in
tongues inferior to prophesying. God puts more emphasis on
prophesying than on tongues. The prophetic ministry is one
in which both God's word as well as the prophet's words are
found. In this case, the living water comes out of one's innermost being (John 7:38). The word comes out of the
innermost being; it is not poured down from heaven. This is
a most fundamental principle in the New Testament.

God puts much emphasis on man. If we study the New
Testament carefully, we can readily identify Peter's writing

as Peter's, James's writing as James's, and Matthew's writing as Matthew's. Every book has its own idiomatic phrases, its own expressions, and its own grammatical structures. God had no intention for each writer to merely transcribe His word. It is His intention for the teaching to be His but for the words to be man's. Since this is the case, a minister of the word has a tremendous responsibility! If we are not up to the standard, what can we contribute? This is the reason that our very person has to be broken. If the person is not proper, what will we bring to the word of God? We should never think that God's word is so ethereal. In releasing His word, God gives man a sentence or two. Then man must release God's word with his own words. He has to use many words to express a few sentences. Consequently, it matters a great deal as to how a man "dilutes" these few sentences with his own words.

In speaking the outer words, we have to realize that there are three prerequisites. The first is light, the second is thoughts, and the third is the inner words. Suppose we are going to have a word with the brothers and sisters, whether it is in the form of a personal conversation or in the form of a message. How are we going to release it? We must first take possession of the few words. These words are, figuratively speaking, the mother of all words. All subsequent words are encapsulated in such words. But because they are too condensed, we have to dilute them before others can receive them. We have to break them down into little pieces, like breaking down a rock into fragments. While we are speaking, we are breaking down or hammering the "chunky" words into smaller pieces and presenting the pieces to others little by little. This is how we release God's word. We have to break down the inner word into smaller pieces and release them little by little. We cannot speak for two hours only to find that the big rock is still in us. Such speaking is useless as far as the release of God's word is concerned. On the one hand, human words are useless, but on the other hand, they are most crucial. This seems to be a contradiction, yet this is a fact. It is useless for us to convey God's word with our own words, no matter how clever and smart we are. Yet when God's word is with us, we can release His word with our own words. Our words can either release His word and magnify it before men, or they can seal up God's word and veil it from men. It is our words that release God's word little by little. The more we speak, the clearer God's word becomes. The utterance of the outer words is for the release and deliverance of the inner words.

We should note the mutual interaction of various factors. In carrying out the ministry of the word, one must first have the inner words. Next he has to convey the inner word through outer words. However, the release of outer words is never simple. The mind also has to function. If it does not function properly, the speaking cannot go on. Yet the mind cannot be set on the words themselves. The mind has to be set on the revelation which has been seen. While one is speaking, how can he be certain that his speaking conveys to others the inner words that are hidden within him? He must exercise his mind to speak what he sees in his spirit. First he must have the light in his spirit. Then he must have thoughts to capture the light. Then he needs a word or two within him. Finally, he has to consider how he should speak. The Lord has given us two things, light in our spirit and the words in our inner being. When we speak, we push out the revelation with our own thoughts, and we release it with our own words. We should not need to force our mind to chase after the revelation, yet our mind should be strong enough to retain the light, and we should be able to release it with our words. Here we find four things—two belong to the inner realm and two belong to the outer realm; two are from God and two are from us. When we combine these four things, we have the ministry of the word. This kind of exercise is very basic. The words we have in our mouth are based on the words we have in our inner being. Our speaking should be a combination of these two kinds of words.

Too much, we have suffered the frustration of losing the inner revelation as we are speaking according to the inner sense. Even as the words are in our mouth, the inner revelation goes away. At other times, we may retain the inner revelation, and the burden for the word may remain in us for two, three, or six months. Yet in releasing this revelation there is not a framework to follow. Hence, on the one hand, we need the Lord to give us the word. On the other hand, as we are speaking, we have to look inwardly for the framework and speak according to this inner registration.

Brothers, we have to see both sides of the issue. Sometimes we have the revelation and the capturing thoughts, yet we do not have the words. We understand the meaning of the revelation, yet we cannot find the words to express it. We are full of thoughts, yet we are short of words. The audience, however, can only understand our words; they cannot understand our thoughts. At other times, we have the words, yet the revelation in the spirit is gone. When men listen to our words, they can only sense manna that has gone stale; that is, the words that we speak do not match the revelation within. The outer words that we release have to match the thoughts within, and others should see the light through such words. The mind is very important, yet the mind is not the organ to receive the revelation. Our cleverness is altogether useless in this respect. If we try to capture revelation with our own clever thoughts, we can only expect great sufferings for God's church. However, we still need the mind. In fact, we need all four things—light, thoughts, the inner words, and the outer words. We need the inner words within us, and we need words in our mouth. While we are conveying the inner words, we have to look for the outer words. These two kinds of words are like two railroad tracks. If we have only one track, the train will not run properly. The outer words have to match the inner words, and the inner words must be translated into outer words.

Many times we sense the shining within us. We understand the meaning of this shining, yet we do not have the crucial words to express it. Such a realization is sufficient for us, but if we try to help others with this realization, the result is like an ox grinding a millstone; we go around in circles without discharging our burden. Many times we have the word within us, but we do not have the outer words. The result is like a railroad with only one track; it is impossible to move the train. God's word cannot be released. We may say many things, but God's word is not released. Revelation alone is not sufficient for our preaching work; the inner word alone is not sufficient. We must have light, thoughts, the inner words, and the outer words. Only when these four things are present and working together will we have the ministry, and only then will the ministry be a ministry of glory.

Speaking according to the Words of the Scripture

In preparing the outer words, we have to pay attention to the words of the Scripture. When we have the inner words and try to release them to others, we often find that we are short of words. For the most part, we aim our utterance in a particular direction and exhaust our words in a few minutes. The inner words are very condensed and compact. Our own utterance is not adequate to release such condensed and compact words. If we repeat the same word once, twice, or ten times, others will be bored by our speaking; they will not appreciate it. Our speaking may be very concise, but it is ineffectual. A man realizes the shortage of his own eloquence when he tries to be a minister of the word. He can talk about many things, but as soon as he talks about spiritual things, he finds that he can do very little. He runs out of resources in no time, while the inner words remain unreleased. He can release his own words, but the inner words remain locked up. This is the reason that we have to be familiar with the words of the Scripture. God uses us as His ministers of the word, yet He knows that our utterance is limited. Therefore, *He* spoke to us in many portions and in many ways (Heb. 1:1). At the most, our thoughts can be expressed one way. But God has spoken to us in many portions and in many ways. This is why we have to be familiar with the words of the Scripture. We have to spend time to study the Bible. During our study, we are equipped with biblical doctrines, knowledge, and teachings. Our speaking must be founded upon the Bible; it must be supported by biblical teachings and biblical truths. These things afford God's children a means and a basis for accepting our words.

After we have received light, thoughts, and the words, we may discover that a few portions of the Scripture identically match the revelation we have received and that many things in these portions are similar to our revelation. We should make a note of these few portions and verbalize the word we received from God with repeated reference to these portions of the Word. Perhaps the word that we received from God is only a few sentences long or at most a dozen sentences long. But we can draw from our experience in the Word to utter the speaking that is within us. This utterance, though short, will pierce men's hearts and enlighten their understanding. This is the reason that we have to be familiar with the Scripture. We have to use the words of the Bible to facilitate our utterance of the revelation. This is not to expound the Bible in an objective way but to explain it in a subjective way. We are not presenting an exegesis; we are conveying the revelation which we have received. We are using the Scripture only because that particular portion of the Word matches our experience. Because Peter's words, John's words, the words of Genesis, or the words of the Psalms match the things we are about to speak, we can use them to present our point. We should ponder how Paul spoke on this subject and how Peter spoke on the subject. We should ponder how David or Moses spoke on the subject. As we ponder, we should consider how the Lord wants us to speak on the subject. These men spoke on the subject in their own way. Now we have to mold our word, the very word that we have received from God, according to their words. We have to do this in all sorts of ways. The revelation and light we received, the burden and responsibility we have from God, form the basis of our speaking. When we repeat the subject over and over again with our own words, the inner words will be released. Light will shine and the burden will be discharged.

Our study of the Bible should not be for exegesis only. A mere exegesis of the Bible is vain. The words of the Bible are given for us to release the burden within us. Without these words, we could not enunciate our burden. Words from the Bible discharge our burden. There may be five, ten, or twenty different portions of the Word that can accomplish this matter. One portion is not enough to release our burden; we have to release our burden in a variety of ways. Suppose we have a burden within, and we try to discharge it through one portion of the Word. We must ask ourselves whether or not our burden is discharged after the application of just one passage. If our burden is still heavy, we may have to use a few more passages to discharge it. But if the burden is not that strong, fewer passages may suffice. After we have found the right passages, we must first try to relieve our burden one way. If the burden remains in us, we should try to relieve it another way. Perhaps we have to use five different passages before our burden is fully released. The ministry of the word is related to the release of the inner word, the weighty word of God, through the release of the words of the Bible. In speaking for God, we must lay hold of the best tool—the Bible. Yet we must issue this warning: The Bible alone is not enough. The mere letter of the Bible is only doctrines. The basis of the ministry of the word is revelation; it is the inner word. However, when this word is released, it must be released through the words of the Bible. If a man lacks inner revelation yet immerses himself in pure Bible exposition, his activity will remain on a very low plane. We cannot borrow Paul's riches and count them as our own. We have to see something ourselves and speak according to what we have seen before we can have the ministry of the word. We must have revelation, the word, and the Scripture before we can speak. If we only have the word within, but not the Bible without, we cannot speak.

THE TEST OF THE MINISTRY OF THE WORD

How do we know whether our speaking is on the right track? As we speak, we have to be attentive to whether our burden is being reduced or whether it is becoming heavier. This is crucial. We do not have to wait until we step down from the platform to find out whether or not we are speaking on the right track; we can sense this as we are speaking. Whenever a word goes out from our mouth, our burden should be reduced a little. Three things—God's word, His light, and our thoughts—constitute a burden. When this burden is discharged, it is discharged through outer words. Hence, every outer word should reduce the inner burden. It would be wrong if an outer word did not reduce the inner burden. One knows within himself whether the message has been delivered properly. If his burden is lessened as he speaks, he can be sure that he has delivered his message properly. If there is no reduction in his burden after speaking for a few minutes, he can be sure that he has taken the wrong direction; he has not said the right thing. It would be better for him to not say anything at all, than for him to go on for another hour without changing direction. He should say, "Brothers, what I just said was wrong," and he should start his message all over again. The more he learns, the less problem he will have in this matter. While we practice serving as a minister of the word, we have to speak for the purpose of releasing our inner burden. We have to learn to come to a message with a burden and to walk away without the burden. If there is no burden before we speak, we cannot speak at all. But after we speak, the burden should be gone. We cannot come with a burden, speak for half an hour or an hour, and then find that our burden is still present. In such a case, God's light has not become the word, and we will only carry the same burden back home with us. Sometimes we can have the strange experience that part of what we say is right and part of what we say is wrong. As a result, part of the burden that we bring to the meeting is discharged while another part is not discharged. We may feel that this is still not that good.

Sometimes the problem can grow worse. Instead of alleviating our burden through our speaking, we only add to our burden and make it heavier. An illustration we use in our speaking may add to our burden. We may inadvertently joke a little in the midst of our speaking, which may stir up uncontrollable laughter in the audience. The result may add more weight to our burden. Many illustrations, jokes, sudden ideas, or distracting thoughts may add to our burden. At the end of our speaking, we may feel that our burden is heavier than when we began. Our eye must be single. We should speak to discharge our burden; we should not speak for the sake of speaking.

One basic principle in speaking is that our eye has to be set on discharging our burden. Everyone carries a burden with the view of discharging it; no one carries a burden with a view to bringing it back to his starting point. Any burden that comes to us must be discharged by proper words. If we feel that our burden is increasing while we speak, we should stop speaking right away. If we do not know how to use the proper outer words, we will have quite a problem with the ministry of the word. If a sentence we utter relieves the burden, we know that we are speaking on the right track. We can repeat the same thing from different angles and in many ways. Then we will feel our burden going away, and we will know that we have said the right thing. Eventually, our burden will be gone. In our speaking, we may have only one or two sentences that we really want to say. The rest of the sentences are to carry forward and support those one or two sentences. If we can deliver these one or two sentences properly and if we can effectively release the inner word within us, our speaking will be in line with the principle of an inspiration.

May the Lord be gracious to us and grant us accurate and life-piercing words. We only need these few words. When these few words are released, we will touch the climax of our speaking. If we speak this way, we will have the ministry of the word.

CHAPTER THIRTEEN

THE SPIRIT'S DISCIPLINE AND THE WORD

When a minister of the word stands up to speak, what is the source of his speaking? A minister of God's word does not just use his mind to think of words to say; his words must come from another source. Let us now examine the source from which he derives his speaking. Once we know the source, we will realize that many things should not come out of our mouth; they cannot be considered as God's word. We must repeat the fact that there is a strong relationship between the ministry of the word and our human elements. We should also remember that in the function of the ministry of the word, God first gives man a word or two, which he then develops into many further words. These many words are based on the one or two words. Their source is the one or two words, and they are built upon the basis of these one or two words. When a minister of the word stands up to speak, he uses his own words, yet he is speaking the word which God has spoken within him. This is the meaning of being a minister of the word. This ministry of the word contains human elements. This is why we have to pay attention to these human elements when we function as ministers of the word. We must realize that the words are being released through man.

When a man speaks from the platform, the kind of person he is will be seen in the kind of words he speaks. Sometimes, God will acknowledge a man's speaking as His own. At other times, He will not acknowledge the speaking. The crux of the whole matter lies in the kind of person a man is. Suppose two persons have received the same light in their spirit and have acquired the same words. The ministry they render, however, may be completely different because the persons are different. This difference results in different ministers of the word. The inner revelation may be the same, and the inner word may be the same, but their ministries may be different because of the difference in their persons. This is the reason that we have to study the source of a man's speaking. Utterance comes from revelation, yet such utterance is very much affected by human elements. The kind of person we are determines the kind of words we will speak. A right person will speak right words, but if a man is poor, his speaking will be low, weak, and childish. He will use human utterances, clever words, and unfocused speech. Thus, his words will not be "spiritual words." If the person is right, the words will spontaneously be spiritual, lofty, and accurate; they will be words that come as a result of touching God. In order to track the source of our outward words, we have to pay attention to our very person. The kind of person we are has a direct bearing on the kind of words we speak.

DIFFERENCES IN THE SPIRIT'S CONSTITUTION RESULTING IN DIFFERENT SPEAKINGS

The kind of person we are determines the kind of words we speak. If God has done some constituting work in us, that is, if His Spirit has operated in us, disciplined us, and dealt with our outward man and crushed it, to the extent that we begin to touch something spiritual and our character begins to change, our speaking will be the speaking of the Spirit spontaneously. The words we speak will be based on the constitution of the Spirit. Without the constitution of the Spirit, there can be no speaking of the Spirit. We cannot utter something of the Spirit by ourselves. There first must be the constitution of the Spirit within us; the Holy Spirit has to rearrange and reconstitute us. Once we were a certain kind of person, but after the Lord has worked on us for years, we begin to experience the Spirit's rearrangement and reconstitution in our whole being. We become like a house that has been remodeled and even reconstructed. We should note that the speaking of the Holy Spirit is based on the constitution of the Holy Spirit. If the Spirit has not done a reconstituting work in us, our words will never be fresh. When the Spirit reconstitutes our whole being, we become new, and the things we speak are new.

This is the reason for Paul's lofty attainment, which is revealed in 1 Corinthians 7. We can learn a singular lesson from this chapter. When the constitution of the Spirit in man reaches a dependable, spiritual, and advanced state, the man is no longer conscious of the revelation he has received. The constitution of the Spirit results in the spontaneous manifestation of revelation. This is why revelation was not an extraordinary thing in Paul. He received light in such an ordinary way that it was almost like his own thoughts. Today men do not have enough constitution of the Spirit. This is why they are so far from God's revelation. First Corinthians 7 is very unique. Here was a brother who was under God and constituted by the Spirit to such an extent that his thoughts and feelings were almost the same as God's. God's revelation was almost the same as his own words; God's revelation was no longer an extraordinary thing in him. Human elements can rise to such a height that they merge with God. According to Paul, his words were his own. He told others that he did not have a command from the Lord and that he was speaking from himself. Yet he was so highly constituted by God that he also could immediately follow this confession with the words, "I think that I also have the Spirit of God" (v. 40). We have to identify the crucial relationship between the person and the word. Here was a man who was fully constituted by the Spirit. When he spoke, God's word was released. It seems as if he released God's word without making reference to special revelation. This is the highest peak that can possibly be experienced by man. Paul's speaking demonstrates the principle that when the person is right, the words are right. When a man is divinely constituted, his speaking is God's speaking. We should pay particular attention to this. A man can be so thoroughly dealt with by the Lord, and his person can be so pure and clean that the Spirit's utterance is released through him whenever he opens his mouth.

We all must pay attention to the fact that the basis of our speaking is the constitution of the Holy Spirit within us. Many people are altogether useless in the eyes of the Lord.

But even among those who are useful to the Lord, we find differences in the constitution of the Holy Spirit. These differences in constitution result in differences in speaking. Two persons can be equally useful to the Lord, and both may have attained equal depth of spirituality in the Lord. Yet their constitution is different. The revelation they receive and the inner word they have may be the same, but the differences in constitution can mean different kinds of speakings. Both can be ministers, even lofty ministers of the word, yet the words that come from their mouths may be different. This is because the human elements they possess are different. John was different from Paul, and Paul was different from Peter. As a result, their speakings were different. These men were all used by God, not in an ordinary way but in the highest way. Yet when they opened their mouth, their speakings were different. When Paul spoke, God's word was within him, but his own words were also in his mouth. Yet his speaking was God's speaking. The same was true of Peter. God's word was within him, but his own words were in his mouth. Yet his speaking was God's speaking. Both Peter and Paul underwent a profound constituting work. When they spoke, they spoke God's word. Yet the outward manifestations of their words were different.

THE FORMATION OF THE WORD

God's word was a person when it was in the Lord Jesus. Today God's word must also be a person when it comes to us. When the Lord was on the earth, He was the Word becoming flesh; God was speaking through the flesh. Today God is again manifesting His word in the flesh; He is still embodying His word in a person. He is still speaking through flesh. This is why God has to deal with our flesh today. He has to deal with our flesh to such an extent that the release of a word from our flesh is the release of the word of God. In order to reach this point, we must have the constitution of the Holy Spirit in us. God constitutes something into us through His indwelling Spirit, and as we ponder over such things and enunciate them, God's word is released. The inward constitution of the Holy Spirit makes God's word our own subjective word. A minister of God's word must allow the Spirit to constitute him to such an extent that the word is no longer objective, but subjective. God's constitution in us through His Spirit has to be so apparent that our mind and God's mind become not only compatible but one and the same mind. God's constitution should be so strong that our word becomes not only similar to God's word but God's very own word. This is the result of the constitution of the Holy Spirit. When our word becomes God's word, we have the ministry of the New Testament. When we find man in this ministry, we find God. When man speaks, God speaks. Since God's word is released through man, what manner of man must a person be, and what dealings must he go through!

Let us consider how God carries out this constituting work within us. The words within us are formed by God Himself; they are created by God through the daily trials and dealings that He arranges for us in our environment. We may be under some kind of dealing for many days or months. They may be days of victory, or they may be days of defeat. We may find them bearable or unbearable, but the Lord's sovereign hand is behind all of them. Day after day, incident after incident, we are disciplined a little at a time. Gradually a word or two becomes clear within us. As we become clearer, we can begin to speak, and this speaking is of our own words. God has created a word or two in us. This is the way words are formed. These words are our words, and they are also God's words. This is very important. This is where we pick up our training. Suppose we experience some dealing by God. In the beginning we may wonder what is happening to us, and we may not have any word at all to describe it. As we pass through the dealing, we do not seem to be clear about anything. But after a while, we begin to feel a little clearer and exclaim, "Ah, this is what the Lord wants. He is dealing with me for the purpose of getting this one thing."

But it is not this simple. We do not become clear all at once. We may be somewhat clear and yet not altogether clear. While tarrying around this hazy zone, there is a gradual clearing away. As things become clearer, we begin to have a word or two. This clearing away becomes the very word we possess. Sometimes the Lord gives us a trial, a very severe trial, and we find ourselves too weak to overcome. We may even say to ourselves that there is no way to get through. But gradually we may feel that there is somehow a way to get through, perhaps even to overcome. We often hobble between a sense of victory and a sense of defeat, and after some days we find that we indeed have overcome. During this time we may feel that we cannot get through, but daily we overcome. When we add up all the times that we are able to get through, we find that in the end we *are* able to overcome without our knowing it. Throughout this process, the word takes form. This word is our own word. We have to realize that this movement between light and darkness is a process through which God forms His word in us. While we are under trials and while our senses move back and forth between confusion and clarity, God is forming His word in us. We may feel that we cannot overcome, and yet we find ourselves overcoming. We may feel that we are about to fall, and yet we find ourselves still standing. Day by day we find the Lord delivering us out of different situations. This deliverance becomes the word which we have within us. The more we go on, the more we become clear, and the more word we have. This is the process by which words are formed in us. The ministry of the word is not something that can be conjured up; it is something formed. The formed word is different from the conjured-up word. While we are groping in darkness, something seems to be clear to us, and yet it goes away in an instant. During those moments of clarity we see a little, and the sum total of all these clear moments gives us a clear registration, resulting in our words. Our words, therefore, are what we have experienced.

To be a minister of the word, we need not only light, thoughts, the inner words, the outer words, and the memory; we also need to pay attention to how we deliver this word on the platform, that is, the word formed out of the discipline we have received. God creates words in us through discipline. The measure of our speaking is determined by the amount of dealings that we have received. We can only speak to the extent that we have been dealt with by the Lord. The amount of experience we have before the Lord is the amount of words that we will have. This makes things quite clear: The Lord is molding us, the person, with the view that eventually we will handle God's word. The Lord is doing a carving work on our person today with the view that our person will eventually become an oracle for God's word. The extent of the release of such a word is strictly determined by the amount of training we receive. Our words are based on the amount of experience we have before the Lord. God's intention is to make us and His word one. It is not a matter of us passing on God's word in an objective way but a matter of God's carving and molding, with the result that our words become God's words.

Let us go on further by posing a question: Where is the light of revelation found? We may say that it is found in the spirit. Why is the light of revelation not seen continuously in our spirit? Why do we see this revelation sometimes and not see it at other times? When does our spirit receive revelation? We receive it as we are being disciplined. We receive light in our spirit based on the dealings that we receive. When we go through dealings, our spirit sees light. The light of revelation comes under the discipline of the Holy Spirit. If the discipline of the Spirit is lacking in a person, the light he receives in his spirit likewise is short. There are definite times and places for us to receive light. We receive light in the spirit, and we receive light during the times that we go through dealings. Hence, every dealing affords us a chance to receive more revelation. If we miss a dealing, we may be missing a revelation. If we receive a dealing from God, it means that we may be receiving a revelation, a new unveiling, from Him as well. We have to know God's hand. Many times the Lord's hand is upon us. He deals with us and touches us little by little, and we yield to Him little by little. The Lord may have to touch us many times before we can surrender a little and before we bow our heads and say, "Lord, I am willing to surrender. I will no longer struggle." When we say this, we have the shining. As the Lord deals with us time after time, we yield to Him time after time. As we yield to Him in this way, our spirit becomes enlightened. As we are made aware of what is happening, we begin to see the light, and the light brings in the word. Hence, God uses dealings to give us light, and He also uses dealings to give us words. The words we use in our preaching should be molded through the divine dealings and trials we experience; they should not be something conjured up by ourselves.

As a minister of the word, we have to make sure that we are making progress in our speaking. If there is progress in our speaking, it means that there is progress in the dealings we are receiving. When we first begin to speak for God, we may not have much to say. No matter how clever we are, how good our memory is, or how much we have received from man, we will be unable to speak effectively. In order for the Lord to give us the word, we first have to yield to His dealings, time after time, little by little. Every dealing brings in a little speaking, and the more God deals with us, the more His speaking is in us. He will speak to us more and more each time. After we go through the dealings, we will have the right words to speak when we stand on the platform. We should pay attention to the process by which the word is formed. The formation of the word is carried out through the discipline of the Holy Spirit.

In 2 Corinthians 12 Paul said that he received a great revelation concerning the third heaven and Paradise (vv. 2, 4). The third heaven is the highest heaven, while Paradise is the lowest place. One is the heaven of heavens, while the other is in the center of the earth. Paul told us that he was lacking in none of these revelations. Yet these revelations could have made Paul boastful. Because he was afraid that others would consider him too highly, he refrained from speaking of them (v. 6). There was also a thorn in his flesh, a messenger of Satan, which buffeted him (v. 7). He entreated the Lord three times for the thorn to depart from him, but the Lord answered, "My grace is sufficient for you, for My power is perfected in weakness" (v. 9a). This was a spiritual revelation from God; it was not mere knowledge. Then Paul said, "Most gladly therefore I will rather boast in my weaknesses....for when I am weak, then I am powerful" (vv. 9b-10). This shows that when Paul received a new revelation, he also received new knowledge. The revelation concerning the third heaven and Paradise might very well have been Paul's highest revelation. Yet he received more help from the Lord's subsequent word than from the realization of the third heaven and Paradise. We have never been to Paradise, and no one has ever come back from Paradise to tell us anything. Neither have we been to the third heaven, and we do not know of the things from that place. Yet for two thousand years the church has been receiving help from the Lord's word to Paul: "My grace is sufficient for you." The church has received more help from this word than from the revelation of the third heaven and Paradise. Where then does the ministry of the word come from? Paul went through the dealings. The Lord brought him to the point where he could boast, "When I am weak, then I am powerful." He knew that God's grace was sufficient for him, and he received the ministry of the word in this way. Paul's ministry of the word was produced under such circumstances.

Utterance comes from discipline. The kind of revelation that is found in 2 Corinthians 12:9 is the result of the discipline of the Holy Spirit. Without discipline, there can be no revelation. Without the thorn, there cannot be the grace. This thorn was a heavy blow to Paul; it was not an ordinary thorn but a buffeting from a messenger of Satan. The word *buffeting* means battering, abuse, oppression, and affliction. Paul was a man of experience. He was not afraid of sicknesses because he had passed through many trials. When he said that something was a suffering, it surely must have been a suffering. He had a thorn, which was the buffeting of the messenger of Satan, who tried to hurt him through the thorn. Yet God granted Paul grace in the midst of such severe discipline, acknowledging, "My grace is sufficient for you." Paul received the revelation to know God's grace and His power, as well as his own weakness. Countless numbers in the church of God have received deliverance through Paul's revelation. It is much easier for us to go on when we know our own weaknesses. As soon as our weaknesses leave us, power leaves us. But if our weaknesses remain with us, power is with us. This is a principle. Such a revelation, such a principle, is received through the discipline of the Holy Spirit. Discipline gives us the light, and discipline also gives us the word. We have to learn to pick up our words one by one, like a little baby learning to speak.

God puts us through many trials which other children of God will eventually experience. Once we learn our lesson, we will have a word for such an occasion. The more we yield and surrender, the more words we will have. Such words come from submission, a submission that is learned through trials. Our very submission brings forth the word. If we do not submit, we will not have the word. But as soon as we submit and prostrate ourselves, we will receive the word. Once we fall on our face, some words will be written and inscribed into us. God ordains that His children go through different kinds of trials. At times God's mercy allows us to go through trials which others have not yet gone through. We are tried first, and then others are tried. When the trials have done their job in us, the word will come to us. Other brothers and sisters may be tried later and may come to the end of themselves, but by then we will have risen up, and we will be able to release the word that has been formed in us during our trials. Our word will become life, light, and power to those who go through the same trials after us. We will once more have the ministry of the word.

We must remember that all ministers of the word have to take the lead in accepting trials. If we do not go through any trials, we will never have any word. If we have not passed through a particular trial, we cannot effectively help those who are going through the same trial. Even if we speak, our words will be empty. What use will these empty words serve? The formation of the word is a process that involves fire. The church has to pass through the fire. God must bring the ministers through the fire first; the fire must pass through the ministers first. Those who have passed through the fire will have the word. The fire will consume them. As they are consumed by the fire, they receive a word from Him. They receive a word whenever they surrender to God. The more they surrender, the more word they have. When other brothers are under the same trial, they will have a word to render help to them. This is the reason we say that the ministry of the word supplies words that are taught by the Holy Spirit. This does not mean that the Holy Spirit merely speaks some words of wisdom through our mouth, but that the Holy Spirit has taught us to express the words ourselves. We are taught by the Holy Spirit, and we have learned the words to say to others by passing through the fiery furnace. Any speaking that involves less than this is vain and empty talk. This is a very basic issue. This is the reason that every dealing involves some basic lessons that we should learn. Every word that we speak must be harnessed by fire. Unless our word is harnessed by fire, it will not do others any good; we will wonder what effect it has upon others. When others are in grief, our comfort will amount to nothing. No outside words will amount to anything in someone's inward being. We can only become useful by passing through God's dealings.

The church has received so much help from 2 Corinthians 12 during the last two thousand years because Paul had a thorn. Thank the Lord for such a thorn. Once a thorn is removed, the effectiveness is gone. The power of 2 Corinthians 12 was manifested through the thorn. Without a thorn in Paul, the whole experience would have been void of any spiritual worth. Power is manifested in the thorn; life is manifested through the thorn. Only a foolish person will try to save himself from a thorn. Once the thorn is gone, the ministry is over, and no word will remain. The power of the word comes from the thorns we experience. Ministers of the word are men chosen by God to take the lead in facing dealings and trials. They in turn also take the lead in their knowledge of Christ. They minister Christ to God's people. They are able to minister to others because they are ahead of the others in their sufferings. They can supply many because they bear more burdens than others. If we have no desire to be a minister of the word, nothing more needs to be said. But as long as we have a desire to be a minister of the word, we have to take the lead to suffer what others have yet to suffer. We have to suffer more than others suffer. God has not made us ministers of the word for the sake of just one person; He has made us ministers for the sake of many people. Therefore, we must be ahead of many in their sufferings, and our sufferings must be greater than theirs. Otherwise, as an individual, we could only render help to another individual; we would not be able to help more than one person in their difficulties or trials.

The amount of riches a minister of the word releases is very much related to the amount of dealings he has received from the Lord. We should not ask God to deal with us slowly, delicately, or leniently. As ministers of the word, we should face dealings that many will have to suffer; we should bear what many will have to bear. Unless we do this, we will not have much to offer others. The utterance of some brothers runs out so easily because they have not received many dealings from the Lord. We can trace the problem to this root. A man must go through many dealings before he can become a minister of the word. If he has experienced enough dealings from the Lord, he will have the right words when others come to him for help. A minister of God's word must be rich in utterance, and in order to be rich in utterance, he must be rich in dealings. Only those who are rich in dealings can be rich in utterance. Those who have gone through a wide variety of trials will be able to meet the needs of the brothers and sisters who are going through a wide variety of trials. Hence, those who serve must not have passed through a few dealings; they must have passed through many dealings. If they can only make claim to a limited range of experience, they cannot meet the need. Many people have needs, and their needs are varied. If we are short in any way, we will not be able to supply them. This means that we need an accumulation of deposits. We must experience many trials, going through what many people will go through, before we can serve them. Without this, we will not be able to serve them in any way when their problems are before us. Thank God that Paul had such a great ministry. His ministry was great because he suffered greatly; he experienced much. This is the reason his ministry was so great. If we want to have a great ministry, we should expect more dealings from the Lord.

THE GOAL OF THE MINISTRY OF THE WORD

What is the goal of ministering to others with the word? The purpose of ministering to others is not merely to deliver them out of their dire situations or to bring them through their trials. We must have a specific goal in ministering to others: The goal is that they would know the Lord. All revelations are revelations of Christ. Unless a revelation is a revelation of Christ, it is not a worthwhile revelation. All revelations are given for the purpose of revealing Christ. We should realize that the ultimate goal of the ministry of the word is to lead men to know Christ. When God puts us in a certain environment or allows us to face certain difficulties, we are faced with a great sense of need; we find that we are forced to seek the Lord. We should remember that every discipline of the Holy Spirit unveils a need to us. The Holy Spirit puts us in an environment in order to show us a need and to show us that we can never meet the need or overcome the situation by ourselves. At such times, our only solution is to know the Lord. Without such a need, a man will not seek to know the Lord. Without his thorn, Paul would not have known the grace of the Lord. The experience of a trial is not just for the sake of passing through the trial; it is for knowing the Lord through the trial. Paul did not say, "All right, I will simply suffer." Instead, he said that he knew grace. This means he knew the Lord. God has to use the Spirit's discipline to create a need in us which can only be satisfied by the Lord; only the Lord can bring us through. Such a need induces us to know certain aspects and attributes of the Lord. Second Corinthians 12 shows us that Paul's knowledge of the Lord's power was acquired through his weaknesses. When he encountered pain, he found grace. The thorn weakened him, but the thorn also led him to the knowledge of grace. The Lord put him in weaknesses in order for him to have the knowledge of power. He put him in sufferings in order for him to have the knowledge of grace. Where there is the need, there is the knowledge. A certain kind of need produces a certain kind of knowledge. If we want to have a full knowledge of the Lord, we have to have a wide range of experience. If our experience is limited, our knowledge of the Lord will be incomplete. Perhaps we have known the Lord in many ways, yet our knowledge of Him concerning a certain matter is not complete. In order to know the Lord, we have to know Him in a complete way. If the discipline of the Spirit is not complete, our knowledge of the Lord will not be complete. If the discipline we receive is short, we will not have the right word to minister to others.

We have to pray that God would train us, that is, put us in all kinds of environments and trials. At the same time we have to give God the opportunity to bring us through such trials. As we yield ourselves to the trials, we afford the Lord the opportunity to give us more knowledge of Himself. When we face a dealing today, we will have a new realization of Christ. When we receive another dealing tomorrow, we will have another fresh realization of Christ. In this way, our knowledge of Christ will increase day by day, and we can minister the Christ we know to the church.

What then is the word? The word is Christ. The word which we receive in our trials and discipline comes from our knowledge of Christ. Today there are thousands and millions of God's children in the church, but their knowledge of Christ is too limited. Some only know one or two things about Christ. There is the need for ministers to be raised up who will give God's children more knowledge of Christ. A minister of the word, through the variety of trials that he experiences, acquires a wide range of knowledge of Christ and is equipped with an abundance of words. These words are given so that he can minister Christ to others. This is the reason that we say that God's word is His Son. God's word is Christ. What we know through the word is what we know through Christ. Today we may find a brother here or there in the church who is short of the knowledge of Christ in one or more aspects. By the mercy of God, we may have passed through a certain experience, and our knowledge of the Lord gained through this experience will enable us to supply him with our supply. Whatever he lacks, we will be able to supply him and fill up his lack. We will be able to serve God's children because we have first learned the right lessons. If our ministry is built upon this foundation, our word will be God's word.

At times, we make use of others' experiences. But it is not a simple matter to use others' experiences, because this results in too much activity in the mind if we are not careful. Many clever people make use of others' experiences all the time; they have no experience of their own. They are blank before God. This does not work. Before one can draw from others' experiences, he himself must have gone through many dealings before the Lord. Whenever we borrow an experience from someone, we have to preserve it and cultivate it in our own spirit. Our own experiences must be preserved in our spirit as well. Anything that is preserved in the spirit is living. Suppose we acquire knowledge about the Body of Christ from God. This knowledge has to be cultivated in our spirit before it can be used to lead others to a knowledge of the Body of Christ. It is all right for us to borrow others' experiences as long as we have something in our spirit first. But if we are individualistic and do not know anything about the Body of Christ and if there is nothing in our spirit, we cannot make use of others' experience. We must be those who are living in the Body of Christ and our experience must be nurtured in our spirit before we can serve others with such a word. If we do not have these things, everything is an exercise of the mind, and it is powerless. We may think that we have delivered a logical message, but we have not touched the real thing. When others listen to us, they do not touch the real thing.

This is analogous to the principle of quoting Scripture. Suppose we have to quote the Scripture today. First we have to touch something in our experience, and then five, ten, or more verses will come to us. However, we must cultivate these verses in our spirit; we cannot cultivate them in our mind. The same is true in our conversation with the brothers. Words which are relevant to the subject should be cultivated in our spirit. We can only minister to others what we have cultivated in our spirit. If we have something but do not cultivate it to keep it alive, it does not do us any good. Even our own experiences from five years ago have to be kept and cultivated in the spirit. If they are kept in the spirit, our spirit can use them when we talk with others about them. The same can be said of the Scripture. If our spirit cannot use it, it cannot become part of our ministry.

Our word must be formed by God within us. The words we speak must be God's word. These words must not be a product of our thoughts or something we have picked up from others. They must be something that God has created and formed within us. God has to try a man with fire for years before a few words can be wrought into him. They are produced through prolonged years of carving and molding. We must realize that such words are the words of the constitution of the Holy Spirit. The Holy Spirit has to work on us for a long time before these words can be produced. These words are a kind of trust or earnest from the Lord. When we experience something from the Lord and we are led through such an experience, some words are formed in us. These words are truly our own, yet at the same time, they are truly God's. It is by this process that our words become God's word. One can only speak such words if he has walked through the depths of the valley. Such words have been washed and tried by God; as such, they are God's word. We must be clear that the source of our speaking is the discipline we have received from God. Our speaking is based on the light we have in ourselves, and the light of the word we have received is based on the discipline of the Holy Spirit. Even our reference to others' experience is based on the discipline of the Holy Spirit. We have to learn our lesson in the depths of the valley before we can announce it on the heights. We must see something in our spirit before it can become light to others. Every word that we speak has to be pressed out, squeezed out, and harnessed from the depths of our being. Whatever kind of person we are, whatever kind of trials we suffer, and whatever lessons we have learned will be reflected in the kind of words we speak.

The word is produced through trials, pain, defeat, and darkness. No minister of God's word should be afraid when God leads him into such circumstances. Once we know this way, we will praise Him, saying, "Lord, You are about to give

me some more words." The first few times we may act
foolishly. We may wonder what is happening to us. But after
a while we should no longer be foolish. We should realize that
some words are produced the first time we go through a
trial. More words are produced the second time a trial comes.
After we go through such experiences again and again, the
words become more abundant and rich. Then, whenever we
face a trial, a suffering, a failure, or a weakness, we will
have a clear voice within, saying, "Lord, You are giving me
more words again." We will become wise in the acquisition
of words. In the church of God, a minister of the word should
take the lead in suffering, not merely in speaking. If we
cannot walk ahead of the church in the discipline of the Holy
Spirit, we have no word to minister to the church. This is a
very serious thing. We must be ahead of the church in the
matter of trials before we can have something to minister to
it. Otherwise, we can do nothing, and all of our ministry of
the word is in vain. We cheat ourselves as well as the church.
The hymn "Let Us Contemplate the Grape Vine" (*Hymns,*
#635) climbs higher and higher with each stanza. At the end
it shows us that the more we sacrifice, the more we can give
to others. If we are not a sacrificing one, we have nothing to
give to others, and we cannot be a minister of the word. The
ministry of the word is a speaking that issues from one's
depth. This is the source of our speaking. Without this, there
is no speaking.

Finally, we have to remember the basic principle which
Paul put forth in 2 Corinthians 1. He said, "For we do not
want you to be ignorant, brothers, of our affliction which
befell us in Asia, that we were excessively burdened, beyond
our power, so that we despaired even of living. Indeed we
ourselves had the response of death in ourselves" (vv. 8-9).
The phrase *response of death* can also be translated as the
judgment of death. What is this judgment of death? Paul goes
on to say that God had a purpose in all these things. It was
to teach him not to have confidence in himself but to have
his confidence in God who raises the dead. This was his
comfort. When other brothers and sisters went through the
same trial, he was able to comfort them. "For even as the

sufferings of the Christ abound unto us, so through the Christ our comfort also abounds. But whether we are afflicted, it is for your comforting and salvation; or whether we are comforted, it is for your comforting, which operates in the endurance of the same sufferings which we also suffer. And our hope for you is firm, knowing that as you are partakers of the sufferings, so also you are of the comfort" (vv. 5-7). This is the basic principle underlying the ministry of the word: taking the lead to suffer in all kinds of trials and then ministering to others what has been learned. We are first comforted, and then we comfort others with the comfort with which we ourselves have been comforted. This is a very basic principle. For this reason, we should never use shallow words in our speaking. Rather, we should speak what we have learned through our repeated trials. Many expressions, words, and illustrations cannot be used, because our speaking becomes shallow as soon as we use them. During ordinary times we have to learn to speak accurately. The Lord has to discipline us until our words echo the words of the Bible more and more. We should learn to use the terms and the expressions found in God's Word more and more. The words of the ministry are words that issue from within through discipline.

The source of the word is the discipline we have received; the word is acquired through discipline. For this reason, we must never despise the discipline of the Holy Spirit. If a word does not have its origin in the discipline of the Holy Spirit, it is a vain word, and the church does not receive any benefit from it. Brothers, do not regard the discipline of the Lord lightly. We must learn our lessons by passing through the fire.

CHAPTER FOURTEEN

THE WORD AND OUR MEMORY

A minister of the word must also pay attention to his memory. In fulfilling the ministry of the word, a man's memory occupies a very important place. Its significance goes far beyond what men ordinarily imagine. This is another matter in which we should exercise ourselves before the Lord.

THE IMPORTANCE OF THE MEMORY

In ministering to others as ministers, we often feel that our memory is too poor. Some of us may have a good memory by birth, but when we serve as ministers, we realize how insufficient our memory is. As soon as we become aware of our poor memory, we discover that it is difficult for us to release our words. It seems as if a veil is covering our mind, and our burden cannot be released. We can only speak what we remember; we cannot speak what we do not remember. In other words, in serving as a minister of the word, how should the outer words match the inner words? How can the inner words be converted into the outer words? How can the inner words support the outer words? Without the supply of the inner words, there are not any outer words. Once the inner words stop, the subject of the outer words is lost. The subject lies in the inner words, not in the outer words. Hence, the outer words must draw their supply from the inner words. Without the supply of the inner words, the outer words dry up. This is where our memory comes into play. The outer words convey the inner words to others through the memory. The memory carries the inner words to the outside world. Whenever our memory fails, our burden cannot be released. We have to see the importance of the memory.

Whenever a minister of the word stands up to speak, he encounters a strange phenomenon: The more he remembers a doctrine, the less he remembers the revelation behind it. This is something beyond our control. Suppose we understand a doctrine, and it is very clear to us today. We may not be able to boast that we remember everything about this doctrine, but we can say at least that we remember a big part of it. But suppose we see a revelation within, capture the light with our thoughts, and also have a few words to articulate what we have seen. It is not so easy to remember these few words. The Lord may give us a sentence, and the sentence may articulate what our thoughts have captured; it may express what we have seen in our spirit, and it may encompass the retained thoughts as well as the light of the Holy Spirit. The sentence may be very simple; it may consist of just five or ten words. Humanly speaking, it should be very easy for us to remember these words. Yet, strangely, the more real a revelation is, the harder it is for us to remember it. This is a fact, not a theory. Our memory fails us after just five minutes of our speaking. Sometimes the order of the words is reversed. Sometimes important words are left out. Sometimes even though we try our best to recall the words, they are gone altogether. Even when we remember the words, the very thing behind the words is gone. At this point we should realize how hard it is for God's revelation to be retained in man's memory, and we should say, "Lord, be gracious to me and help me remember."

We need the aid of our memory to transmit the inner words to the outside world and to express them in outer words. However, because our memory often fails us, the inner part cannot aid the outer part. The more we speak, the farther the outer words drift from the inner words. After we finish a message, we may realize that the inner words were not released at all. This is a very painful experience. We may think that jotting down some notes on a pad may help. At times this may be useful, but at times this may not be useful at all. It is strange that even as we read what we have jotted down and try to recall it, we may realize that we know all the characters and all the words, yet we cannot remember the very thing that the words are trying to convey. This is when we find our memory failing us. If what we see is merely a doctrine, it can easily be communicated to the outside world. The more doctrinal a point is, the easier it is for us to remember it. But if it is a revelation, it will not be that easy for us to remember it. If we try to express and convey the revelation we have within, we find that we have forgotten what we have seen just a moment ago. We remember the words, but we have forgotten the very things behind the words. The trouble with us is that we often forget what we have seen when we stand on the platform. Throughout our speaking, we speak about something else; we do not speak of the things we have seen. The result is a loss to the ministry. Hence, a minister of the word must have a good memory.

We need two kinds of memory, the outward memory and the memory of the Spirit. We need to use these two kinds of memory properly before we can be a minister of the word. The outward memory is the memory of the outer man. It is the memory that resides in our mental faculty. This memory occupies an important place in the testimony of God's word. But there is a second kind of memory, the memory of the Holy Spirit. The Lord Jesus refers to this memory in John 14:26: "But the Comforter, the Holy Spirit, whom the Father will send in My name, He will teach you all things and remind you of all the things which I have said to you." This is the reminding of the Holy Spirit. It is the Holy Spirit who makes us remember such things; we do not remember them by ourselves. We should spend some time to find out about the memory of the Holy Spirit before considering the outward memory.

THE MEMORY OF THE HOLY SPIRIT

First, our spirit sees something; second, our thoughts capture it; and third, we have a word within us. What is contained in this word? This word contains thoughts, and it also contains light. God gives us a sentence or two. These sentences contain thoughts as well as light. What should we pay attention to before God? We should know what the word of revelation is. A revelation is a seeing, a removal of the veil.

The light shines through, and we see what is beyond the veil. Initially, we see what is beyond the veil, even though we cannot articulate it. This light appears to us like the flashing of a camera. God then gives us thoughts to capture the light; the light is converted into the thoughts. Finally, He gives us a word or two which encompass the entire revelation. One word from God unlocks all the significance behind the light. We can say that the word of revelation is a word of "seeing." We can say that it is a word, yet this word is an inner seeing, an inner revelation; it is not merely a word. When this word is in us, it is, at the same time, a "seeing." When it is in us as light, we do not understand what it means. When it is converted into thoughts, we can see its meaning. When it becomes a word, we can grasp it in our thoughts as well as utter it in our mouth. This is the word.

What is the word? The word is a revelation that has become articulated thoughts. A word does not mean just a word alone; it is not just three, five, eight, or ten sentences. It is something within us, an utterance of what we see. Originally, seeing is a function of the eyes; it has nothing to do with the mouth. But when God gives me a word, the word includes light. I can be very clear within, but I cannot articulate what I see. Today the word enables me to articulate what I see. Therefore, we have to be clear that the word is not just one or two sentences. It embodies a seeing, and it is an articulation of our seeing. When we have both the word and the seeing within us, we can call the word our own. God first shows us something in a clear way, and then He gives us a word. The word explains what we see.

The word can only be retained in the memory. We have two kinds of memory. One is a faculty which retains the word. The other is a faculty which retains the seeing. One retains the word; this is the outward memory. The other retains the seeing; this is the memory of the Holy Spirit. The problem today is that our outward memory often functions to remember the word, but the Spirit's memory is gone. We do not remember the seeing. We remember the few words, but we forget the seeing. This is where the problem lies with revelation: It is not like doctrines which can be memorized word for word. There is nothing more to doctrines than simple recitation. Doctrines remain in the outside realm, but the ministry of the word touches life. The more doctrinal something is, the easier it is to remember; it can be repeated easily word for word. However, the inward vision is related to life, and the more something is related to life, the easier it is to forget. One can remember the words verbatim but lose the vision of the thing behind the words. This is what happens when the memory of the Holy Spirit is gone. We must bear in mind that the word that God has given us must be nurtured in the memory of the Holy Spirit. Only then will the word remain living. Once the word is separated from the memory of the Spirit, it becomes something physical and is no longer spiritual. It is very easy for a spiritual thing to turn into a physical thing.

It is very easy for the inner word to degenerate into something dead and outward. It is very easy for a spiritual word to degenerate into something outward and physical. Spiritual words must be kept alive in the Holy Spirit before they can have an effect on us. Words of revelation must be kept alive in the Holy Spirit before we can derive benefit from them. If a word of revelation is not nurtured in the Holy Spirit, a person can remember the words without remembering the revelation. For example, we all know that sin is ugly and evil. Some see this the day they become a believer. Others see this at the time of their revival. Some see the evil of sin the day they hear the gospel. Others, who were given to a dissipated living, do not see the evil of sin until three to five years after their salvation, when they experience a great revival of the Spirit. Once, a brother became conscious of his sins and was very sad. He prostrated himself and rolled on the ground from eight o'clock in the evening until the next morning. The rest of the people had left the meeting, but he was still rolling on the floor. It looked as if he had touched the gates of hell, and he was crying, "Even hell is not big enough to swallow my sins." That day the Lord opened his eyes to something; he saw something in his spirit. Afterwards, he related what he had seen in his spirit to others. He told them about the evil and abomination of sin. Another brother testified that when this one talked about sin, others could feel sin like a thick, black cloud overshadowing them. In his consciousness sin was a thick, black cloud; nothing could be worse than it. When he spoke and articulated the inward revelation, others received the help. But after two or three years, the vision became blurred. He could still say that sin was like a thick, black cloud. When he stood up, he could say the same words, but the picture was gone; the revelation of the Spirit was gone. The revelation was no longer as clear and strong in him as before. Formerly, he would be in tears when he spoke about the blackness of sin. But when he spoke about its blackness now, he could laugh. The taste had changed. The words were the same, but the memory of the Holy Spirit was gone.

Romans 7:13 says, "Sin through the commandment might become exceedingly sinful." One day the Lord may show you how evil and sinful sin is. The very word *sinful* is enough to scare you. But when you preach about it after a few days, it is possible that you still remember the word *sinful,* but the picture, the image, is gone. When you see the sinfulness of sin, both the word and its picture are present. But when you stand up to speak about the evil of sin, the word is present but the picture is gone. We call this picture the memory of the Holy Spirit. In serving as a minister of the word, we need the memory of the Holy Spirit. Such a memory reminds us not only of the words but also of the picture in our speaking. Without such a memory, we may remember the words, but the thing, the picture, is gone. Whenever we stand up to speak, we have to ask the Lord to grant us the memory of the Holy Spirit so that we will convey not only the words but impart the very thing behind the words as well. Unless we have this memory, we can speak on the evil and sinfulness of sin ten or twenty times without knowing what sin really is. We can only impress others with the sinfulness of sin when the memory of the Spirit reminds us of its sinfulness. While we speak about it, we should not only have the words but the picture as well. What is God's word? It is *word plus picture.* Brothers, do we see this? God's word must be supplemented by the picture. In fact, God's word is word plus picture. Word without the picture is not God's word. If we have the wrong picture behind the words, the words alone are not enough.

Take another example. Suppose we are preaching the gospel and the subject is the Lord's love. While we are speaking on love, we may have the picture in front of us; our speaking is based on the picture. This is good. But many times the one who is speaking on God's love does not believe in God's love. How can he expect others to believe in it? We need the memory of the Holy Spirit. The Spirit reminds us of the picture; He causes us to remember the very thing called "love." When we speak on that thing, we hit the right spot. The more we speak about it, the more we strike life. Life is struck; it is released. Without the memory of the Spirit, we may have all the right words, but we miss the very thing itself. The phrasing is right, but the thing is gone. This is useless. In preaching God's word, we have to look to the memory of the Holy Spirit to remind us of the revelation in addition to having the inner word that the Spirit gives to us. When we speak according to this inner word, whether it is once or twice, life will be released, and others will see what we have seen. It is useless for us merely to pass on letters. The Spirit must first remind us of the word before we can speak it.

Some of us were saved through John 3:16. But what if we memorize John 3:16 to see whether it will work again for others? It will not work even if we recite it ten times to others. The Holy Spirit opened our eyes at one time to this verse. John 3:16 is only useful inasmuch as this seeing, which brought about our salvation, is retained in our memory and as we are reminded of this thing. The only thing that works is the memory of the Holy Spirit.

Many people found the Lord to be very loving and precious when they received forgiveness of their sins. They saw a revelation within, and they found the Lord to be very clear to them. The forgiveness which they experienced was great; therefore, the love was great (Luke 7:47). They saw something, and they had the word in their mind. They had both the thoughts and the word. One day they spoke on the platform for an hour or two. The word within was released, and everyone felt happy and received help. After some time, they repeated the same speaking again. The words were still there; they remembered them all. The outer words were not missing, but the more they spoke, the more they realized that they did not have the real thing. It seemed they had forgotten that very thing they once talked about. They could not recall what it was. The words were still there, but the love was gone. They were short of the memory of the Holy Spirit. Every revelation has to be preserved in the memory of the Holy Spirit. A minister of the word must be a person with a good memory of the Holy Spirit. The stronger this memory is, the better it is for him. His ministry of the word will be so much richer because he will have so many more living deposits within him. But if his memory of the Spirit is poor, he will have to repeatedly study all the revelations God has given him. This is a pity. A man must not only know the revelation of the Holy Spirit, but this revelation must be enriched continually. Perhaps we were saved thirty years ago. At that time the Lord gave us a revelation. Later He gave us another revelation and yet another one. The revelation became greater and greater. At the time of our salvation, we saw the basic revelation. Later the revelation became deeper and greater. A minister of the word must have the memory of the Holy Spirit; that is, he must nurture the revelation he receives in the memory of the Holy Spirit. When he receives a fresh revelation, he has to keep it and nurture it in the memory of the Holy Spirit. Then everything he receives will be kept alive.

Let us come back to the illustration of the sinfulness of sin. This must be a fresh vision in us. If it is fresh within us, we will be a minister of the word when we release it sentence by sentence. If it is not fresh within us, we can speak about the sinfulness of sin on the platform, but others will receive only stale manna; it may be a day old, a year old, or even ten years old. We will not be serving as ministers of the word in that case, and our word will amount to nothing. When some brothers give a gospel message, others can see that they have the memory of the Holy Spirit. When others preach, others can see that they do not have the memory of the Holy Spirit. No one can pretend. If a person has it, he has it; if he does not have it, he does not have it. The same principle can be applied to higher and deeper revelations. Revelation is kept alive in the memory of the Holy Spirit. In order to be a minister of the word, our word has to be nurtured in the memory of the Holy Spirit. If we have the memory of the Holy Spirit, this memory will become operative as we speak and convey the inner word to others. The strange thing is that when we see something in the spirit, we may forget about it the very first time we try to use it to minister the word. We cannot speak what we want to speak. It is understandable that we might lose the acute sense of sin which we felt ten or fifteen years ago. But while we are speaking on the platform, we often forget what we saw the night before. Our outward memory is useless in retaining the revelation of the word. We cannot depend on our outward memory to capture the revelation. Revelation can only be retained in the Holy Spirit.

Consider another illustration. Suppose a person realizes the great difference between pressing upon the Lord and touching Him. He sees the great difference between physically and spiritually touching the Lord. When he sees it, he is very clear and very happy about what he has seen. After two or three days, when he visits a sick brother, he tries to tell him the same thing. Yet he finds that he is going around in circles. The more he speaks, the colder and emptier his words become; his endeavor is completely futile. With sweat upon his brow, he tries as hard as he can to remember what he once saw, but to no avail. The only reason for his failure is that his revelation has not been nurtured in the memory of the Holy Spirit. If the words of revelation were nurtured in the memory of the Holy Spirit, he would have no trouble using them in his ministry of the word. Hence, we need the revelation, the thoughts, the inner words, and the outer words, and we also need the memory of the Holy Spirit. Without the memory of the Holy Spirit, the inner words and the outer words do not function. No one can be a minister of the word by his own natural strength. It does not matter what kind of person we are. As long as we trust in our natural strength, we are completely useless. Only a foolish person boasts about himself. What do we have to boast of if we cannot even remember what we saw yesterday? We rack our brains to recall what we saw yesterday, and we still cannot remember a thing. No matter how hard we try, our memory still fails us. In order to support and supply the outer word with the word of revelation, we have to maintain the word of revelation within the memory of the Holy Spirit. Only then will the words we speak be what the Lord wants us to speak, and only then will they be spiritual, not physical. Unless the words of revelation which we have received are preserved in the memory of the Holy Spirit, we will find our spirit sagging as soon as we speak.

When the Lord works in us, it is easy for us to be a minister of the word. But when the Lord does not work in us, nothing is harder than assuming the ministry of the word. If a man remains loose and forgetful, and if he is undisciplined in his thoughts and words, he is useless in the ministry of the word. There are strict requirements for the ministry of God's word. The Lord has to work on us very much before He can use us. If we allow ourselves to relax a little, we may still be able to do other things, but we will not be able to be a minister of the word. We have to ask the Lord for grace. We have to ask Him to grant us the memory of the Holy Spirit so that we can remember the words we have seen. Revelation is within the word. If we have the memory of the Holy Spirit within us, we will remember the word. We will remember not only the word of revelation but the revelation of the word. When we supply the outer words with this word of revelation, we will know what we are talking about as soon as we open our mouth. While we speak, we will see, and spontaneously we will become ministers of the word. If while we are speaking, we do not see the inward things, we panic. We become confused and do not know what to say. Brothers, we have to acknowledge the futility of a clever mind in this endeavor.

OUTWARD MEMORY

Next, we have to consider the outward memory. Sometimes the Lord uses our outward memory. At such times the outward memory becomes necessary. But sometimes the Lord does not want to use our outward memory. At such times the outward memory is useless to Him. Why is our outward memory necessary at times and useless at other times? I cannot explain this; I can only state the fact. This is a fact for which I can give you no explanation. Sometimes we have the word within; we have the word of God's revelation, and we also have the memory of the Holy Spirit. We are very clear within, but we still need to exercise our own memory. The Holy Spirit reminds us of things; He does not create a separate memory for us. The memory of the Holy Spirit means that the Holy Spirit reminds us of things. John 14:26 says, "He will... remind you of all the things which I have said to you." God's Spirit is living within us. When He gives us a revelation, this revelation is kept alive in the Holy Spirit. When we speak, God may give us two words. These two words are the key words. If we remember these key words, amazingly the memory of the Holy Spirit will remain. But if we forget these two words, the memory of the Holy Spirit will also be lost. Sometimes when the Holy Spirit reminds us of these words, we are afraid that our memory will fail, and we write down these crucial and important words. Often as we recall these two words, the picture within comes back, and we see the revelation once again. This shows us that the Holy Spirit uses our outward memory. Sometimes we jot down a few words, and just a glance at them makes us inwardly clear. Yet sometimes we are not clear within even after we look at the words. During these times, it is clear that the Holy Spirit is not using our outward memory.

Hence, we can say that the outward memory can be both useful and useless. Sometimes the Lord shows us something. Yet after a while, only the outward memory is left; inwardly we do not see anything. There is nothing that we can do about this. Under normal circumstances, we should write down the words we have received. The more revelation we receive from God, the more we need our outward memory. The less revelation we receive from God, the less we need our outward memory. The stronger our inward memory is before the Lord, the more our outward memory and inward memory will be purified. As the things in our outward memory and inward memory become more purified, we will retain things both in our outward memory as well as in our inward memory. In the beginning our inward memory may not match what has been retained in our outward memory. Do not be discouraged. The things we retain outwardly may sometimes be visible to us and sometimes be gone from us. But as our experience advances, we will find these two kinds of memory becoming more and more one; they will merge to become one memory. We will find that, along with the outward remembrance of the words, there is also the inward remembrance of the words. This is the reason that we have to humble ourselves before the Lord. We have to pray much, look to Him much, and be ready at all times. When we are clear about what we see, we can speak to others about it. We must always preserve the inner words in the revelation of the Holy Spirit before we speak it out.

Sometimes you may give a good message, and everyone may applaud you. But within you know how good the message really was. At the time of your speaking, you could not recall the very thing that you were impressed with. The outward memory did not match the inward memory. You said the right things, but the revelation was not there; it had faded into the background. We must learn this lesson before the Lord: A minister of the word must have light, inner thoughts, the inner words, the outer words, and the memory of the Holy Spirit, as well as the outward memory. The memory of the Holy Spirit should lie between revelation and the inner words; it should be ready always to supply the inner words. The outward memory should be placed in between the inner words and the outer words; it should be ready always to supply the outer words.

Let us consider these three steps: light, the inner word, and the outer words. (For now we will not consider the thoughts.) The memory of the Holy Spirit should lie in between the first and the second items. Our own memory should lie in between the second and the third items. The memory of the Holy Spirit should lie between the light and the inner words so that the memory of the Holy Spirit can supply the inner words with light. The inner words have to be fed by the light of the Holy Spirit. Without the feeding of the light, the inner words will die; they will become something physical, not spiritual. The memory of the Holy Spirit supplies the inner words with light so that the inner words will continue to thrive in the environment of light. Then we have to use our own words, which we acquire by exercising our own memory to supply the outer words with the inner words. When this happens we will have the speaking.

In exercising our own memory, we have to remember that the outward memory can never replace the function of the inner memory. In fact, the memory of the Holy Spirit often has no use for the outward memory.

Another thing we have to realize is that sometimes the outward memory can even become a barrier to the memory of the Holy Spirit. The outward memory is not only unqualified to substitute for the Spirit's memory, but at times it actually can frustrate the Spirit's memory. Sometimes the inner word within us is shining and living, and the Holy Spirit reminds us of this shining. Yet outwardly, we forget the few crucial words. The utterance is gone, and we cannot go on. Many times there is no problem inwardly; the problem lies in outside factors. The crucial words are lost, and the speaking is gone. When we become more experienced, we see that our memory sometimes aids the Spirit's memory, while at other times, our memory blocks the Spirit's memory. The Spirit's memory has to use our memory. The Spirit cannot use another memory besides our own; it has to use our memory. Suppose we are busy with outside affairs all the time and cannot remember many words. We are either too careless or too anxious. Even though the Lord has given us three or five words, we can forget them all and be unable to remember one thing. Even though we cannot remember these words, nevertheless, we may speak for an hour. The taste, however, is gone. This is a serious matter. This is the reason that we sometimes have to write down the revelation we have in a few words. The few words will refresh the seeing, and the entire revelation within us will come alive again as we read these words.

Every time we serve as a minister of the word, the Holy Spirit may want to say many things. We cannot emphasize one part while overlooking another part. For example, the Holy Spirit may want to say three things, yet we may miss two of them. The two things that we have missed become a burden to us. As long as we miss one thing, we cannot be considered as a qualified minister of the word. Within one revelation, God may need to release more than one word or cover more than one subject. He may want to bring up two or three subjects. If we forget them or skip over them, we will feel the weight upon us. Therefore, we have to write down the three or five words. These three or five words can evoke more meaning than just the meaning of the words themselves. The Lord may want us to mention three or five subjects. We should write down every one of them so that nothing is missed. If we miss the last point, we barely may be able to get by with the rest of the speaking. But if we miss the first point, the whole meeting will be ruined.

Ministry of the word is a very serious matter. We must never offend the Spirit. We may think that it does not matter much whether or not we speak well. It seems as if we can afford to miss one out of five sentences. No! If we miss the very thing that we are supposed to release, we will feel the weight upon us increasing. If we miss something, we will feel its weight, because we have not communicated what God wants to convey to His children. Consequently, our burden increases.

A minister of the word should never fail. We must remember that if the Lord wants us to say three things, we have to say three things. If the Lord wants us to say five things, we have to say five things. If we cannot release them all, our burden will increase. If we release all the points except one, the light will be veiled, and we will feel the weight and the bondage. This is the reason that we must learn to exercise ourselves to have a good memory before the Lord. We must guard against any failure of our memory. May God grant us a clear understanding of the way of the ministry of the word. Our outward memory is merely a slave to the Spirit's memory; it is merely a servant. But if this servant becomes unfruitful, the Spirit's memory is not able to function well. Our memory needs to be renewed so that it can become useful to the Spirit. Every minister of the word has to pass through the proper dealings before becoming useful. Our mind must be dealt with to the extent that it can become useful. Our memory also must be dealt with to the extent that it can become useful. The thoughts and the memory are very much related to the ministry of the word. Once our memory fails, revelation is locked up and eventually dies.

THE MEMORY IN THE QUOTING OF SCRIPTURE

We should also pay attention to the matter of quoting the Scripture. In delivering God's word, we have to follow the example of the apostles who quoted from the Old Testament. When we speak on a certain subject, we should quote from the Old and New Testaments. In speaking God's word, we must have the written Bible as our basis. We should base our speaking on the Old Testament as well as the New Testament. But there is a problem today: If we are not careful, we can be led astray by the Scripture. In quoting from the Old and the New Testaments, we may get carried away by the quotations. We may miss what we intend to speak in the first place, and when we return home, our burden becomes even heavier. This is not a simple thing. Many times while we are speaking, we have no control over our memory. It is easy for us to speak on an Old Testament passage or a New Testament passage and then get carried away by it. We wonder why we feel heavier and heavier as we speak. When we return home, we feel condemned; we feel that we have wasted time. We have expounded the Scripture and explained the doctrine, but we have not discharged the burden that God has given us. Therefore, in our speaking, we have to learn to continually check whether or not the burden is unloaded. We may say this or that, and we may quote from the Old Testament and the New Testament, but all these are peripheral to the purpose of bringing out God's present word. Unless there is God's present word, there is no need for us to speak at all. If we do not have God's present word, we would do just as well if we came together and studied the

Scripture together without any special speaking. We must not be satisfied with just repeating something in the Old Testament and the New Testament; we must release our own words as well.

The ministry of the word is a very subjective thing. We have to speak God's past words, and we have to speak God's present words. We must not only speak about the Old Testament and the New Testament; we have to come back to our own words. We can say something through the Old Testament, and we can say something through the New Testament. But we also have to say what we need to say. Our words have to be strong and rich. We should release what we want to say sentence by sentence. As each sentence is released, we touch the right spot, and more life is released. The burden is gradually discharged, and it is fully discharged when the message is done. We may feel that our utterance is short, but our burden is discharged; we have done what we needed to do. Following this, we will see the fruit in others. One thing is certain: Where there is the discharge of a burden, God's children will see the light. If they do not see the light, it is their problem, not ours. But if we cannot discharge our burden, then the problem lies with us, not them.

We must realize before the Lord that a minister of the word should always be burdened with words. Speaking is for the discharge of a burden. In order to discharge a burden, we must have the Spirit's memory. Without the Spirit's memory, we cannot discharge our burden. Even when the Spirit's memory is fresh, we must still be careful not to be carried away by the truths of the Old Testament and the New Testament. We should always remember that our burden is to bring God's present word to men. We should not merely expound the Bible, while forgetting what we are supposed to do. If we forget the words that we are supposed to speak, we will find that we still have not said that very thing even after we have said everything. It is possible that there may be a hindrance from Satan. In any case, our thought has to be rich, and our memory has to be rich. We have to be rich in everything before we can release our burden through our speaking.

CHAPTER FIFTEEN

THE WORD AND OUR FEELINGS

In previous chapters we have said that a minister of the word needs four things. Two of these things, light and the inner words, are of God, while the other two, thoughts and memory, are of the minister himself. Before a minister of the word opens his mouth to speak, he needs to have two things available to him—his own thoughts and his memory. But this is not all. While he is speaking, he also needs two more things—proper feelings and a proper spirit.

THE SPIRIT BEING RELEASED THROUGH FEELINGS

In reading the Bible, we find one outstanding feature in all the writers of the books: Their feelings were never a hindrance to them in their ministry of the word. In their speaking, they expressed their feelings. We must realize that the release of our spirit often is affected by our feelings. If a man's feelings cannot be expressed, his spirit cannot be freed. Whether or not a man's spirit is released has very little to do with the will or the mind. It has much to do with the feelings. The spirit is mainly expressed through our feelings. When our feelings become a hindrance, the spirit is blocked. When our feelings are cold, the spirit becomes cold. When our feelings are dry, the spirit is dry. When our feelings are calm, the spirit is calm.

Why do God's children so often confuse the spirit with feelings? God's children can most readily discern the spirit from the will because there is a great difference between them. They can discern the spirit from the mind because this difference is also great. But it is not easy to discern the spirit from feelings. It is easy to confuse the two because the spirit does not flow independently; when it flows, it carries feelings with it. The spirit does not express itself through the mind or the will but through the feelings. This is the reason that many people find it difficult to differentiate between the spirit and the feelings. Although the two are totally different, the spirit being one thing and the feelings another, the spirit is nevertheless expressed through the feelings. The light bulb is the place where electricity is expressed. Although electricity and the bulb are two different things, the two cannot be separated. In the same way, the spirit and the feelings are two different things, yet the former is expressed through the latter. For this reason we cannot separate the spirit from the feelings. But this does not mean that the spirit is the feelings or that the feelings are the spirit. For those who have never learned the spiritual lessons, the spirit and the feelings are one and the same thing. This is like some people who consider that electricity is the same as the light bulb. In reality, electricity and light bulbs are two entirely different things. When a minister of the word speaks, his spirit has to be released. But the release of the spirit is related very much to his feelings. If his feelings are not proper, his spirit cannot be released. The electricity in the power company can be very strong, but without a light bulb no light will be seen. In the same way, no matter how wonderful our spirit is, the spirit is frustrated if our feelings are poor. The spirit is released through the feelings. In order for the spirit of the minister of the word to be free, it must have suitable feelings to express itself. If the feelings do not obey the spirit or follow its instructions, the spirit is blocked. For the purpose of releasing the spirit, a man must have proper feelings. Now let us consider the kind of feelings that are proper.

Man has a will, but the will is the coarsest part within him. Man also has a mind, which is more refined than the will, yet the mind is still coarse. Man also has feelings, which are the most delicate part in him. When a man makes a decision, he may do so in a definite way. Even though man is capable of thinking, his thoughts are not necessarily refined. But in man's emotions and feelings, we can find a soft and tender spot. In the Old Testament, particularly in the Song of Songs, the finer parts of man are signified by scents. Scents can only be detected by the nose, and the sense of smell is a very delicate function. Smell represents the finer sentiments. The Bible uses the nose as a symbol of feelings. Although man's feelings are delicate, not all feelings can be used.

A minister of the word has to use his feelings. Every time he speaks, he has to put his feelings into the words he is speaking. Without this, his words are dead. Before a minister of the word opens his mouth, he must have memory and thoughts. But after he opens his mouth, he first should have feelings. If his feelings cannot match his speaking, his speaking amounts to nothing.

The Lord Jesus once illustrated this point to His disciples, saying, "But to what shall I liken this generation? It is like little children sitting in the market places, who call to the others and say, We have played the flute to you, and you did not dance; we have sung a dirge, and you did not mourn" (Matt. 11:16-17). If a man has feelings, he will dance when others play the flute and mourn when others sing a dirge. In other words, a minister of the word cannot speak one thing but feel just the opposite. This altogether disqualifies a person from speaking for the Lord. We cannot speak a word of grief without having any feeling of grief. If we do not have the feeling of grief, we cannot be a minister of such a word of grief. The feelings that we are speaking of are not a kind of performance. Any performed feeling is an imitation; it is like acting in a play. A minister of the word should not perform his speaking in an artificial way. When a minister of the word speaks, he should be full of feelings for the words he is speaking. Every word of his should be full of feeling. If the words are sorrowful, he should feel sorrowful. When the spirit is sad, the feelings should be sad as well. Some words are joyous, and he should feel joyful. When the spirit is joyful, he should have the feelings of joy.

We must remember that it is not enough to just release the word; the spirit must be released as well. However, when the spirit is released, it conveys our feelings also. Therefore, if our feelings are not up to the standard, our words will be short of the spirit. When our feelings are too rough, they are useless in the release of the words. The feelings are the most delicate part of man. If our feelings are rough and insensitive, we cannot use them, and our speaking will be without the spirit. Whatever words we are speaking, we must have the spirit to match the words. If the spirit is different from the words, the two become incompatible, and the words will suffer a loss. The result will be nothing but failure. When we release certain words, we have to convey a certain spirit. In other words, we need the proper spirit for the proper words. We cannot speak one kind of word while having another kind of spirit. No one can be a minister in this way. The kind of spirit we have must match the kind of word we speak. But when the spirit is released, it cannot express itself; it must be accompanied by feelings. If our feelings are unusable, or if they are heading in a different direction from that of our spirit, the spirit is unable to do anything. Hence, our spirit must match God's word, and our feelings must also match God's word.

FEELINGS BEING RELEASED TOGETHER
WITH THE WORD

While a minister of the word is speaking, it is not enough for him to release words alone. If the obstacles mentioned above are not dealt with, nothing will happen even if one has light, thoughts, the inner word, the memory, and the outer words; all of these will be vain. It is a big problem for our feeling to be different from the feeling in God's word. Today we should not try to touch the feeling of the Bible in an outward way. Rather, we should speak with our feelings when we exercise our inner being to speak from the Bible. God's word embodies God's feelings, and He demands that we have the same feelings. When we speak, our feelings must match our words. Our feelings should be reflected in our words. Only then will our feelings touch the audience. In other words, when we speak with our feelings, the Holy Spirit reaches others through our feelings.

What is the problem today? The problem is that some have the revelation and the word, but they do not have the fruit. Why do some have the revelation and the word but not the fruit? The only explanation is that their spirit is not released, and their spirit is not released because their feelings are not released. When their feelings are not released, the Holy Spirit does not have a channel through which to release Himself. Hence, even when we have the light and the word, we can still be fruitless if our feelings are absent. We must remember that feelings are needed to release the word. We have to have light, thoughts, the inner word, memory, and the outer words. But when we speak, we must have feelings as well. The Holy Spirit touches men through feelings. Of course, trying to touch others with feelings alone is just a performance. It only conveys death; it is not the ministry of the word. We can touch others with our feelings because both our spirit and the Holy Spirit are working already. In other words, our feelings must match our speaking before both can be released in a powerful way. Only then will the Holy Spirit operate in others when the word is released. It is a great frustration indeed when the first hindrance we encounter in our speaking is ourselves.

When some brothers stand up to speak, the first hurdle they face in discharging their burden is themselves. They try very hard to release what they want to say. Yet they have one problem: their words do not seem to go very far. There are hurdles; the words are not easily released. The word cannot find a proper channel for its release. The biggest hurdle with these ones is themselves. While they speak to the brothers about the Lord's love, they do not feel the Lord's love at all. Such a feeling is not in them. It is not a matter of whether or not they have seen the love of the Lord, but a matter of whether they have the sense and the feeling of the Lord's love as they are speaking. A brother may have seen the sinfulness of sin, but when he stands up to speak, he may not feel the sinfulness of sin. His words and his feelings do not match. He is short of the proper feelings. When a brother stands up to speak about the grief of repentance, but does not have the feeling of such grief, his words are not released in a proper way. If he does not have feelings for it, his audience will surely not have feelings for it. We minister the word to others because they do not have the feeling, thoughts, and light. We have seen the sinfulness of sin, but they have not. If we want them to see the sinfulness of sin, we must have feelings about it when we speak. Only then will a word on the sinfulness of sin affect them, and only then will our word convey the proper feeling to them. We have to reach their feelings, and we have to speak until they see the same thing that we see. If we are short of feeling or our feeling is not usable, others' feelings will not be affected. George Whitefield was very effective in speaking about hell. One day while he was speaking on hell, men held on to pillars in fear of slipping into hell. His word on hell was full of feelings. It was as if hell was opening up for the sinners right before their eyes. Because he spoke with such feeling, his spirit went out with the words, and the Holy Spirit went out as well. This is the reason men were so touched that they held on to the pillars for fear of slipping into hell.

If a man is very careless with his speaking, he will not be conscious of the limitations of his feelings. He will not realize that his words are vain and that his speaking is useless. If we are serious about being ministers of the word and serious about speaking to an audience, we will find that our feelings often are inadequate. We will realize that the thing that hinders us the most is our feelings. This first hurdle frustrates us. We may need to say a very strong word today, but the more we speak, the weaker we feel; our feeling cannot match our speaking. Our words are harsh, but not our feeling. The more we speak, the less serious the matter sounds. Our feeling cannot catch up with our words, and all that is left is shouting. Many brothers only know how to shout; however, their shouting is not for others but for themselves. They cannot do anything else, and so they shout. Whenever they shout, others immediately know that they are short of feelings. When many people speak, half of their energy is spent on struggling with themselves. They spend half of their energy on themselves because their feelings are so short. They have to speak until they have the feelings first. They have to speak until they come up to a desired level before they are able to convey the same word to others. Words that are meant for others have to be spoken to the ministers first because they are a barrier to their word. It is a serious problem with many people to find, after stepping onto the platform, that they are in fact a barrier to their own words. They want to pass on God's word to others, yet they do not have such a feeling before God. Their feelings do not match their words. As a result, their words are blocked. We must see that a minister of the word must have usable feelings. If he does not have them, he is not qualified to be a minister of the word. If his feelings are not adequate, his words cannot be released; they will be blocked inside of him. This is a serious thing, a very serious thing. This is where much of the problem lies. We have the word, but our feelings are different from the word. We realize the seriousness of the word, yet our feelings do not match it in seriousness. When the word is released, our feelings should be released at the same time. Yet we find out that our feelings are absent. If a man speaks without any feeling at all, no one will believe him. It would be useless even if he shouted at the top of his voice. While he is speaking, he does not feel the things he is speaking. In fact, he may even find the whole exercise amusing; he may feel that he is performing. How can one expect others to believe such a word? We can only expect others to believe our word if we believe the word ourselves and have a feeling for it ourselves. If the more we speak, the colder and more unnatural we become, and if we realize that our feelings really do not match our word, we can be certain that our spirit is not released, that the Holy Spirit is not released, and that our word has no power.

THE CULTIVATION OF TENDER FEELINGS

We should not merely know how to apply our feelings. We also should know how to take the right way to acquire feelings that are proper and usable. This leads to a consideration of our basic experience, which is the breaking of our outer man. In the previous discussion of the minister as a person, we paid special attention to the breaking of the outer man. Unless the outer man is broken, the Lord's word cannot be released. Unless the outer man is broken, a great part of it can never be used by the Lord. We have to repeat this point.

We need to see how the Lord breaks our outer man and how
He prepares our feelings for the ministry of the word.

God deals with a man by arranging all kinds of circumstances to buffet him. This buffeting naturally produces
wounds and pain. When a man receives wounds and pain, his
feelings are hurt, and they become more tender than before.
Man's feelings are the tenderest part of his outer man; this
part is more tender than the will or the mind. Yet even this
tenderness is not enough for God. It is not tender enough to
satisfy the demand of God's word. In order for God's word to
be released through us, we must be full of feelings for His
word. In order for God to use us to be ministers of the word,
our feeling has to match the word's feeling. The feeling of
every minister of the word must match the word he ministers.
Every minister of the word has to be equipped with such
feelings—feelings the word demands. The feelings for the word
must be rich enough. A speaker must have the sense that
when God's word is released, his person is released as well.
Otherwise, the word will not be powerful in others, and it will
not be powerful in him.

After one goes through God's dealings, he realizes how
crude his feelings are in the eyes of God. Although the feelings
are the most tender part of a person, these feelings are still
crude and are useless in the eyes of God. If our feelings are
not tender enough when God's word is released through our
mouth, we will find that some of it is padded with feelings,
while some of it is void of feelings. In painting, a painter
has to mix the paint powder well. If the powder is not well
blended, some areas will be left untouched. If the paint is
well mixed, the whole surface will be evenly covered. This is
true of the feelings of the minister of the word. Those whose
feelings are crude will miss the mark in eight out of ten
sentences. Those whose feelings are fine will match every
word with their feelings. In the Bible the Lord's life is typified
by fine flour. This means that our Lord was very fine in His
feelings. It is a horrible thing when brothers say things
without having any feeling about them at all. Their feelings
are unusable. Their feelings cannot match their words; they
are not fine enough. Their feelings hardly are expressed in

one or two out of ten sentences. We have to remember that unrefined feelings cripple the release of God's word. We need the Lord to work on us until our feelings are fine and tender. We must be broken before our feelings can be tender before the Lord. In the Bible we find the writers of the Scripture not only full of experience of life and thoughts of the Holy Spirit but full of spiritual *feelings* as well. The ministers of the word in the Bible released their word with much feeling for the word. Today in serving as ministers of the word, we have to release the word with feelings. If our feelings cannot match our word, our audience will not take our word seriously. If God's hand has never touched us and broken our outer man, naturally our feelings are not tender in the eyes of God; we do not have any wound or hurt. If we are sensitive in a certain matter, it means that we have a wound and a hurt in that matter. The grains of wheat must be ground into powder before they can be fine. We must have wounds and hurts before our feelings can be tender. The more wounds and hurts we have, the tenderer we become. As the pressure is applied, the one grain is enlarged to three, five, seven, or one hundred grains. The feelings become finer. We should not expect to be fine in our feelings if we have not suffered any wound or bleeding from God. There is not such a thing. We must have wounds, and we must go through dealings.

As soon as we touch some brothers, we know that the Lord's work is not deep enough in them. If a brother is disciplined and has learned to walk somewhat properly, has advanced somewhat in his conduct, and has made progress in the study of the Scripture as well as in other areas, yet has failed to become tender in his feelings, he is missing something before the Lord; there are still some parts in him that God cannot use. No matter how much a person's outward behavior changes and no matter how much light he sees within, his training is still too superficial and shallow if he is lacking in feelings. When a man touches the work of the Lord's cross, his entire person is broken. His strong will is no longer stubborn, his arrogant mentality is no longer arrogant. His will is broken, and his arrogant mind is also subdued. At the same time, his feelings become more and more refined. The Lord can deal with a person's will with one great shining of His light. A man may think that he is clever and resourceful, and the Lord can bring down his exalted mind in one great shining. However, the feelings cannot be dealt with through one shining. Tenderness in one's feelings is the result of an accumulation of countless numbers of dealings. One's feelings do not become tender until he has passed through certain circumstances. If we are sloppy in certain matters, the Lord will arrange circumstance after circumstance to deal with us. After one circumstance goes away, another one comes. Time after time, we are ground and pressed like grains in a mill. Eventually, we will be pulverized into fine flour.

Before the Lord we need a stricken spirit. What is a stricken spirit? Since the spirit is expressed through the feelings, a stricken spirit has the feeling of being stricken. The Lord desires that we live in a stricken spirit; He desires that our feelings be fine and tender. Such tender feelings are not in us; we acquire them through being stricken. The Lord wants us to live in a stricken spirit, which means that He wants us to have the feeling of being stricken. We should be so broken by the Lord that the feeling of His chastisement is fresh with us, and His discipline should still be fresh in our memory. The Lord has to work on us so much that we fear and tremble in our feeling, that we no longer dare to be cavalier or lazy. Every time God works on us, chastises us, and deals with us, our feelings become finer and more sensitive. This is the deepest lesson in the breaking of the outward man. The breaking of the feelings may not be as drastic as the breaking of the will and the mind, but it is much deeper.

If we live in a stricken spirit and if there is a wound in us, we feel the pain. This pain spontaneously makes us fearful; our feelings are refined by the pain. As we are dealt with repeatedly, we become genuinely happy when our hearts are happy and genuinely sad when our hearts are sad. When God's word comes to us again, we will sense the feelings of the word, and our feelings will match the word. This is a glorious thing. The purpose of chastisement is to make us compatible with God's word. When He speaks or expresses a desire again, our feelings will match His feelings. The Lord is disciplining us. He repeatedly tries us until we have a wound and a scar in our body. We were once coarse and insensitive, but after discipline, we begin to have feelings. As soon as God's word comes, we feel something. As soon as He moves, we are sensitive to it. At least during the period immediately after our discipline we can match God's word. As the Lord increases His discipline in us, we are broken, and all our feelings come up to His standard. A minister of the word must come up to the standard of the Lord's word in all his feelings. After we have gone through such discipline in our feelings, we discover one interesting thing: We not only speak God's word, but we feel His word as well.

What we feel inwardly is expressed outwardly. Peter "lifted up his voice" when he spoke at Pentecost (Acts 2:14). He lifted his voice because his feelings were strong. I am afraid some of us have never lifted up our voice in our speaking. The only explanation is that our feelings are not strong enough. Peter was full of feelings as he spoke, and because his feelings were so strong, he was able to lift up his voice when he spoke. God's word has feelings, and it does not come out like words from a dictating machine. It is pressed out by strong feelings. Paul exhorted the church in Corinth "through many tears" (2 Cor. 2:4). I am afraid many people have never shed tears in their messages because their feelings are too short. Lifting up one's voice or shedding one's tears are not big things in themselves. But if a person has never lifted up his voice or shed his tears, something is wrong. There is no special merit to lifting up the voice or shedding tears. But there is definitely something wrong with those who have never lifted up their voice or shed tears; the feelings of such ones have never been broken by the Lord. If a man's feelings have been finely ground, he will rejoice when God's word calls for rejoicing and weep when God's word calls for weeping. This is not a performance. Do not try to perform. If it is a performance, an experienced person immediately will see through the farce and artificiality. We must never be artificial. Artificiality only corrupts God's word. What we are saying here is that we must have proper feelings. We have to have the same feeling as God's word. Joy and sadness are opposite examples. When the Bible speaks of joy, the proper reaction is to rejoice, and when it speaks of sadness, the proper reaction is to grieve. Some people are so bound up in themselves all their lives that they are always cold. They do not rejoice when others play the flute, and they do not mourn when others weep. Their feelings cannot meet the need, and God's word is frustrated through them.

Why do so many people have feelings that cannot be used at all? Why does the Lord bring them through so many experiences? It is because the root of man's feelings lies in the person himself. The problem with feelings is different from the problems with the will and the mind. The problems with the will and the mind are more complicated. The problem with feelings is simply that they are centered around the person himself. Many people expend all of their feelings on themselves. They have little difficulty feeling for themselves. If a man expends all of his feelings on himself, he does not have any feelings for others. Some brothers are dull and insensitive to everything; they seem to be indifferent to everything. Yet they are not insensitive or indifferent to themselves. A brother can be rude to every other brother, but if someone is rude to him, he is offended. This brother has expended all of his feelings on himself. He loves himself and cares for himself. When he suffers, he feels it. When he has problems, he weeps, but he has no feelings whatsoever for others' affairs. Brothers, if the Lord does not conquer our feelings completely, we will be useless in the ministry of the word. The Lord often lays His hand on us through the discipline of the Holy Spirit with the purpose of turning our feelings toward others. We need to direct all of our feelings into the service of the ministry of the word. We have no time to spend our feelings on ourselves. Our feelings have to be tender all the time. Once they are exhausted, they become useless. Many people are obsessed with themselves; they think that they are the center of the universe. All their feelings revolve around themselves. God has to deliver them out of their shells. We do not have an unlimited supply of feelings. If we exhaust our feelings, we will not be able to be a minister of God's word. God must discipline us and deal with us until we do not have feelings for ourselves and until our feelings become tender. The foundation of tender feelings is a freedom from self-centeredness. The Lord has to break down our feelings so that we will no longer be self-centered. The more we are ground and the finer we become, the more our feelings will become useful.

A minister of the word has to have feelings that are fine and rich before God can make use of them. We must remember that our words are only as rich as our feelings. The amount of riches in our word is determined by our feelings. Our inward feelings dictate the number of words we speak. Sometimes we have many words, yet our feelings are not strong enough to match them. At such times, our words are bound by our feelings. All ministers of the word have to remember that their words can only go as far as the breaking they have received from God. The words cannot go beyond the person's condition. Some people have trouble with their mind. Others are short in their feelings. They are still short in God's breaking work. A spiritual man is rich in all kinds of feelings. The more spiritual a person is, the more feelings he has. Never think that the more spiritual a man becomes, the more insensitive he becomes. The more lessons a man learns from God, the richer his feelings will be. If the feelings of a sinner were compared to the feelings of Paul, it would be easy to see that Paul was superior both in his spirituality as well as in his feelings. The more dealings a person receives, the more feelings he has. When our feelings are enriched, we find the right sentiment to match the words we speak. When the feelings match the words, God's word finds the free outlet He desires. If words are spoken yet feelings lag behind, the two are out of step, and the utterance will not be satisfactory. We feel that something is wrong. We may try to say more, and we may try to raise our voice, but something still is wrong because our feelings do not match our speaking.

If a man desires to be a minister of the word, he must subject himself to strong dealings. Once he turns away from a dealing, he will fall behind. We must be dismantled before the Lord. Unless we are broken, we cannot accomplish any work. Without discipline, there is no work. Even if we were the wisest men in the whole world, we still would be useless. It does not matter how clever or knowledgeable we are. Only those who have been broken are useful. This is a very serious matter. Our emotions and feelings must go through repeated dealings before they can become useful to our speaking. If the Lord has dealt with our self-love once or twice, when we speak about self-love, our feelings spontaneously will match our speaking. There will be no hindrance whatsoever. If our pride has been dealt with, when we speak about pride and about the Lord resisting the proud, our feelings will match our words. In other words, our feelings can match our words only to the extent that they have been touched. Our feelings must be totally and universally stripped before they can serve us in the release of the word. This is the only way for us to prepare ourselves for the ministry of the word. Our feelings must match the word. The extent of our feelings will determine the extent of the speaking that we can render. Every time our words touch something higher, our feelings have to be made finer. May the Lord be gracious to us, and may all of our feelings match our words.

CHAPTER SIXTEEN

THE WORD AND
THE RELEASE OF THE SPIRIT

THE RELATIONSHIP
BETWEEN THE WORD AND THE SPIRIT

Now let us turn to the matter of the word and the release of the spirit. Whether or not the spoken word is received as revelation or merely doctrine depends very much on whether the minister is releasing his spirit. Whether or not others hear just words or hear the words and see the light depends on whether the minister's spirit is released. Whether or not a person falls on his face at the word or remains unchanged depends on whether the minister can release his spirit. The words may be right and feelings may be present, but if the spirit is not released, others will only touch a perfect doctrine or a high teaching. It is something that they can understand, but they do not touch God's word. The word can be released without the spirit at all. It can be spoken in a very common way. If a serious word is spoken with a common, indifferent spirit, the word will become very common. But when a message is released with a strong spirit, the message itself will become strong spontaneously. The words may be perfectly right in themselves, but there is also a matter of the kind of spirit that accompanies the release of these words. This depends on whether or not the minister of the word has released his spirit. A minister of the word can release his spirit in an ordinary way or he can release it in a strong way. He can even let out his spirit in an explosive way. The quality of the word depends on the way the spirit is released. The result that the words produce in others depends not so much on the words themselves but on how the spirit is released. While a minister is speaking, he can release his spirit or he can withhold his spirit. He can release it in a strong way, or he can release it in an ordinary way. This decision is in the hands of the minister. A minister of the word has to learn to push out his spirit during his speaking.

There is a close relationship between the spirit and the word. When the spirit is affected, the word is affected. When the spirit is wrong, the word is wrong. It is difficult to clearly explain how the spirit affects the word. All we can say is that man's spirit is very tender and fine; it must not be tampered with or offended. In preaching God's word, one may have everything in place. But if the spirit is not ready, there is no way for the word to be released. A man must release his spirit before he can release God's word. Every experienced preacher of the word knows what it means to release the spirit. If it is windy, rainy, and dark outside, and one hesitates to open the door of his house to go out, someone else must give him a push to help him go out the door. This is how the spirit is pushed out. When we stand up to speak in the meeting, it is possible that our spirit will not move, and we will have to push it out. If we do not push it out, there will be a marked deterioration in our speaking. Often when we push a little to release the spirit, the words become much more powerful. Others will not only hear the words but will touch the very thing behind the words. They will not only touch our words, they will touch our spirit as well. Sometimes a person can understand every word of a message, and he can even repeat and recite the message to others; however, he cannot repeat the spirit. At other times, when a person hears a message, he not only hears the words but touches the spirit as well. If a man does not touch the spirit, the word will have no effect on him.

The same can be said about reading the Bible. Some people only see words when they read the Bible, while others touch the spirit of the Bible. When some read the Bible, they only see Paul's word but do not discern his tone. They cannot discern whether the tone is high or low, soft or loud. They do not know whether it is a tone of sadness or a tone of joy. When others read the Bible, they see Paul's words as well as discern his tone. They know the sadness in Paul's prayer or words. They also know whether Paul was speaking in anger or with joy. They touch Paul's spirit. We may read through the book of Acts sentence by sentence, but we may not touch the utterance within the word. Paul cast out a demon from a slave girl (16:18). If we do not touch the spirit, we will only know that the demon was cast out; we will not know what exactly happened. We will not know whether Paul was speaking with a loud or strong tone of voice, because we have not touched the spirit. We must get into the spirit of the writers of the Bible before we can know the Bible they have written. The Scripture these ones have written is an expression of the kind of spirits they have. If we only touch the word without touching the spirit, we cannot read the Bible.

Similarly, we must experience God's dealings before we can release our spirit in our speaking. If we have never been dealt with by the Lord, or if the dealing is not deep, pure, or clean enough, our spirit can never go out with God's word. Even if we try to push our spirit out, there is nothing for us to push. We may push out doctrines, but we can never push out the spirit that lies behind God's word. We have to remember the meaning of preaching. Preaching means the release of the word. But this is not all; preaching also means the release of the spirit. When a minister of the word releases the word, he is releasing his own spirit at the same time. His spirit is released through his speaking. Spontaneously, the Spirit of God is released through the spirit of man. The Holy Spirit is released together with man's spirit. If man's spirit is not released, the Holy Spirit is not released. This poses a great problem to the speaker. We need to remember that listening to a message has nothing to do with listening to the words; it has to do with touching the spirit.

We need to realize that when the word is released, that is, when the ministry of the word is released, not only is the word released, but the spirit is released as well. The listener should not touch just the word but should touch the spirit as well. If a man only touches the word without touching the spirit, what he has is something very common and mundane. If we have not touched the spirit, we will be indifferent to even God's own speaking. Only when we touch the spirit do we touch life. The Lord said, "The words which I have spoken to you are spirit and are life" (John 6:63). We have to touch the spirit before we can know the meaning of the word. In preaching God's word, we must take care not only of conveying the right words but of releasing our spirit. It is a fact that a man cannot release his spirit continually. One has to pay a certain price to release his spirit. A minister of the word often cannot afford to pay such a price. This is the reason that no man can release his spirit continually. Of course, the stronger our spirit is before the Lord, the easier it is for us to release it; we can release it again and again. It is difficult to believe that a man can stand up and speak for God and yet never once release his spirit. At least once or more than once, he has released his spirit, forcing his spirit to go out with his words, and others have touched his spirit. No one prostrates himself before words alone. A man is humbled because he has touched the spirit. If all we have are words, these words will easily become doctrines. Even a word of revelation can easily become a doctrine. If we preach a word of revelation and release our spirit at the same time, others will touch not only the word but the spirit as well. God's Spirit reaches others by passing through our spirit.

THE TRAINING OF THE SPIRIT

The exercise of the spirit of a minister of the word depends on two things. First, there is the training of the spirit; second, there is the willingness on the part of the minister. Whether or not a minister can exercise his spirit to minister to the church and the extent to which and the areas in which he is able to exercise his spirit depend entirely on the amount of experience he has related to these two things.

First, let us speak of the training of the spirit. A minister of the word cannot release his spirit more than what he has learned to release. The extent to which his spirit is released is determined by the amount of training he has received from God in his spirit. If a brother has not received much training, we cannot expect him to exercise his spirit to any great extent. But if he has received strict and repeated trainings in his spirit, it will be easy and spontaneous for him to exercise his spirit in the ministry of the word. His exercise will go as far as his training carries him. A man cannot release a spirit that he does not possess. His limits before the Lord are the limit of his spirit. This is a very basic lesson.

God spends a great deal of time during our lifetime to train our spirit so that it can become useful. He has to train us to such an extent that we can use our spirit freely and copiously. The Lord arranges our circumstances with a view to breaking us; He puts us in unbearable environments. Just like Paul, when he went through his experiences described in 2 Corinthians, we may find these environments to be severe and harsh. He said that he was excessively burdened beyond his power and despaired even of living (1:8). The environments the Lord prepares for us are always greater than what we can bear and what our strength can handle. Every thorn that we suffer is an unbearable, unendurable, and insurmountable thorn to us. When the Lord puts us in these environments, two things are produced. On the one hand, the Lord breaks our outer man through these environments. Our mind is torn down at times; our emotions are torn down at other times. Even more, our will is totally broken. We are left with no choice but to yield totally to the Lord and to confess our failures and inability. This is the negative part of the result. On the other hand, under the discipline of the Holy Spirit, something positive is produced by God. Do we remain flat on the ground as we are being torn down, or do we eventually rise up? Are we defeated by the thorn, or do we eventually overcome the thorn? Do we say that we are excessively burdened beyond our power and despair even of living and then do nothing more about it, or do we look to the One who raises the dead and rise above the fall? We must remember that the Lord always puts us in environments which are beyond our power, environments which drive us to despair even of living and which strip us of all hope. In such hopeless environments, we gradually learn to trust in Him, to look to Him, and to rely on Him.

It is very easy for us to talk about trusting in the Lord at ordinary times! How common is our speaking concerning looking to Him at such times, and we thoughtlessly speak of relying on Him! Yet only when the Lord puts us in a hopeless situation do we begin to learn to trust in Him and to rely on Him a little. As we begin to touch a little of God's grace and power, we unconsciously find ourselves overcoming. We realize that even our trusting is a believing that is exercised in the midst of weaknesses, that our looking to Him is done in fear and trembling, and that our trust operates in the absence of any assurance whatsoever. We may think that this faith, trust, and reliance on Him are feeble and not of much use. Yet it is in the midst of such weaknesses that we acquire a little faith, a little trust, and a little reliance on Him. Unconsciously we touch a little grace and a little power. Under such circumstances we find mercy to overcome, and our spirit is trained. This is a matter not only of the breaking of the outer man but also of the training of the spirit. It is not merely a definite and negative breaking but a definite and positive building up. It is here that we find circumstances that we can overcome and circumstances that the Lord has called us to overcome, and it is here that we find the Lord raising us up above our problems. Unconsciously we overcome them. Satan can try his best in these circumstances to attack us, yet our feeble trust, our feeble waiting, and our feeble faith bring us to God's power. Here we are able to say to Satan, "You have done all you can. Humanly speaking this is beyond my power, but thank the Lord, I have overcome. He has given me hope. He is the One who raises the dead, and He is the One who strengthens the weak." Through such an experience, our spirit is strengthened a little. It receives a certain amount of training, and it is enriched a little. Through this, our spirit acquires some useful deposits and accumulates some strength.

The Lord's work in us does not happen just once. He works in us repeatedly and in many ways. As He operates in us repeatedly, our spirit becomes stronger and stronger. God not only breaks our outer man through the environment; He also builds up our inner man. He not only tears down our outward man; He also builds up our spirit. We rise above our trials through the rising up of our spirit. We never come out of a trial without our spirit first coming out of it. As our spirit learns something, receives some dealing, and passes through some training, our entire person also rises up out of the trial. Daily the Lord is building us up. When we are put into trials, we are pressed on all sides. But when we come out of the trials, the environments are beneath us, and we transcend above our surroundings. When we are in the trials, we feel weak. But when we emerge from them, we are strong. What goes in is death; what comes out is the resurrection life. No trial can lock us in, and we are different when we emerge from a trial. We cannot remain the same through a trial. Either the trial ruins us and makes us useless vessels, or we emerge from the trial on a more glorious plane. A trial either makes us better or worse. All those who cannot pass through the trials are unfit for any use. All those who withstand the trials and overcome them have a mark of victory with them the rest of their life. They have been delivered out of their circumstances, and the Lord will grant them similar victories when they encounter similar situations. When a new environment comes along and new difficulties arise, they will experience new victories. In other words, their spirits have learned something new; they have undergone some new training.

Whenever we go through a trial, we go through it with the view of eventually transcending it. The more trials we have, the more strength we find to meet the trials. Through this process our spirits are strengthened. Whenever we go through an experience, our spirits are strengthened. The more experiences we go through, the stronger our spirits become. Through the discipline of the Holy Spirit, the Lord breaks our outer man again and again. When the outer man is broken, the inner man is empowered to overcome all obstacles. When the hammer falls on us, it breaks and shatters our outer man. But the same hammer becomes something which our spirit overcomes. When the Lord puts us in an environment, our outer man is broken. Our outer man cannot withstand any trial. Whenever a trial comes, our outer man is broken. The more trials we have, the more our outer man is broken. At the same time, the spirit prevails over these environments. The environment prevails over our outer man, but our inner man prevails over the environment at the same time. Through this process we are delivered from the environment and eventually overcome it. This is what happens when we go through trials. The same thing is repeated whenever we face a trial: The Lord first gives us a trial and puts us under it. We experience the breaking of the outer man, but the experience does not stop there. Our inner man rises up to overcome the environment, and we emerge on the other side. The trial which overcomes our outer man is eventually overcome by our inner man. Whenever we go through an experience, our spirit receives some training. It becomes more aggressive; it learns a little more of the Lord's grace and His Spirit. In other words, it becomes stronger than before. When our spirit is trained and becomes strong, we will have a usable spirit in our ministry of the word.

On the one hand, a minister of the word must experience the breaking down of the outer man. On the other hand, his spirit has to be trained to be strong and useful. This work can only be accomplished by the discipline of the Holy Spirit. When we go through a trial, we have to remember that such a trial makes us different in the end. Either we will become stronger or become worse. Either we will murmur against God in our trial and remain defeated or we will come out of it in full victory. We should refuse to come out of it in defeat. Second Corinthians 12 shows us that when a thorn comes, God gives us the grace to overcome the thorn. In the past we knew a little about grace, but we did not know the kind of grace that comes with the thorn. Every trial comes with its thorn-laced blow so that we can experience the thorn-laced grace. What we knew before was a thornless grace; what we know now is a thorn-laced grace. We are like a boat that floats in two feet of water. As long as the water remains two feet deep, we can sail through it quite easily. But if there is a rock that is two feet high in the middle of the stream, the boat cannot go through. At such times we need to ask the Lord to raise the water level by two feet. When we know more grace, our spirit becomes stronger. Paul said that he would "rather boast in...weaknesses" (2 Cor. 12:9). Whenever a weakness comes, we are empowered, and we can serve as a minister of the word by this power. Different ministers of the word have different degrees of spiritual power because they experience different kinds of building work. The words of the ministers may be the same, but their spirits are different. If we want to use our spirit, it must first become strong. We may be trained, but the extent to which we have been trained determines the extent to which our spirit can be used. This extent varies in different people. The degree to which our spirit is trained determines the extent to which we can be used as a minister of the word. Whenever a minister of the word encounters a trial or an affliction, he should realize that God is using it to prepare him to be His minister. We should not be so foolish as to think that it is best to escape. The more we run away, the less things will work out for us. We should always remember that without the thorn, there will never be the grace or the power, and the sphere of our service will be very much confined. We may still speak, but we will not have the spirit to release the word. We may have the word, but we must still have a properly functioning spirit to accompany the word.

WILLINGNESS ON THE PART OF THE MINISTERS

The exercise of a minister's spirit is something that demands his life. He has to put his life on the line. When a person serves as a minister of the word, he must not only have a useful spirit, but he must be willing to sacrifice and expend his spirit. Every time a person serves as a minister of the word and ministers the word to others, he has to exercise his spirit by pouring out his life, just as the Lord Jesus did when He poured out His life. The night the Lord prayed in the garden of Gethsemane, He said to the disciples, "The spirit is willing, but the flesh is weak" (Matt. 26:41). With the disciples, there was only willingness. With the Lord Jesus, there was not only willingness in His spirit but a readiness to pour out His life. This is the reason His sweat became like great drops of blood falling down upon the ground (Luke 22:44). In other words, one's spirit is exercised by the pouring out of his very life. One has to exhaust all his energy, being spent to the point of experiencing spiritual fatigue and spiritual death. Whenever the spirit is released, it challenges the weaknesses and death in others. There is a price involved in releasing the spirit in this way; it is a release of burden, a release that results in pain and fatigue. The release of the spirit requires a sacrifice, whether in private talks or in public speaking. We have to release our spirit because many people are spiritually weak. Our spirit has to be pushed to the forefront to confront these spiritual weaknesses and to destroy them. We must wrestle with these elements and pin them down. When our spirit is released, we will find that many people have spiritual death, spiritual coldness, spiritual stubbornness, and spiritual dryness. We have to push out our spirit in order to suppress and overcome their death. We have to transcend their death and swallow up their death. As soon as we are filled with the word, we will see that those sitting before us are filled with darkness; they cannot see. We have to release our spirit in a strong way, as if we are storming the stronghold of darkness and confronting the attack of darkness. We are preaching God's word on the one hand, and we are confronting the attack of the forces of darkness on the other hand. Such death and darkness will try to swallow up our spiritual energy. While we are standing before men, we have to release our spirit. We have to overcome their darkness and break through their shadows. This is a work that requires sacrifice. It is spiritually exhausting, and it demands a high price. While a minister of the word does not necessarily have to pay this high price every time, he must be willing to pay such a price.

In order to exercise the spirit in this way, a person must first have a proper functioning spirit. Actually, one can only exercise his spirit to the extent that it has been trained. He cannot do anything beyond this extent. But whether or not he can even exercise his spirit to that extent depends on his willingness. Sometimes a person experiences great pressure before the Lord. If he is willing to pay the price to break through, he will break through. But if he is not willing to pay a great price, he may choose to release his spirit in a common and easy way. It is not an easy thing for a minister of the word to stretch his spirit to the limit. A man may exercise his spirit very much, but he may not be willing to stretch it to the ultimate limit. It is spiritually exhausting for a brother to push his spirit to its limit or near to its limit. It is, therefore, not unusual to find a minister who is reluctant to push himself to his limit.

Those who do not know anything about paying the price for the release of the spirit will not know what I am speaking of here. A man who realizes the burden that must be borne in releasing his spirit will know what I am speaking of. A person who has never lifted two hundred pounds has no idea how heavy two hundred pounds are. Only those who have lifted two hundred pounds know how much energy is needed to lift such a weight. Whenever a person fulfills a spiritual ministry, whenever he exercises his spirit, he carries a burden that seems to demand all of his energy. In the exercise of the spirit, the amount of one's willingness before the Lord is a controlling factor. If a man is willing, he can push the word out. The more he is willing, the more strongly the word will be released. In speaking from the platform and in conversing with the brothers privately, the strength of the word that is released depends on the amount of the spirit that is pushed out. In serving others with the word, the spirit is under the minister's own control. A minister can withhold the spirit, or he can release his spirit. As he is speaking, he can either make his message strong or weak. If he is willing to sacrifice himself, he will strengthen the meeting. If he is not willing to sacrifice himself and is not willing to pay the price, he will make the meeting a common thing. The decision to make a meeting strong or weak is in the hand of the minister of the word.

For those who have never been trained, the work of the Holy Spirit is beyond one's grasp. For those who have received dealings from the Lord, and in whom the Lord has done a deep work, the result of a meeting is determined by the ministers themselves. The amount of the Holy Spirit's work is determined by the amount of sacrifice the ministers pay. If we are not afraid of exhaustion in a meeting, if we are not lazy, and if we are not affected by the audience or held back from paying the price or taking the dealings, we will release our spirit in a strong way. When the word goes out, the spirit will go out as well, and the word will have a strong impact on others. But if we are exhausted, lazy, or reluctant to do anything, we can say the same thing in a hurried way, but our spirit will be bound. The words are the same and the speaking is the same, but the spirit will not be released. Or it will be released only in a limited and weak way. Others will touch the word, but they will not touch the spirit. They will only hear the sound, but the words will not have any impact on them. The words may be accurate, but they will be weak.

In the ministry of the word, there is not only the manner of the delivery of the word but also the matter of willingness on the part of the deliverer. Are we willing and happy to push out our spirit? If we are willing, the word will spontaneously have a strong impact on others. If we do not push out our spirit, the words will not be strong. Words often are common because the spirit does not break out; rather, it flows out slowly. A gushing spirit knocks down others along the way. The prayers of some brothers can only be described as a breaking forth of the spirit. Their entire spirit bursts forth. Anyone standing in their way is knocked down. The words may be the same, but the spirit is different; it charges forth, and no one can stand in its way. Whether or not a person's spirit is released depends on whether he is willing and ready to pay the price.

A worker has to learn to speak accurately, but this is not all. While he is serving, he has to learn to push out his spirit. If he is willing to pay the price, he can push out his spirit in a strong way. When the word goes out in this way, the spirit follows. The release will be strong, and no one can stand in its way. If, however, a man has been wounded in some kind of way or is going through some experiences, his words may produce no effect at all. The more he speaks, the worse things become and the less effect his speaking produces in others. His words may be the same, but the wound and hurt in his spirit frustrate his speaking. Under these conditions, it is not easy for a man to see God's light. Where there is injury, the spirit is bound, and words become hollow and weak. Words can only be strong when the spirit is pushed out. The spirit has to be in the word. The spirit has to move, and it has to be released through the word. We can say that the spirit must be packaged in the word and released through the word. When one is willing to pay the price to release his spirit through the word, others will see the light and touch the reality.

The release of the spirit is one spiritual facet in the ministry of the word. In fulfilling the ministry of the word, one must do his best to release his spirit. In order to release the spirit in a high way, one has to exert all of his energy. All of the emotions, thoughts, memory, and utterance of a person must be made available and ready. There should be no interrupting thoughts; every thought should remain silent, focused, and available. The memory also has to wait on the spirit. Not a single feeling should run astray. In other words, all of one's energy, memory, utterance, emotions, and feelings must wait on the Lord; every part of his being must be dedicated to the Lord's use. All the activities of the self must stop; only the spirit should remain alert and ready for His use. This is like an army with myriads of soldiers and horses on a battlefield who anxiously wait for a command from the general. We have to use our mind, but our mind cannot be the master; it should only be a servant. We have to use our emotion, but our emotion cannot be the master; it should only be a servant. All of the body's energy and strength must be headed up under the spirit. Only then will the spirit have the liberty to release itself.

If a minister of the word cannot find the right word at the critical moment, his spirit will suffer. If he cannot find the right feelings at the critical moment, his spirit will also suffer; it will not be released. No work requires a higher degree of concentration than the release of the spirit. In order for the spirit to be released, every part of a person's being has to be focused. This does not mean that every part of a person has to be released independently. No! They should be released in conjunction with the spirit. Whatever we say should be what the spirit wants to say, and whatever terminology we use should be the terminology of the spirit. Consider again our earlier illustration. The myriads of soldiers have to wait for the commander's word. If he wants a soldier to do something, the soldier has no choice. If he wants to direct another, that one has no choice either. When we order our spirit to be released, it has to be released. If our thoughts are a little relaxed, confused, or our memory fails a little, our spirit will be in jeopardy; it will be injured.

A minister of the word should learn not to injure his spirit in any way. When we speak, our entire person has to be made available. No part of our being should lag behind; we cannot afford to let any part drag along. No part can afford to wander off and wait for its retrieval. Every part must be on full alert so that the spirit can be released to its fullest extent. This involves a high price. Because such a high price is involved, a minister of the word may not always exercise his spirit to its maximum extent even though it is possible for him to do so. When he is willing, his spirit will be used to a greater extent. When he is not willing, his spirit will be used to a lesser extent. When he is willing, he can bring more blessings to others. When he is not willing, he will bring less blessings to others. The amount of blessing that others receive depends on the amount of his willingness. Blessing in the ministry of the word is determined by the ministers. If we are willing to give others blessing, they will receive blessing. If we want others to be stumbled, they will be stumbled. If we want a great light to shine on them, they will fall on their face. Everything depends on the amount of growth we have in God. The more lessons we have learned from God and the higher and deeper these lessons are, the more often we will be used, and we will be used to a higher and deeper extent. The more we learn from God, the more things we can do. If we have learned only a little from God, we will be able to do very little. We determine how much light others will receive. We determine whether or not others will fall on their face. We determine how much spiritual reality others will touch. The Lord has entrusted this matter to the ministers.

PUSHING OUT THE SPIRIT

Every genuine minister of the word knows what it means to push out the spirit. As he speaks, he has to exert his strength, not his fleshly strength, but another kind of strength. He has to push out his spirit. It seems as if he has to exert all his energy to press out his spirit. The spirit is a force within, and while he speaks, he pushes out this force and releases it. When the word goes out, the spirit is pushed out and released at the same time. When a person pushes out his spirit, those around him will touch something. Whether his audience hears a doctrine or God's word depends on how he pushes out his spirit. If he pushes out his spirit voluntarily and willingly, his listeners will not hear just a message; they will touch something behind the word. But if he does not push out his spirit in his speaking, others will not touch the very thing hidden behind the word. The ministry of the word sometimes becomes very common because there are too many words and too little spirit. One can speak much yet push out his spirit only a little. After an hour or two, he may have pushed out his spirit for just a short amount of time; the rest of the time he may not have pushed out his spirit at all. This is very common. If we push out our spirit with all of our might, we have the ministry of the word. A strong ministry of the word is one in which the amount of words equals the amount of spirit, that is, the two are the same. When the word is released, the spirit is also released. Whenever there is the word, there should be an equal amount of spirit to go with it. The spirit should push the word along. This constitutes a good and strong ministry of the word. The audience in this case touches the released spirit and hears the word. Whether a minister of the word is common or powerful in his utterance depends on his willingness. It also depends on his training. If he is not well trained or if he is not willing, his words will be weak. His utterance is strictly controlled by him. His training constitutes what he has, and his willingness constitutes what he wants to do. On the one hand, a man may have something, but he does not want to give it away. On the other hand, a man may want to give something away, but he does not have that very thing. We must have what we want to give, and we must want to give it. However, we must first have the training before we can have the willingness.

It is proper for the spirit to match the word. However, there are exceptional cases when the amount of spirit exceeds the amount of words. Sometimes one faces special circumstances in which special needs arise, and God may allow one's spirit to go beyond his words. Even though the words can only say so much, the spirit can cover much more. This, however, is very rare, and it is very difficult to achieve. Our spirit will not exceed our words every time, but there are times in which it will. The significance of the ministry of the word lies in the release of the spirit, while the significance of the reception of the word lies in the touching of this spirit. The ministry of the word is a service in spirit. While we speak, we exercise our spirit; when the spirit is released, we have the ministry of the word. The ministry of the word is not merely a release of words but a speaking that is coupled with the spirit. The ministry of the word is a matter not of opening the mouth but of having a definite word within and then pushing out the spirit through the word. Whenever we have the word without the spirit, we have doctrine; we do not have God's word. May all the ministers of the word see that a message is not just a message but the pushing out of the spirit through the speaking of the word. If we only have the word without pushing out the spirit, we do not have a ministry. No minister of the word can function with a dormant spirit, because the ministry of the word is the release of the spirit. God's intention is not just for men to hear the word but for men to touch the spirit of the word. The spirit rides on the word and goes out with it. God wants us to touch His Spirit; He does not want us to merely touch His word. His Spirit is released through the word. Every minister of the word must be able to speak and, at the same time, must be able to push out the spirit behind the word. Whenever we speak, we have to push out our spirit. This is the ministry of the word.

A powerful ministry of the word, that is, a powerful utterance, consists not only of the pushing out of the spirit but even of an explosion of the spirit. This means that when the word is released, the spirit explodes. The spirit is not released in an ordinary way but in a way of explosion. When this happens, men fall on their faces before God. If a man functions as a minister of the word in this way, he can decide whom he will touch on a certain day, release his spirit, and touch that person in exactly the way that he has prescribed. He can predict whom he will shower his spirit upon, and his spirit will come as a shower to that person and soak him thoroughly. This is possible. When he speaks, he will release his words, and any opposing, cold, and stubborn spirit will be subdued. It is possible for the spirit to be released in an explosive way. When the spirit is released in this way, others will touch something and will fall down no matter how stubborn they may be. We have to pay attention to the amount of spirit we release during our speaking. The release of our spirit cannot exceed the capacity we have within us. We can only release as much as we have. The measure of power is limited by the capacity we have; we cannot force ourselves to do more. It is not a matter of our words, our voice, or our attitude. Resorting to these things is just performing. We should never pretend to have a certain attitude or a certain tone of voice when we are void of the spirit. We should realize that a man can be subdued only by the release of the spirit. No one can stand in the face of the spirit.

What is the meaning of the release of the spirit? We will mention a few points.

The Release of the Spirit
Being the Release of the Holy Spirit

What is the release of the spirit? The release of the spirit means the release of the Holy Spirit. The Lord has entrusted the Holy Spirit to the church. His intention is for the church to be the innermost being out of which will flow rivers of living water of the Spirit (John 7:38). The church is the vessel of the Holy Spirit. We must realize what is the work of the church today. The church is the vessel of the Holy Spirit. God has not poured out His anointing oil indiscriminately on the whole world; He has poured it out on the church. The church now anoints men with this anointing oil. The meaning of the church being a vessel of the Holy Spirit is not that it is an instrument used by the Holy Spirit but that it is a vessel to contain the Holy Spirit. The church is a vessel, which means that the Holy Spirit is contained in the church. But how is God's Spirit contained in the church? The part in us that contains God's Spirit is simply our spirit. All Bible students acknowledge this. The type in the Old Testament is very clear. The dove sent out by Noah could not descend on the old creation; it could only descend on the new creation (Gen. 8:6-12). In our entire being, only the spirit is of the new creation. Hence, the Holy Spirit can only remain in our spirit. Exodus says that the holy anointing oil could not be poured on the flesh (30:31-32). No part of the flesh can contain the Holy Spirit; the spirit is the only place that can contain the Holy Spirit. Ezekiel 36 says this in a more explicit way: "A new spirit will I put within you....And I will put my Spirit within you" (vv. 26-27). The "new spirit" is our spirit, while "my Spirit" is the Holy Spirit. If we do not have a new spirit within us, we cannot possibly have God's Spirit. We must have a new spirit before we can have His Spirit.

The meaning of pushing out our spirit is to release the Holy Spirit together with our spirit. All Bible students know that in many instances in the Greek language it is hard to differentiate between the human spirit and the Holy Spirit. The word *spirit* is spoken of most frequently in chapter eight of Romans. Yet in Romans 8 it is hard to tell which occurrence of the word *spirit* refers to the human spirit and which refers to the Holy Spirit. In English there is a distinction of capitalization, but in Greek, there is no distinction of capitalization. Man's spirit is already united to God's Spirit. The more training we receive, the more released our spirit becomes. The Holy Spirit is released when our spirit is released because the Holy Spirit dwells in us. Hence, the release of the spirit does not refer just to the release of our spirit, but to the release of the Holy Spirit as well. The extent of the release of the Holy Spirit depends entirely on the release of our spirit. The Holy Spirit is limited by our spirit. When we speak to a brother or to an unbelieving sinner, our spirit determines the degree of the release of the Holy Spirit. The matter hinges on the vessel; there is no problem with the anointing oil.

Brothers, we should not be so foolish as to put all the responsibility on the Holy Spirit. Today the Lord has placed the responsibility on the church. Matthew 18:18 shows us the authority of the church. John 20:23 says nearly the same thing as Matthew 18. Both speak of the Lord forgiving the sins of those whom we forgive and retaining the sins of those whose sins we retain. How can this be? This is because we have received the Holy Spirit. The Lord did not say, "I have given you the Holy Spirit. When you recognize the Spirit's forgiveness of someone, you should forgive him yourself as well. When you recognize the Spirit's retaining of someone's sins, you should retain his sins as well." The Lord only told the church to acknowledge the Holy Spirit. After it has acknowledged the Holy Spirit, it can then forgive someone, and the Lord will forgive that one. It can retain someone's sins, and the Lord will retain his sins. Today the authority of the Holy Spirit is at the disposal of the church. How great is the responsibility of the church! If God acted alone, it would not matter much whether or not the church failed a little. But God has entrusted everything to the church. The church cannot fail. If authority rested solely with the Holy Spirit, the success or failure of a minister would not be of much consequence. But the Holy Spirit has bound Himself to the minister. If the minister fails, the Holy Spirit has no way to go on. If God kept all authority in His hand, it would not matter much whether or not we stumbled or failed. But today God has not kept the work of the Holy Spirit in His hand; He has put this work in the hand of the ministers. When the spirit of a minister is released, God's Spirit is released. If his spirit is not released, God's Spirit is not released. God is willing and happy to entrust His authority to the ministers, giving them a free hand. Only the most foolish person will think that he can act hastily; only the foolish ones are nonchalant. We must remember that the problem today is with the ministers of the word. Whether or not the Holy Spirit can be released is in the hand of the ministers.

The Release of the Spirit Being
the Release of Power

The release of the spirit is also the release of power. Whether or not a stubborn man will be subdued depends on the amount of spiritual power that is released. If our spirit is strong, he will be subdued. As long as a person is not completely closed (which makes it impossible to do anything), he will be subdued when your spirit is released in a powerful way, even if such a person is very stubborn by nature. We should never put all of the blame on others. Nine out of ten times the problem is probably with us, not with others. If our spirit is powerful enough, we will subdue them. The more power our spirit releases, the more others will be subdued.

The Release of the Spirit Being
the Release of Life

The release of the Spirit is also the release of life. When the spirit is released, the Holy Spirit is released, power is released, and life is released. Whether or not others will touch spiritual reality when they listen to us depends on the release of our spirit. Whether or not they will touch life also depends on the release of our spirit. If we merely release the word, others will only touch doctrine; they will not touch the Holy Spirit. But when we stand up to speak and willingly and voluntarily push out the Holy Spirit, others will not only hear doctrine; they will touch life. Whether or not others touch the outward shell of the word or the life within the word depends on whether we have pushed out the spirit.

The Release of the Spirit Being
the Release of Light

This is not all. The release of the spirit is also the release of light. Light first becomes the word in us, and then it becomes light in others. First, light becomes the word in us, and then through our spirit the word becomes light to others. Whether or not a man sees light is not his responsibility (with the exception of those who are prejudiced) but the responsibility of the minister. Whether or not a man opens his eyes is his own responsibility, but having opened his eyes, whether or not he sees light is the responsibility of the minister. A man is responsible only for opening his eyes; the minister is responsible for giving him the light. If a man decides to close his eyes, nothing can be done about it. But if a man opens his heart, eyes, and spirit and does not see anything, the responsibility rests with the minister. If the spirit of the minister is strong in the release of the word and if the Holy Spirit goes forth with the word, the word will become light to others. God's light is embodied in His word. In delivering God's word, we release the spirit, and we also release the Holy Spirit. When this word reaches man, it becomes light. If a man kneels down and prays after hearing the word, saying, "Lord, grant me light," he has only heard doctrine; he has not heard God's word. God's word is light. When one hears God's word, he sees light. A man should not need to kneel down and pray after hearing a message. He should not need to say, "I understand this message, but I do not have the light. Lord, give me the light." If one has to ask for light after he has understood a message, it means that the message and the light are still two separate things. This is where Christianity has failed: Doctrines do not bring light. Everything is clearly explained, but nothing avails. Everyone can say it, but no one can apply it.

We must remember that when a man hears God's word, he sees light. If a man hears God's word but does not see light, the responsibility rests on the shoulder of the speaker. We often put the responsibility of seeing on the shoulder of the listener. This is wrong. Other than exceptional frustrations and closedness on the part of the listener, the speaker has to be responsible for the lack of light in a message. Many people have an open spirit, a seeking heart, and an open mind; they want to receive the light. If the light does not come, it means that something is wrong with the ministry of the word; the frustration is with the minister. If the spirit is active while the word is released and if the Holy Spirit operates while this is going on, the word will become light to the hearer. A man will no longer need to ask for light. He will not need to kneel down and pray, "Lord, I have heard this word. Now give me the light." As he hears the word, he will receive the light. Some ministers should repent before the Lord. They have no light to give to others; it is locked up in them. This is a problem on the part of the ministers. It is most unjust for ministers to blame the poverty in the church on the brothers and sisters. The brothers and sisters are responsible for opening their eyes, while the ministers are responsible for giving them light. Whenever the spirit of the ministers is released, light is released.

A minister can determine the amount of light he will release. He can determine before the Lord how much light he will give to others on a certain day. He should be a man who has passed through dealings. When he pushes out his spirit, he should push out what he sees, the revelations in his spirit and the light within him, together with his own spirit. He has to push out his spirit, like a man being pushed out through a door. He has to push out the light. He must release the light not only in a way that seeks understanding but in a way that causes men to fall on their face. Often, a minister is prepared to release "light" only for the purpose of helping others to understand. As a result, others may understand but have nothing more. A worker often pays attention only to the audience's understanding; his only motive and desire are for his audience to understand his word. But if he is willing to pay the price before the Lord, he will push out his spirit in such a way that his word will release light. The light will be so strong that others will understand not only the words, but they will be subdued by it as well. They will fall in the face of such light. Light can make a man fall down on his face. Once a man sees light, he will fall down; he will prostrate himself on the ground. This is something the ministers should do before the Lord. If there is an adequate willingness on the part of the ministers, light will be released in a strong way.

PRESSURE AND THE RELEASE OF THE SPIRIT

There are underlying principles to the release of the spirit. The amount of spirit that is released by a person depends on two things: the amount of his willingness and the amount of pressure that he sustains. As we come to the meeting, God may give us a certain amount of pressure. If the pressure is heavy and abiding, we can be certain that God wants our spirit to burst forth. As the pressure builds up, our words are squeezed out. We are pressed, and our spirit has to be released in a particular way in order to relieve this pressure. Hence, pressure brings about exceptional release of the spirit. Whether or not our spirit is released in an exceptional way depends on the amount of pressure we are under. When we talk to a brother, we may find that he is in ignorance and darkness, even boasting in his darkness. He dwells in darkness, yet he considers himself very highly. God will give us a certain oppressed feeling as we talk to this brother. We will feel extremely agitated. When God's pressure increases within us, we will be provoked and irritated. This cannot go on for long; soon we will have to open our mouth. As we speak, we will not speak in an ordinary way; our words will come out in a burst. This bursting forth is an intensified release of the spirit. Whether or not the spirit is released in a strong way depends on the amount of pressure we experience. Suppose this arrogant and self-assured brother is sitting in front of us. The pressure within us will build up and swell as we listen to him. As we are feeling sorry for this brother, our spirit breaks forth in a burst. The question today is whether or not inwardly we have the willingness to speak the word that is within us. If we are willing and the pressure within us is strong enough, the word will burst forth in the form of a rebuke. If the release is strong enough, others' arrogance will be subdued. Of course, if we do not have a willingness, nothing will happen. I wish all the brothers would see that our spirit is empowered whenever we exercise it. Whenever we exercise our spirit, it becomes stronger yet again. The more we exercise, the more our spirit will become useful to us. As our spirit is empowered again and again, the Lord will have a way with us.

This is what happened to Paul when he cast out the evil spirit. The slave girl cried out for many days, "These men are slaves of the Most High God" (Acts 16:17). One day, Paul became fed up, and he said to the spirit, "I charge you in the name of Jesus Christ to come out of her," and the spirit came out (v. 18). Many people can only lift their voices; they cannot lift their spirit. This is fruitless. The principle of miracles is the same as the principle of speaking. Paul was provoked within; the pressure was too much. When he commanded the spirit to come out, it had to come out. When there is enough of a build-up of the burden in the spirit, words will burst forth. When the light is strong, the release will be strong. We must be pressed by the power of the spirit to the point of being fed up. When this happens, the release of our word will change others. In the same principle, a man can only rebuke others when he experiences pressure in his spirit. When the Lord came out of Bethany, He saw a fig tree that was barren, and He said to it, "May no one eat fruit from you forever!" (Mark 11:14). This came out of the pressure in His spirit. The word was released under spiritual pressure. As a result, the tree withered from the roots. We should note, however, that a minister of the word is not free to release this kind of word everywhere. We can speak such a word only when we are provoked, angered, disturbed, irritated, and agitated. This is the principle of works of miracles. This is also the principle of words of rebuke. When our inner being breaks out and our spirit is released, others will be subdued.

Ministry of the word is the ministry of the spirit. A man receives the word when he touches the released spirit. When a man touches this spirit, he will fall on his face. When the spirit is released, power is released from within, light is released from within, and life is released from within; the Holy Spirit is released from within, and the pressure is relieved. The only thing that works is the release of the spirit. Everything else is vanity. Our mind, words, memory, and feelings all help us in the release of our message, but it is our spirit that is the necessary ingredient. We can only speak as our spirit is released. When we have all these things, we have the ministry of the word.

THE PURITY OF THE SPIRIT

Our word must be backed up by the spirit. But in order to release a spirit that is pure and clean, we have to go through dealings. One thing is certain: The kind of spirit that we have determines the kind of expression of the Holy Spirit that we bear. The kind of nature that we have dictates the aspect of the Holy Spirit that we express. The manifestation of the Holy Spirit is different in different persons. Just because we have the same Spirit does not mean that we have the same manifestation. The Spirit who flows to others bears the characteristics of the channel through which He flows. When the Holy Spirit flows, He carries along with Him the characteristic of the person who bears the flow, and He reaches men in this way. Therefore, the Holy Spirit is expressed in one way through one person and in another way through another person. One person can have one kind of ministry while another can have another kind of ministry. The Holy Spirit was expressed through Paul in one way and through Peter in another way. The same Holy Spirit was manifested in Peter and in Paul. It was the Holy Spirit in both cases, but the manifestation in Peter carried Peter's flavor and characteristic, and the manifestation in Paul carried Paul's flavor and characteristic. This is very clear. The Holy Spirit does not annul the human elements in each person. God never annulled the human elements within each writer of the Bible. When one person is filled with the Holy Spirit, he has one kind of manifestation. When another person is filled with the Holy Spirit, he has another kind of manifestation. Not everyone has the same expression and manifestation. When the Holy Spirit fills a person, He carries the very characteristic of the person himself.

Brothers, do you see our responsibility? If the Holy Spirit reached others through the word alone, without any relation to our human nature, we would have no responsibility in the matter. If we only had to carry the Holy Spirit with us and convey it to others, without any involvement of our human elements, we would not have much responsibility; we would only need to carry Him. But the experiences of many saints show us that the Holy Spirit reaches other men with the special characteristic of the bearer. Since this is the case, our spirit needs to be pure; it has to be dealt with. Otherwise, others will receive improper elements. We have to realize that the human factor is a great matter. The Holy Spirit does not operate independently or in an unprocessed manner. Our nature has a role to play. The Holy Spirit does not annul our nature; rather, He is released with our nature. The Lord said, "If anyone thirsts, let him come to Me and drink. He who believes into Me, as the Scripture said, out of his innermost being shall flow rivers of living water" (John 7:37-38). The Lord's word indicates that one must first drink the water, and then the rivers of living water must flow out of his innermost being. J. N. Darby points out that the innermost being refers to the deepest part of our being. It is out of the deepest part of one's being that the Holy Spirit flows; the Holy Spirit flows out together with the person. When this water reaches a person, the Holy Spirit carries this person's characteristics with Him, and flows to others this way.

Therefore, we have to learn to take the dealings. When the cross comes to us, it should not come in vain. As the cross works on us, we receive more carvings and dealings, and our being is purified even more. Every trial brings more purification. The more fire we have, the more cleansing we receive. The more trouble we suffer before the Lord and the greater such trouble is, the more our spirits are purified, and the purer will be the expression that the Holy Spirit assumes. A particular aspect of our character often goes through some dealings, but the work is not complete, and there are still impurities. As a result, others touch the Spirit of God at the same time that they touch the impurities. When we come across a minister of the word, we often find that he has God's word, and his spirit is released. Yet, at the same time, his own person is too conspicuous; he is not broken enough. The breaking he has received is not thorough enough. The Holy Spirit is released through him, but at the same time his own characteristics are released as well. Brothers, our responsibility is too great! If the Spirit of the Lord worked absolutely independent of man or if the Holy Spirit rejected anyone who is flawed in any way, the matter would be much simpler. It would be easy to tell the difference between the work of the flesh and the work of the Spirit if the Lord put us aside as soon as we were off just a little. But the trouble today is that the work of the flesh is still within us. Even though our spirit is not pure enough, God does not reject us; He still uses us. Many who are proud are under the illusion that they are useful and that they have passed the test. They are wrong. God often uses a person even though there is still weakness in him. We have to realize that the more God uses us, the greater our responsibility is. If God would not use us, we would have much less trouble. But the Lord often uses us even though He knows that we are unqualified. The Holy Spirit does not operate independently today. He is not being released apart from man. This is a deep principle in the work of God. When the Holy Spirit reaches out, His reaching is done in conjunction with man's spirit. The Lord takes man up, together with all of his characteristics, in His release.

We should be in fear and trembling all the time. Even though the Lord may use us, we must not forget that we are still unqualified. We have to remember the gravity of our responsibility. If something is wrong with us, the flaws that are in our spirit will be mixed in with the word of the Lord. One day the Lord will shine His light in us, and we will prostrate ourselves before Him and say, "Nothing that I have said in the past was up to Your mark." Anyone who receives any light will be deeply conscious of his past failures. Indeed, God's Spirit may have accomplished some amount of work through us, but our person is still wrong; we remain an impure vessel before the Lord. We are not a perfect vessel. In the hand of God we are a contaminated vessel, and we need deeper dealings. When a man receives the light, he discovers his shortcomings; he realizes that his very person is unusable. When the word is released, the spirit must also be released. Therefore, we need to ask for mercy and grace so that everything would be under the discipline of the Holy Spirit. Every day we must learn to accept the discipline of the Holy Spirit. Without this, our spirit will not be useful. The Lord may want to make us a minister of the word; He may be working in us every day. All the dealings, trials, and occurrences in our environment are for the purpose of increasing our usefulness in the Lord. All things work together to make our spirit purer and more perfect. They work together to bring about a purer flow when our spirit is released and to increase the usefulness of our spirit. Today God may grant us mercy and allow His Spirit to be released through us, and we may think that we are now a great

servant of the Lord. We may be puffed up. We may think
that all is well, without any realization that His selection
was merely provisional in its measure.

We must realize that the training of a minister of the
word is a daily matter. It is also a lifelong work. The words
we speak may not improve, but our spirit can improve.
Perhaps the words we speak are the same as the words we
spoke ten years ago. But when we speak the same words
today, our spirit is different from the spirit we had ten years
ago. A young man must never think that he can give the
same message as an older man. He can speak the same words,
but he does not have the same spirit. Some brothers repeat
the same things they spoke twenty or thirty years ago. The
words are the same, but the spirit is different. We should
never be concerned with whether we have the same words
but whether we have the same spirit. While we can speak
the words of some older brothers, it is not easy to have their
spirit. It is not enough for a minister of the word to have the
word alone; he must also have the spirit. The Lord said, "The
words which I have spoken to you are spirit and are life"
(John 6:63). When a minister of the word stands up to speak
for the Lord, not only must his words be pure, but the release
of his spirit must be pure as well. It is not a matter of
whether or not we can say the words, but of whether our
release of the spirit is pure.

The issue is not our eloquence. What is at stake is the
kind of spirit we convey when we speak. One realm justifies
a man as long as he is clever, eloquent, and wise. But another
realm demands nothing less than the Lord's chastising hand
and the discipline of the Holy Spirit. The two belong to two
entirely different realms. The second kind of word can only
be "beaten out" through the hand of the Lord. Words are
beaten into existence; they are wrought into one's being.
Every day the Holy Spirit "beats" the word into a person's
being. If we are going to preach a message today, it is not
enough to simply deliver the word. We may think afterwards
that our message was wonderful, and we may feel very good
about ourselves. We may think that we can continue to preach
the same message. We may think that our words are not

much different from those who have the genuine ministry. Yet none of our speaking will result in anything. In fact, we are living in a different realm. Others might have told us about a truth, and we might have received it. Since that time, we may be speaking about the same truth, but our speaking does not lead us anywhere. The words can be the same, but if we do not have the proper spirit, there will be flaws in the release of our spirit. The Lord's words are spirit and life. This is why our spirit must be dealt with by the Lord. Our person must be carved and molded before our spirit can be released in a proper way. When the word is released and the spirit is released, praise the Lord, the Holy Spirit is released as well. This is the way of the ministry of the word. Without such a release, we will be like scribes teaching the Ten Commandments. The trouble with this kind of teaching is that everything is doctrinal, didactic, and expositional. If the spirit is not involved, everything is vanity. God has to work on us until our spirit is released whenever the word is released. Sometimes there is the need of extraordinary release. But not every instance requires such extraordinary effort; only a few times do we need such special outbursts. During these times the Holy Spirit bursts out and operates in a strong way. Unless we have such an experience, the message we preach will not match the preaching of the apostles.

We must understand the responsibility of the church today. God has entrusted His Christ to the church with the intention that the church would communicate this Christ to others. God also has entrusted His Holy Spirit to the church with the intention that the church would communicate this Holy Spirit to others. God also has entrusted revelation and spiritual blessings to the church with the intention that the church would communicate the same to others. This is God's intention. This is God's plan. The church is the Body of Christ on earth. Just as a body expresses a man, the church expresses Christ. The desires of the head are expressed through the body. Without the body, the head cannot express itself. Similarly, without the church, Christ cannot express Himself. In this age God is blessing men through the church. As such, the church carries a heavy responsibility. We should never think that everything is in heaven today. We can never forget Pentecost, and we can never forget the cross. The situation today is entirely different from that in the Old Testament. Malachi 3:10 says, "Bring the whole tithe to the storehouse that there may be food in My house; and prove Me, if you will, by this, says Jehovah of hosts, whether I will open to you the windows of heaven and pour out blessing for you until there is no room for it." This was the principle in the Old Testament. The blessing was in heaven. But today the blessing has come to earth. The Spirit will rapture the church from earth to heaven. Protestantism has forgotten the position of the church, while Catholicism has tried to usurp God's blessing with carnal hands. Today we have to ask God to open our eyes to see that all spiritual blessings are now in the church. The church can now dispense these blessings to others.

Today the church is in the business of dispensing. The book of Ephesians shows us clearly that the blessings have descended while the church has ascended. All the spiritual things are now in the church. What is a minister? A minister is one who dispenses these spiritual riches to others. The church has enjoyed and received all these riches. All the riches of Christ are now in the church. Today the church dispenses to others the Christ it has received. A minister is one who dispenses to others the Christ he has seen and received. We must never be so fallen as to consider everything to be far away. Many people pray as if the church has never ascended to the heavens. They beseech as if the Holy Spirit has never descended to the earth. That is not the church. Romans 10:8 says, "The word is near you, in your mouth and in your heart." Brothers, if we have the light, we can transmit the same divine light to others. If we have God's word, we can convey the same word of God to others. The matter depends on whether or not we are willing and happy to do this.

For years God has been looking for sanctified vessels to transmit His word. This does not mean that God will not use us unless we are perfectly sanctified. For the past two thousand years, countless fleshly hands have touched God's work, and countless carnal hands have contaminated His work. Brothers, within us, we know very well what we were ten years ago. We can only say that we were carnal men. Yet God still used us. We know very well what kind of a person we were twenty years ago. We can only say that we were filthy and sinful men. Yet God still used us. We should never be so foolish as to think that we are useful to Him just because God has used us. More and more we are realizing the gravity of our responsibility. "O Lord, even while we are being used, the self is contaminating, defiling, and corrupting Your word. We have mingled our sin and filthiness with Your work. There is little separation now between the work of the Spirit and the work of the flesh. Lord, we have sinned. Forgive us. Be merciful to us."

The Lord has committed Himself to the church. His way is with us. Today God dispenses all that He is to others through man's spirit. We should pray that our spirit would be acceptable to the Lord. We cannot boast of our work in the past. We have no reason to remain in our impurity; we have no reason to remain in our carnality or fleshly ways. We must remember that God has entrusted Christ to the church. He has entrusted the Holy Spirit, His word, and His light to the church. Today the church can dispense light to men; it can dispense the word, Christ, and the Spirit to men. The trouble is with our impurity and our mixture. We must realize our responsibility. When we speak well, everything will be well. When we do not speak well, everything will not be well. The responsibility is entirely on our shoulders. The word has to go out. The Holy Spirit has to go out. The spirit has to go out, and light has to go out. A man must be brought to the point where he can become a sanctified vessel.

If we realize what the church is, we will spontaneously realize what a minister is. A minister is one who dispenses to others through the word what God has entrusted to the church. The responsibility of a minister is greater than any other kind of responsibility. If the flesh remains an impure mixture in us, we do not have a way to go on. We will only destroy God's work and damage it. God needs men, yet we cannot be His servant or His minister. May the Lord have mercy on us. We have to know the proper way to go on. When our word goes out, light has to go out with it. We have to dispense such a strong word to others so that they can do nothing but see the light and fall on their face.

CHAPTER SEVENTEEN

A FEW THINGS TO PAY ATTENTION TO IN OUR SPEAKING

Serving as a minister of the word is an altogether new thing to us; we have never done such a thing before in our life. We are like newborn babes who have never learned to speak. We have lived on this earth for many years and have been speaking for all these years. Yet we have never known this kind of speaking before. In order to speak this way, we have to start from the beginning. In learning to be a minister of the word, we should forget about our previous speaking and preaching experience. This kind of thought is a distraction. The ministry of the word is very new to us; it is different from any of our former training, understanding, and practices. No one can be careless in this matter. We cannot depend on past experiences. We cannot consider the ministry of the word to be the same as our ordinary speaking. As far as being a minister of the word is concerned, we are babies; we have to learn everything from the beginning. A baby has to learn every sound of the alphabet when he learns to speak. Today we are like babies; we have to learn everything from its very foundation. The flesh has characteristics in its speaking, and the spirit also has characteristics in its speaking. We cannot rely on any past experiences of speaking and preaching. If we try to bring in these elements, we will change the nature of the word. We have to be like a baby, learning everything afresh. Many terms and expressions have to be picked up. Many thoughts have to be acquired afresh. Even the way we behave ourselves has to be taught and learned in a fresh way. No one should bring in anything old. But neither is it a matter of introducing something novel. As a matter of fact, this kind of speaking is so new and unfamiliar to us that everything related to it has to be acquired afresh, bit by bit and piece by piece.

When God gives us a word, we can say that it is a hard task to release it on the one hand. But we also can say that it is a very easy task to release it on the other hand. This is like prayer. In one sense this is the easiest thing to do, because a new believer can pray the first day of his Christian life. In another sense one can spend his whole lifetime learning how to pray. The same is true of learning to be a minister of the word. On the one hand, it is a difficult skill to acquire. On the other hand, while one is learning to be a minister, God will show him that the whole endeavor is not that hard after all.

Let us now consider a few things we should pay attention to in our speaking.

GUARDING THE SPIRIT FROM ANY INJURY

In speaking as a minister of the word, we have to take care that our spirit is not hurt or injured. We should not speak for the sake of speaking. Our speaking must be accompanied by the release of the spirit. It is a total failure on the part of the ministry of the word to release the word without releasing the spirit. It is absolutely impossible for anyone to try to release his spirit without the word. One must have the spirit and the word at the same time. The word is released because the spirit is released in the process. It is the spirit that touches men and moves men. It is also the spirit that opens men's eyes. At times the spirit is so prevailing that it even subdues men. The release of the word is actually a release of the spirit. If our spirit cannot be released, it is useless for the word to be released by itself. If there is any hindrance in us, we will have just the word without the spirit. Sometimes, even though we do not know what is wrong with us, our spirit is injured. Our spirit is extremely delicate; as such, it is very easily injured. The feeling of the spirit is very sensitive. It is so delicate that it goes beyond our normal sensitivity. We may not feel something, yet the spirit has felt it already. Once the spirit is injured, we are left with a word that is void of the spirit. In speaking we have to be very careful not to injure the spirit. Several things can cause injury to our spirit. Let us consider them one by one.

First, we may be touched by some sin or defilement before we speak. When we speak, the spirit does not follow because it is injured. It is difficult to say what kinds of sins or defilements will injure our spirit. We can only say that with many sins and defilements, a slight touch, contact, or contamination, can injure our spirit. We do not have to actually commit these sins. As soon as we open our mouth, we know that we cannot go on. Before a minister of the word opens his mouth, he has to pray for forgiveness and cleansing. He should confess all of his known sins and defilements before God, and he should seek cleansing and forgiveness for them. He should seek cleansing and forgiveness for the sins and defilements that he is not aware of as well. He has to exercise diligence to avoid these things. He should guard himself and exercise care to turn away from these things. The spirit's feeling is more sensitive than a person's other feelings. A man may not realize that he is contaminated by certain sins and defilements for three to five days. Yet his spirit has detected some warnings already. He may have the right words and the right thoughts; every inward and outward factor may be in place. Yet, despite his efforts to push out his spirit, his spirit seems to remain inert. He does not seem to be able to get his spirit moving. He has a difficult time trying to locate his spirit as he is trying to push it out. These signs indicate that the spirit has been defiled by sin and is debilitated.

Second, the spirit must be watchfully attended to before it can be released. As soon as our mind wanders, moves out of focus, or fails to catch up with our thoughts, our spirit is injured. Our mind has to attentively wait on the spirit before the spirit can direct the mind freely. When our mind wanders, our spirit becomes very heavy and bound. This is another cause of injury to the spirit. Some ministers of the word cannot use their spirit because their spirit is injured, and their spirit is injured because something is wrong with their mind. We have to learn to preserve our mind solely for the spirit's use. Our mind has to attentively wait on the spirit, like a servant waiting on his master. The more experienced we are, the more conscious we are of this need.

Third, in order for the spirit to be strong and undamaged, we have to use the right words whenever we speak. We cannot use the wrong words, the wrong examples, or the wrong order of outline. Once we make a mistake in two or three of the crucial words in our speaking, our whole message is spoiled. These few words injure our spirit, and at the end of the whole message, our spirit remains bound. (Of course, there are times when the situation is less serious, and one or two wrong words do not lead to an injured spirit. At these times, we can still release our spirit.) Sometimes we also may give an illustration which is out of place as far as the spirit is concerned, and the spirit is injured again and bound. Or we may tell a story that is not according to the Spirit's utterance. In such a case, again the spirit is injured and bound. A whole passage may not be according to the Spirit; that is, we have not touched the leading of the Spirit in speaking it. Again the spirit is injured and bound. We must remember that it is very easy for the spirit to be injured. If we do not pay attention to this matter but insist on speaking carelessly, we will find it impossible to push out our spirit. We may want to release our spirit, but we do not have the power to do so. This means that we have injured our spirit.

Fourth, our attitude can also injure our spirit. Many people come to the meeting with much self-consciousness. Self-consciousness is something that easily injures our spirit. While a person is speaking, he may be very conscious of himself. He may think that his audience is very demanding, and that a few are even quite threatening. While he is speaking, he has many feelings about himself. This is self-consciousness, and it bottles up the spirit so that it cannot be released freely. Once the soul reigns, self-consciousness rises, and the spirit loses control.

We must realize that there is a difference between spiritual fear and soulish consciousness. We need to have a spiritual fear, but we have no need of soulish self-consciousness. When we meet together in a certain place, we should be filled with fear, but we should not be filled with a soulish self-consciousness. We know that we cannot make it and that we have no strength in ourselves to do anything. When we come to the meeting, we come in fear and trembling. Such a fear turns our eyes to God, to look to Him, to trust Him, and to rest our faith on Him. Soulish self-consciousness is different; it looks at men. A spiritual fear turns our eyes to God, while a soulish self-consciousness turns our eyes to men. Once soulish self-consciousness arises, our spirit is injured and debilitated; we are unable to push out our spirit any longer.

An evangelist must be free from self-consciousness before he can preach the gospel. All gospel preachers throughout the ages have been men with no self-consciousness. The less self-conscious a preacher is, the more powerful his spirit is. As he stands to speak, he has no feeling for the heavens, the earth, or men. Though these things are all before his eyes, he speaks what is in him. He is oblivious to others' approval or disapproval. This freedom from self-consciousness is the basic qualification of a preacher of the gospel. It lifts a person's spirit up; when he preaches, men will turn. A minister of God's word must learn to free himself from any self-consciousness before he can function effectively. If a man is sensitive about many things while speaking God's word, if he is afraid of men or afraid that others will not listen to him, this fear will damage his spirit. When he stands up to speak, his spirit is not released. His spirit is not strong enough to meet the need. Those ministers of the word who fail to practice this wilt away easily. If a preacher of the gospel feels that his audience is older, more prestigious, or more educated or knowledgeable than he is, he will not be able to deliver his message well, no matter how hard he tries. The more he speaks, the less boldness he has. Once an evangelist reckons others to be great, he will reckon himself small. But if he magnifies the gospel, others will be subdued. A preacher of the gospel must be able to release his spirit. When we convey God's word to others, any sense of inferiority lowers God's word, and our spirit becomes weak and empty. Although words may come out, the spirit is not released.

In order for a servant of God to have the ministry of the word, he must not have any feeling of inferiority. A fear of men is not a mark of humility but a soulish sense of inferiority. This kind of inferiority is soulish. It is far from spiritual humility. Spiritual humility comes when we see ourselves under God's shining and are humbled. Soulish inferiority, however, comes from introspection which, in turn, comes from self-examination and a fear of men. A man with an inferiority complex may be proud and arrogant at times. None of these expressions relate to true humility. Soulish self-consciousness is a kind of soulish inferiority complex. It damages the spirit and puts it out of function. Therefore, when we stand before men, we need to be in fear and trembling as well as bold and assured. We need both. If we are short of one aspect, our spirit will be injured, and once our spirit is injured, we are not able to serve as a minister of the word. Whenever we speak as a minister of the word, we have to learn to preserve our spirit from any injury. Once our spirit is injured, we can no longer use it.

THE SPIRIT AND THE WORD NOT BEING OUT OF TOUCH

When a minister of the word opens his mouth, he may have four or five passages he wants to cover. He may have four or five verses he wants to speak or four or five things he wants to say. The order of the verses matters a great deal in the release of the spirit. The Spirit may want to place a passage at the end of his speaking, while he may put it at the beginning of his speaking. In such a case the spirit will not be released. One problem in our speaking is that our words frequently lose touch with our spirit. Some words should be spoken at the beginning, but we speak them at the end. Some words should be spoken at the end, but we speak them at the beginning. When this happens, the words are released without the spirit; the spirit is set aside. Words go forth, yet the spirit does not go along.

In our speaking, there are times when our words should make a turn. The subject should be changed from one to another; the thoughts should be turned from one to another. It is not uncommon that a man blunders at such turns. As the turn is made, the words and the spirit become separated. The word turns, but the spirit does not follow. The word has made the turn, but the spirit remains in the original place. The word and the spirit become separated. The word has gone on to the next point, but the spirit remains in the same place and has not moved forward. Hence, when the speaking turns from one passage of the Scripture to another, we must exercise care not to make any mistake. Once we make a mistake, the word and the spirit will lose contact with each other. If a certain passage of the Scripture should be used, yet we miss it, the spirit is unable to make the turn, and it loses touch with the word. The word and the spirit are separated; they are not joined together. This is a serious problem.

Those who are less experienced before God are stumbled mainly by injuries in their spirit. Those who are more experienced before God are stumbled mainly by the dislocation between the word and the spirit. At the beginning of one's training, the problem is mainly with the injured spirit; the cause of bondage in the spirit is injury in the spirit. When a man becomes more advanced in the Lord, his problem no longer relates to injury in the spirit but to the separation between the word and the spirit. It is not an easy thing to keep the spirit and the word together. A speaker often has a bad beginning, and the spirit and the word are separated from the very beginning. In speaking, one has to know which word comes first and which word comes next. If he reverses the order, the words may come out without the spirit. The easiest place for the word to lose the spirit is at the turning points. When we make a turn with the word, our thoughts and feelings may not be agile and rich enough to follow the turn. As a result the word goes on, but the spirit lags behind. The words may be released smoothly, yet the spirit is left behind; it cannot follow the word and loses contact with it. When we speak, we have to learn to release both the word and the spirit so that the two do not lose touch with each other. As soon as we find that something has gone wrong, we have to turn our words back to the point of departure. The spirit is very sensitive. Sometimes when we return to the point of departure, the spirit still will not come back. Having cast it aside once, it is not only out of touch with the word; it is injured as well. There may be nothing wrong with the words in our mouth, but the spirit is not present. The sense of the spirit is very fine. We must exercise care, not speaking rashly or negligently. We have to pay attention to this matter. We have to look to God for mercy that our words make the right turns and that they do not lose contact with the spirit. Whenever we speak to the brothers and sisters, we have to turn with the spirit. Whenever we make a wrong or improper turn from one subject to another, we fail to keep our whole message in the spirit. Hence, as soon as we learn about the mistake, we have to turn our words back. Sometimes the more we try to turn the words back, the harder it gets. Sometimes it is better to just cut off an entire portion of the speaking. After a while we may find the direction again. We may find the anointing and the utterance again. Then when we speak in that direction, the spirit is released once again.

Whether or not a minister of the word can make the right turn in his speaking depends more on the Lord's mercy than on man's planning. It is difficult for us to dictate how strong our words will be or how much we can keep our entire message in the spirit. Most of the time, however, it is God's mercy that we make the right turn. We do not make a right turn because we have knowledge or experience. We may not know when we have made the right turn, but we surely know when we have made the wrong turn. Once we make the wrong turn, we know within two or three minutes. As soon as we know that we are wrong, we have to stop immediately. We should never try to save our message. We are ministers of the word. When we feel that our words have gone off on a tangent, we have to turn back. Whenever we are wrong, we can sense it immediately. But when we are on the right track, we may not realize it until much later or when we step off the platform. Sometimes we are at a crossroad; we do not know if we are right or wrong. It takes a while for us to know whether we are right. After a while, we know whether we are right or wrong. If we go on for a few minutes more, we know that something is wrong. We realize that the word and the spirit are two different things; they are separate. Words are going forth, but the spirit is not following. The spirit is very delicate. As soon as something is wrong, it stops. Even if we can find the spirit, we are not able to release it. We feel a great resistance in pushing out the spirit. We realize that we only have the word; we do not have the spirit. As soon as we find out our mistake, we should turn back.

How can a man tell if his words are right or wrong? He can tell by the way the spirit is released. If his spirit is released while he speaks, the words are right. If his spirit is not released, they are wrong. This is the restriction the Spirit places upon us. We have said before that we do not know immediately when we are saying the right thing. When we stand at the crossroad, we do not know immediately what to do. After speaking for a few minutes with both the word and the spirit moving together, we know that we made the right turn a moment earlier. One does not know immediately whether the spirit and the word are moving along together. This is the reason we say that the whole matter has more to do with God's mercy. The more we realize this, the more we have nothing to depend on. When we function as a minister of the word, we can do nothing except look solely to God's mercy. By ourselves, we cannot guarantee that we will speak by the Spirit of God for longer than five minutes. It is easy for us to turn, and it is easier for us to make the wrong turn. Human wisdom, knowledge, and experience cannot help in this matter. If we are under God's mercy during ordinary times and we learn to look to the God who is full of mercy and commit ourselves to Him, we will find that our words will be right spontaneously. But if God does not grant us mercy, we cannot keep ourselves in this way all the time. This is not something that a servant can dictate; it is something that only the Master can dictate. This is not something we can do; this is something that only the Lord can do. It does not matter how much experience we have had in the past or how much knowledge or training we have received from God; we have to commit ourselves unreservedly to the Lord's mercy. Otherwise, we may be right for three or five minutes. But as soon as we make a turn, we are off again.

Before the Lord a minister of God's word must see that his release of the word is not just for the sake of releasing the word; he is releasing it to release his spirit. The purpose of releasing the word is to release the spirit. No minister should think that his responsibility merely lies in the release of the word. The responsibility of the minister is to release the spirit. Speaking the word alone does not constitute the work of the minister; the work of the minister involves the discharge of the spirit through the word. A fundamental test that a minister of the word can apply to himself is to ask how much of the spirit was released after he delivered his message. The more the spirit is released, the more the speaker is relieved; he knows that the Lord has used him. He does not have to worry about the fruit because the Lord is responsible for the fruit. Whether or not someone is saved or has received help is a matter that is in the hands of the Lord; it is not in our hands. The result or the success is the Lord's business; this should not be of concern to us. We are the servants. For us there is only one subjective fruit—the assurance, as we are speaking or after speaking, that the Lord has graced us and has granted mercy to us to discharge our burden.

The joy of a minister of the word is not in the number of words he has spoken, the nodding of the audience, or the help that others profess to have received. The joy of the minister of the word lies in the release of his spirit in his speaking. Once the spirit is released, the burden is gone, the heart is lightened, and he knows that he has fulfilled his responsibility and done what he should do. If the word is released without the spirit, the burden remains. He can raise his voice, strain his throat, and exhaust his energy. But he remains a total failure because his spirit is closed and bound. A man speaks to discharge his burden. He has to let the spirit flow. The more the spirit flows, the more the speaker is relieved, and the more he is relieved, the happier he is. When our spirit is released, we have God's word. If our spirit is not released, our word is not God's word; it is only an imitation of His word, not His very own word. Whenever God's word passes through us, the spirit surely accompanies the word.

We should pay attention to the release of the spirit. Only foolish ones set their eyes on their fruit. Only foolish ones take in the praises of others or appreciate their own words. Foolish ones think that it is unnecessary to touch their spirit. A man has to remain in foolishness, darkness, and total blindness to appreciate and be content with his own words. Such a person has forgotten the fact that his words are altogether vanity if they are void of the spirit. We must pay attention to the release of the spirit in our words. If we pay attention to this, the word and spirit will be together. If we neglect this, the two will be separate. Once we are not watchful, the word and the spirit lose touch with one another. On the negative side, we have to watch out for the separation which is caused by the lack of watchfulness. On the positive side, we have to insure that the word and the spirit are joined to one another. This can only be accomplished through God's mercy. Every word must be accompanied by the release of the spirit. As long as the spirit is released, the speaking is right and others touch something high. On the one hand, we have to be watchful, but on the other hand, we have to look to God for His mercy. By ourselves, we do not know how to make a turn. As soon as we make a turn, we lose our bearing. But if God continues to grant us mercy, we will not lose touch with the spirit when our words make a turn. If a brother takes pride in his own preaching, it can only mean one thing: He is merely a preacher; he does not have the ministry of the word. He can go home feeling great and elevated, but he does not have the ministry of the word. A foolish man is a proud man. We must remember that only God's mercy can keep the word and the spirit together.

THE SPIRIT FOLLOWING THE WORD,
AND THE WORD FOLLOWING THE ANOINTING

There are two ways to speak. The first way is to put the spirit into the word and then to push out the word with the spirit. The second way to speak is to follow the anointing. The spirit takes the lead, and the word follows the anointing. When the spirit and the word are joined together, there are these two different ways to release them.

As we are speaking, God may want to say something. He
puts this something in our spirit. When we release this word
in our spirit, we release our own spirit at the same time.
We pack the spirit into the word, sentence by sentence, and
then send this word out. This is one way. In this way, we
are the servants. As ministers of the word, we exercise our
will to pack the spirit into the word and then release and
push out this word. When the word is released, the spirit is
released with it. As one speaks with his mouth, he inwardly
pushes with his own strength. As he speaks, he pushes out
the word with his spirit, and the spirit goes with the word.
While the word is going out, he packs his spirit into the
word and delivers them together. When such a word reaches
man, the spirit also reaches man. By God's mercy, this kind
of speaking can be very strong; the spirit can be very strong
as well. While the mouth speaks, the heart pushes the spirit
on. This is one kind of speaking.

Another way of speaking is to find the power and anointing
coming upon us as we speak. Before we speak, the anointing
goes before us. Under the brooding and sway of this power,
we speak according to the anointing. The anointing flows out,
and our words follow the anointing. This means that we have
to learn to follow the anointing. As our spirit senses something, we should follow this sense with the word. As more
senses come, we should follow with more words. This kind of
speaking enables the spirit to flow out in a continuous way.
The advantage of this kind of speaking is that we cannot go
wrong easily. The anointing is always before us, and the word
always follows. When we speak under the influence of the
power of the anointing, the word follows the anointing. It
may be less spectacular, but it does not easily err.

These two ways of speaking are different. The ways in
which the speaker addresses the audience, according to these
two ways, are also different. According to the first way, the
speaker can set his eyes on the audience and look at them.
He can study their faces and conditions while he is pushing
out his word with the spirit. According to the second way, the
speaker cannot look at the audience. His entire focus should
be on his spirit, his very own spirit. He should detect where

the anointing is flowing and turn his words in that direction. He should stand at the door like a watchman. As soon as the anointing comes, he should follow. He should follow the anointing and not be concerned with others' expressions, attitudes, and reactions. He should follow the anointing sentence by sentence under the influence of the power of the spirit. This way of speaking pays no attention to the audience. As soon as the speaker turns his attention to the audience, he is frustrated from following the anointing.

Those who are learning to speak by the spirit have to learn to speak according to these two ways. Sometimes when the Lord wants us to speak, He first activates our mind by His mercy to utter some outer words. At the same time, our spirit bursts forth through these same words; we pack our spirit into these words and shoot them out in a burst or an explosion. At other times the Lord wants us to focus all our energy on waiting inwardly. Our entire being, including our thoughts, should be focused on our spirit and in a state of waiting. As the Lord gives us the anointing, we are led along the way step by step. The anointing is before us, and by God's mercy, our mind produces a word that matches the sense of the anointing within. Then we can release this word. The anointing is always before us, and our words follow behind it sentence by sentence. We are not concerned at all about our audience. Our eyes are set on no one. Although we see faces, we have no feeling toward them. All of our feelings are focused on the anointing. All of our thoughts and attention are focused on the anointing. The anointing takes the lead, and our words follow it sentence by sentence. Such a release of the spirit also brings God's children to the Spirit. In their ministry, the ministers of the word should experience both conditions; they should bring God's children to the Spirit through both of these ways.

A message should be delivered under the leading and guidance of the anointing from beginning to end. However, at critical times, the speaker has to give an extra push to his spirit. This is the best kind of ministry of the word. The speaking by the anointing occupies the bulk of the message. The speaker follows the anointing and delivers his message sentence by sentence. He is not concerned about the reaction of his audience, and he does not care who is sitting in front of him; he is faithful only to follow the anointing. When he finds where the anointing is, he finds the "seam" through which he can squeeze out his word sentence by sentence. He knows within himself that his words are following the anointing. As he is releasing his word this way, he may want to bless his audience; he may want to discharge the blessing with a strong impact. In this case he may want to change his way of speaking and speak in a way that discharges his spirit. On the one hand, he needs the power of the anointing. On the other hand, he has to pack his word with the spirit and discharge his spirit this way. When this happens, he will witness the Lord's grace. Others will receive revelation when he wants them to receive revelation. There is no need to wait. Others will fall on their face when he wants them to fall on their face. Others will see when he wants them to see. The lowest kind of ministry of the word is the kind which merely helps others to understand. The highest kind of ministry of the word is one which opens men's eyes and causes them to fall on their face. In order for others to advance from merely understanding with the mind to an opening of the eyes and then to a falling on their face, the speaker has to be willing to pay a price. Everything depends on how much he is willing to pay. If he is willing to pay the price, others will receive something. When there is the anointing of the Spirit as well as the pushing of his own spirit, others will see something through his speaking, and they will fall down on their face. The crucial factor is the kind of price the speaker is willing to pay. For a minister of the word, the basic issue is the matter of the exercise of the spirit. We must pay full attention to this matter. The outer man must be broken because the spirit can realize its function only to the extent that the outer man is broken. The Holy Spirit pays constant attention to the breaking of the outer man in His disciplining work. We have to allow the Holy Spirit to work on us. If we do not rebel against the discipline of the Holy Spirit and if we do not fight against it according to our own will, the Spirit will subdue our outer man, and our inner man will become useful

to Him. This is the reason the breaking of the outer man is
so crucial.

THE MIND UNDER THE CONTROL OF THE SPIRIT

In our speaking, we must also pay attention to our mind.
Whether a word should be spoken first or last is a decision
that rests with the mind. In our service as a minister of the
word, our mind occupies a very important place. If our mental
faculty is versatile, we can place a word at the beginning of
our speaking or at the end. Either place will fit, and the
spirit will be released during the speaking. But if our mind
is not so versatile, nothing works. In such a case, whether
the word comes to our mind at the beginning of the speaking
or at the end, the spirit is not released in our speaking. Every
minister of the word has to guard his mind carefully from
any damage. He has to treasure his mind like a pianist
treasures his two hands. Some people are too careless with
their mind; they can never be proper ministers of the word.
We have to allow the Lord to freely direct our mind; we cannot
allow our mind to go wild. We should not allow our mind to
dwell on illogical things, vain things, or unimportant things.
We must protect our mind like a pianist protecting his two
hands. We should not set our mind on low or base things. If
the Spirit cannot use our mind when He calls for it, we are
frustrated from serving as a minister of the word.

This does not mean that the mind is the source of our
speaking. If a minister of the word bases his activity on his
mind, such activity should be condemned and destroyed to
the uttermost. The thought that a thorough study of the
Scriptures will qualify a man to teach is an abominable
proposition. Any thought that is independent of the spirit
should be destroyed. Any message that is based on the mind
as the source should be annulled. But this does not mean
that we should annul the function of the mind. Every book
of the New Testament is written with rich expression of
thought. Paul's Epistles, such as his Epistle to the Romans,
are full of thoughts. Yet the thoughts are high and lofty. The
book of Romans does not originate from the mind; it
originates from the spirit. Yet the thoughts contained in that

book flow out with the spirit. The source must be the spirit, not the mind. We must take good care of our mind so that it can be available to God when He needs to use it.

We should not indiscriminately condemn our mind. We should condemn the mind as the source. It is wrong for a man to preach according to his mind. The proper way to preach is with the spirit by the help of the mind; no one should condemn this. The more spiritual a message is, the richer the thought behind it should be. All spiritual messages are full of thoughts. When the spirit is released, there is the need for rich and adequate thoughts to support it. We should give our thoughts the proper place. In our speaking, our mind has to decide the order and the way that the words are to be expressed. If a word comes to our mind first, we should speak it first; if it comes to our mind last, we should speak it last. We should speak according to where our mind leads us. We must realize that our spirit does not control our speaking directly. Direct control by the spirit would mean that we are speaking in tongues. Rather, the spirit directs our speaking from behind our thoughts and understanding. This is the meaning of the ministry of the word. Our understanding must be available for the spirit's use. If it is not available, our spirit is blocked, and there is no medium between the spirit and the word. The proper medium between the spirit and the word is the mind. This is the reason that we have to carefully guard our mind before the Lord. The mind must be renewed daily. We must not allow our mind to habitually remain in a low place. Some peoples' minds are habitually low, and the Spirit cannot use them. We have to preserve our mind. It is as we touch the ministry of the word that we know the depth of the meaning of consecration. Many people do not understand the meaning of consecration. Consecration means that our whole being is made available to God. In order to make everything available to God, every part of our mind must be made available to Him. Every day we have to exercise care before the Lord; every day we have to guard our mind from becoming low. If it remains low all the time, we will not be able to pull it up when we have need of it. We have to train our mind every day so that it will be available for the Scripture's use. This is the only way to insure that our mind does not become a hindrance to the spirit. God must be able to direct our mind at will. By His mercy, He will direct our mind. He will let our mind recall what we should say. The things that should be spoken first will come to our mind first, and the things that should be spoken last will come to our mind last. Our words will be controlled by our mind, and our mind will be controlled by our spirit. If our spirit can direct our mind, everything will be right. It will be right if a word is spoken first, and it will be right if it is spoken last. It will be right if we speak more, and it will be equally right if we speak less. If the mind is proper and functional, the word will come out in any case.

THE CLIMAX OF THE WORD AND THE CLIMAX OF THE SPIRIT

In our speaking, it is easy for us to know the climax of our speaking because our mind easily can identify it, but it is not easy to know the climax of the spirit. The climax of the spirit is something that is unknown to our mind. This is the reason that it is not easy to tell the climax of the spirit.

While we are standing on the platform and speaking, how do we know how far God wants to go? How do we know what height the Lord wants to attain? How do we know which points the Lord wants to magnify? How can we know when the Lord wants to climax His speaking? In his speaking, a minister of the word has to pay attention to the difference between the climax of the word and the climax of the spirit. If our condition is right, we should clearly know the particular word that God has given to us whenever we open our mouth to speak for the Lord. We should also know the high peak in our speaking. This means that most words are ordinary words, but some words are especially high; they touch the climax of our speaking. We should know where this peak lies when we are speaking. While we are speaking, we should take care of the peak. The purpose of our speaking is to bring in the climax. But we should realize that the climax in the spirit may not coincide with the climax of the speaking.

Sometimes the climax in the spirit does coincide with the climax in the speaking, but this is not always the case. This makes the matter rather complicated. It would be a simple job for the minister of the word if the climax of the word always coincided with the climax in the spirit. When we know what the peak of the speaking should be, we aim our words at that peak and climb up gradually until we reach that peak. When the peak of the speaking is the same as the peak in the spirit, the matter is very simple. All we have to do is aim our words at the peak. Our spirit will be released and the anointing will be released. The degree to which the spirit is released will be as powerful and strong as the word that is released. Not much difficulty will be encountered in such a release. But sometimes the climax of our speaking does not coincide with the climax in the spirit.

When God gives us a ministry, He gives us the word at the same time. But when we serve the church with this word, the strange and peculiar thing is that even though there is a high point to our speaking, the spirit does not like to release itself at the high point of the speaking. The climax of the speaking may be here, yet the climax in the spirit has not arrived. Sometimes, the climax in the spirit has arrived, but the climax of the speaking has not come. It is true that the spirit has to be released. But it is released with a focus that sometimes is the same and sometimes is different than the focus of the word. Sometimes as soon as we touch the heart of our speaking, the spirit is released in a strong, powerful, and explosive way. But this does not happen every time. Often the center and climax of the speaking have not arrived; only a few simple words are said, and they may be said indifferently. Yet the spirit is released. In other words, the spirit is released before the climax of the speaking is reached.

We have to tell the difference between the peak of the word and the peak in the spirit. We have to learn to direct our words with our mind so that when the spiritual climax is reached, we have one or two words that can serve as the leverage for the speaking of the ministry. As a rule, the climax of the ministry should be the climax of our speaking. But the strange thing is that when the word reaches the peak without the spirit, it is hard to push out one's spirit at such times. It may not be an absolutely impossible task because the spirit will move a little when the word reaches the peak, but it is sometimes impossible to push out the spirit in a very strong way. Perhaps a few minutes or even ten to twenty minutes have to pass after the high point in the word, when the minister has returned to an ordinary utterance, before the spirit rises up and moves out in a strong way. In our preaching we should pay attention to these two things: the high point in the word and the high point in the release of the spirit. The two may coincide. But they can also happen at different times. They may occur at the same time, or one may occur first and the other follow.

What should we do when the high point of the word and the high point in the spirit are different? A minister of the word should remember that at such times the mind has certain duties to perform. In fulfilling the ministry of the word, one has to have a flexible mind; his mind must not be dull. While a minister of the word must have his mind focused on the word, his mind also must be available to the Holy Spirit. It must be so flexible that it can handle any unexpected event. It is not uncommon for a minister of the word to encounter unexpected things. God may speak something different at the last minute; He may want to add something, and the Holy Spirit may move in a different direction at the last minute. But suppose his mind is set like a piece of wrought iron on what he is going to say. When the spirit tries to lay hold of the word, the mind may not be pliable enough. If it is too rigid and dull, the speaking becomes restricted. He can reach a high point in his speaking, but the spirit does not reach the high point. As a consequence, the ministry becomes common and powerless. It is not easy to point out this phenomenon. Perhaps this will become clear to us in the future. Nevertheless, we have to remember that the mind of a minister of the word has to be devoted solely to the word on the one hand, but the mind always must be flexible and agile before the Lord on the other hand. When the Holy Spirit points to a different direction, the mind must turn with Him. In this way he will not miss the spiritual climax that God wants to achieve.

When we stand up to speak for the Lord, our mind must be pliable and open to the Lord. Only then will we know what God is trying to do. We must be prepared mentally to meet all unexpected circumstances. While we are speaking, we should test the Holy Spirit to find out whether our speaking is in the right direction. We should test our own spirit and test God's Spirit as well. If we find that there is some amount of release of the spirit after a few words, we should exercise our mind to facilitate the release of the spirit. We may find that the spirit becomes more released when we speak a certain sentence. We should speak more along this line to release more of the spirit. While we are speaking, our mind should be keen to touch the high point in the spirit. Once our mind touches the high point, we should be ready to speak another sentence to release the spirit. A third and fourth sentence, which will release the spirit further, should follow. In other words, whenever the word comes to a point where the spirit is released, the mind should not turn in another direction, and the speaking should not move away. The mind and the word must move along the same line. The more one speaks, the more the anointing flows, and the more the spirit is released. The word will become stronger and stronger until it reaches the climax in the spirit.

Sometimes the climax in the spirit coincides with the climax in the word. But sometimes they do not fall in the same place. Sometimes the spiritual climax comes before the word has reached its climax. We can do nothing about this. But if the climax of the speaking has come and the climax of the spirit has not, we have to consider what needs to be done in order to release the spirit in a strong way. We have to exercise the utmost care at such a juncture. It is as if we were looking for a lost needle, probing in every direction as with a magnet. When the magnet comes close to the needle, the needle will be swooped up. A speaker has to test with his words. If the spirit does not move when he speaks one way, he has to change. If the spirit remains quiet after he tries another way, he has to change again. He has to watch when the spirit begins to move. An experienced person will know as soon as the spirit moves at his word. As soon as the right word is uttered, he has a registration within that he has said the right thing. It may be a very fine and delicate move, yet he knows. As he speaks with his mind, he is testing whether or not the Spirit likes his utterance. When the Spirit approves his speaking, he may have a very faint sense initially. But as he pursues along the same line, the spirit will be released more and more. At this juncture, his mind should direct his words along this line and strengthen his speaking. He must not turn in a different direction. He should move his speaking in the same direction. The more the word continues in this same direction, the more the spirit is released, and the more he will touch the spiritual climax of his speaking. We have to learn to test the Spirit with the word. We have to know what kind of word brings out the climax of the Spirit and what kind of word frustrates it. The more we touch the peak, the more the spirit will flow, and the more anointing there will be. The more our word hits the right spot, the more anointing we will have, and the more our word will bring us to the spiritual climax, the apex. When we sense the Lord's Spirit and blessing, we can be assured that we have touched the heart of our speaking; this is the spiritual climax of our speaking. If our spirit is strong, we can sustain this climax for a long time. If our spirit is not that strong, we will have to turn after a while; otherwise, the climax will shrivel away. The length of time depends on how strong our spirit is. If the spirit is strong, the climax can be sustained for a longer time. If the spirit is not strong, the climax will fade away quickly. We cannot try to sustain it by force. This is entirely a matter of the spirit. When the spirit is gone and the word is left to itself, the speaker should terminate his speaking on this point.

For this reason, our mind must be in focus and be pliable before the Lord. It must be absolutely in focus, and it must also be absolutely pliable. It must be so focused that it is aware of nothing else. Yet, at the same time, it must be so gentle that it can accommodate any unexpected event. We should be on the alert that the mind does not become so rigid that we fail to touch the Lord's present word and His climax. Our mind has to be exercised to catch up with God's word and the Spirit's move. If we do this, our word will catch up with the climax of the spirit when we function in the ministry of the word.

A PERFECT MEMORY

When we speak as a minister of the word, we have to exercise our mind. We typically speak whatever comes to our mind; whatever we think of, we speak. Our mind controls our words. Yet our mind must have some substance; it must not be full of vanity or aimless thoughts. The basis of our thoughts is our memory. The raw materials from which we formulate our speaking come from whatever we have learned previously, whatever our mind is occupied with, whatever we have experienced and seen in the past, and whatever breaking work we have experienced. These materials are collected from the Lord. The work that the Lord has done and the breaking work that He has accomplished become the building blocks. We spend our whole life accumulating experience, discipline, teachings, and knowledge of the Scripture. These become accumulated deposits within us. When we stand up to speak for the Lord, God's Spirit will direct our mind to search through our memory to put all the things we have acquired to use. In other words, the Holy Spirit directs our mind, while the mind directs the speaking. The mind supplies the speaking with the raw materials, and the raw materials come from the memory. If we do not have any experience, we have nothing in our memory; we cannot remember what we have never acquired. We can only remember what we have acquired. A certain thing that we remember may supply our mind with the right word to support our speaking. Behind the speaking there must be a good mind and good thoughts, which come from one's memory. These thoughts are not extemporaneous or imaginary thoughts; they are acquired through one's previous experiences.

Speaking is based on the mind, the mind is based on the memory, and memory is based on experience. When we stand up to speak, we can only draw from the resources we have collected throughout our life. The experiences we collect throughout our life are like goods in a storehouse. The Lord has brought us through many experiences; we have learned many lessons and seen many truths. All these are stored in the warehouse of our experience. When we open our mouth to speak, our speaking is built upon our experience. But how does our speaking build upon our experience? Our speaking is only related to our mind. We may want to say something, and as we are considering what to say, our mind will go to our memory storehouse. The storehouse of our lifetime experiences can only be accessed and retrieved by our memory. The memory is like the manager of the storehouse; it alone can retrieve what we have known and experienced. The mind then organizes these materials and releases them through our speaking. Here we see the importance of the memory. We must put the director and the materials together. Every ministry of the word begins from the Holy Spirit. But when the Holy Spirit speaks, He speaks through our mind. When the Spirit wants to say something, He first considers what the mind can afford Him. Whatever the Spirit wants to say, the mind must come up with the word. If the Spirit wants to say a certain thing first, the mind has to recall that thing first. Brothers, more and more we are realizing that our mind is not adequate for His use. We cannot recall what the Spirit wants to say, and we think of things that the Spirit does not want to say. This is a proof that our mind is not adequate for His use. A minister of the word only needs to speak once for Him; he will be humbled immediately. He will realize that he cannot make it by himself. He cannot recall what the Spirit wants, and he can recall what the Spirit does not want. His mind is like a flywheel that is misaligned with another wheel. On certain days he feels fine. Whatever the Lord wants to say comes out of his mouth spontaneously; he has the right word to convey the Lord's utterance. During these times, his mind is like a flywheel that is well aligned. When the Spirit moves, his mind matches the move and follows the Spirit. But this does not happen all the time. The mind often does not function that well. The Spirit may want to say something, but the mind is too dull to think of the right words.

We must realize that the Holy Spirit dictates to our mind, while our mind dictates our words. If the Holy Spirit cannot dictate to our mind, our mind cannot dictate our words. When our mind dictates our words, it also requires the help of the memory. The mind does not come up with words of its own; it only recalls words. These words are not imagined or intangible. They are stored in the storehouse. We must first have a verse in our storehouse. The Lord must have dealt with us in a certain way already. When the need arises, the Lord will cause us to remember such a thing. Therefore, as we are preaching, we have to exercise our memory. The Holy Spirit directs the mind, and the mind searches through all our experiences in our memory and then releases them as the word. This speaking becomes a good ministry of the word. A healthy memory is very useful. It comes in handy and affords a person whatever he needs. In the ministry of the word, the Holy Spirit uses man's mind to recall what he has learned. Without any effort on our part, the Spirit can call to mind something we have learned or seen and then place it in our mind. Our mind sees it once more and speaks it out. Many things are retained in the form of just a few words. If the mind is undisciplined, it is not able to recall these words, and the spirit is frustrated from being released. As long as one part of our being malfunctions, the spirit does not flow. We can still preach, but the spirit is not released. The release of the spirit requires the cooperation of a fully functioning mind and a fully functioning memory. As long as something is wrong with our mind or memory, we cannot function properly. This is a very serious matter.

Suppose we know what the Lord wants us to say. It may be something long that cannot be expressed in one word. Perhaps seven or eight words are required. The Lord wants us to speak these words, but we are afraid that we will forget them. Therefore, we try hard to remember them. When we come to the meeting, our mind is set on these seven or eight words. We tell ourselves that we have to remember them. Our heart is set on them, yet we often find that our memory does not serve us on that day. Our spirit is not released. The mere retention of the word in the mind is useless; such a word is powerless. When it is released, the spirit does not move. With a minister of the word, the functioning of the memory has to be something very spontaneous. If we try to muster it artificially, it will turn the other way when the Spirit calls for it.

A minister of the word needs not only a perfect mind but a perfect memory. Memory is like an electrical connection; as long as one end is broken, the electricity is cut off. When a certain part in our memory is blocked, the Lord's Spirit does not flow out. As long as our memory is slightly cut off from the source, we are through. If we try to make our memory or mind the source, we are through. When the Holy Spirit is the source, our mind and memory can become very useful. It is when the Holy Spirit shines from within us that we realize how short our mind is. When light is lacking in our spirit, we become very proud of our mind, memory, and eloquence. These faculties may seem to be functioning very well. But when we are enlightened by the Holy Spirit, we realize the uselessness of our mind, memory, and eloquence. This is the reason that we have to pray; we have to pray that our memory would become the memory of the Holy Spirit and that God's Spirit would be able to use it when He has need of it. When we speak, we may or may not be able to recall certain crucial words. The difference here is very great. If we recall these words, the utterance will be released, and the spirit will be released. But if we cannot recall these words, we will feel a burden like a big millstone upon our back. This burden will weigh heavily upon us, and both the word and the spirit will be quenched.

We have to exercise total concentration in making ourselves available to the Spirit. We have to gather everything that we have experienced in our life, all the discipline that we have learned, all the things we have read and heard, all the revelation we have seen in our life, and all the teachings we have learned from the light. We have to put them all before the Spirit and make them available to Him. They must be gathered together and made available at the same time. Originally, we were like a house with all the windows open to the distracting noise and color outside. Now the windows should be closed, allowing no outside influence. All the things we have acquired in our whole life should be at the Spirit's disposal. Every time the ministry of the word is released in a strong way, the Holy Spirit takes up everything of our life and uses it within a period of five or ten minutes. Ministry of the word involves a price. Every release of the spirit involves a price. The outer man has to be shut out; all the windows to the outside have to be shut. We have to focus all of our memory; our whole being has to be kept under strict surveillance. At the critical moment, we must make everything available to the Holy Spirit. When this happens, we will have a powerful ministry of the word. There cannot be any disruption, distraction, or carelessness. We have to maintain our memory in top condition; our memory has to be on full alert every time we speak. We have to gather up everything in a way that has never been done before during our entire life. We should collect all the things of our life and make them available to the Holy Spirit all at once. This is the duty of the memory in the ministry of the word.

In order for the memory to have the adequate materials, we have to learn many lessons before the Lord and experience many things. Ministry of the word is based on the discipline of the Holy Spirit. Without the discipline of the Holy Spirit, we do not have the supply, and we have nothing to say. We receive the supply through the discipline of the Holy Spirit. As we increase our deposit gradually and continuously, there is room in our memory storehouse to keep the inventory. But if we have only received a little discipline from the Holy Spirit, we will have few lessons to draw from. There will be little place in our memory to direct our inventory, and we will have nothing for the Spirit to draw from. Therefore, the riches of the ministry of the word depend on the wealth of discipline that the minister receives. The more the minister learns his lessons and receives discipline, the more room his memory possesses to maneuver the goods, and the more materials his mind has from which to generate the words. In serving as a minister of the word, we must have substance to our words; we cannot speak vain words, and we must have enough memory to apply everything that we have learned in our lifetime to our speaking. If God's Spirit is directing the speaking, everything we have learned in our life will be used.

THE FEELINGS MATCHING THE WORD

A minister of the word must also exercise his feelings. We must realize that the spirit flows out of us only when our feelings match our words. If there is a little reservation in our feelings about the word we have received from the spirit, the word will not come out, and the spirit will not be released. We often have reservations in our feelings. What does it mean to have reservations? We may feel ashamed of something, or we may fear men's criticism, cold shoulders, or opposition. We may discount our words or hold back the feelings we should have concerning our word. We hold back something and dare not match our feelings with our word. When we speak, we have to let go of our feelings completely. If we do not let go, we will have reservations, and as long as we have reservations, the word will never be released. No matter how hard we try, the spirit will never be released. If the word calls for tears, we have to shed tears. The word often calls for tears, but the speaker will not cry. When this happens, the feelings and the word do not match.

Man's outward shell is very hard. As long as a man does not let go of his feelings, his spirit is not released. The most prominent mark of the outpouring of the Holy Spirit is the letting go of our feelings. There are two ways to let go of feelings. The first is through the outpouring. The second is through the breaking. The release that comes through the outpouring is an outward release. We ourselves must still learn to let go before the spirit can be released. Breaking and discipline enable a man to let go, even when he is not experiencing the outpouring. A young brother who has never received any deep revelation needs the outpouring; this outpouring will loosen him up. But he should not trust in this kind of release through the outpouring. He should accept all kinds of discipline day by day, until his outward shell is broken. This brokenness is indeed precious. One should be released not only when he has the outpouring of the Spirit; his feelings should be broken even when he does not experience any outpouring. In other words, if the discipline of the Lord's Spirit is severe enough and if the shell of feelings is broken, we will have whatever kind of feeling the word requires of us. We must match the word with our feelings. If our word is released without our feelings, the spirit most likely will not flow out. Sometimes God's word calls for tears, yet we cannot cry, or His word calls for shouting, and we cannot shout. This is because the self poses as a primary obstacle to the word's release. Our feelings are affected by men around us, and our feelings cannot match our words.

Sometimes, in order to release the spirit in a strong way, a man has to shout and cry. The Lord Jesus once cried out. John 7:37 says, "Now on the last day, the great day of the feast, Jesus stood and cried out." On the day of Pentecost, Acts 2:14 says, "Peter, standing with the eleven, lifted up his voice and spoke forth to them." When the pressure of the Spirit is heavy upon a man and his feelings are pressed, he is forced to speak in a loud voice. His outward feelings and inward feelings become the same. When Peter and John were released from prison, the brothers gathered together and lifted up their voice to God (4:23-24). They suffered dire persecutions. They asked the Lord to look upon them and to grant them boldness to speak His word on the one hand, and to stretch out His hand to heal on the other hand so that signs and wonders would take place through the name of the Lord. Paul was the same. When he saw the lame man at Lystra, he said with a loud voice, "Stand upright on your feet" (14:10). This shows us that when the ministry of the word is released, the word must be matched by corresponding feelings.

If we do not let go today and if we still have reservations in our feelings, we will find reservations in the spirit as well. The spirit will not be released. In the case of the Lord Jesus, in the prayer of the first church, and in the cases of Peter and Paul, strong feelings were released. They all spoke with a loud voice. When our spirit is released, it must be accompanied by strong feelings. We are not encouraging anyone to preach by shouting. We are saying that when the spirit is strong, the voice can be loud. If the spirit is not strong, the voice can never be loud. If we are inwardly void of feelings, even filling the whole room with our voice is useless. When some people sing, the louder they sing the less spirit they have. The same is true with some preaching. An artificial loudness will not work. Artificiality is useless in the ministry of the word. The inward reality must be released. We should never try to imitate the spirit in an outward way. When our word is released, our feelings must be released as well. This is the reason that we must be broken. If our outward shell is broken, we can shout as we please, rejoice as we please, and sorrow as we please. We do not have to act out these feelings; they flow out from within.

If the Lord cannot get through in our feelings, He will not be able to get through in others' feelings. Others are cold, dry, and contradicting. When we speak, we have to break through their feelings. If the Lord cannot get through in our feelings, we cannot expect Him to get through in others' feelings. If the Lord cannot make us cry, He cannot make others cry. If the pressure does not produce tears in us, we cannot expect it to produce tears in others. We are the first hurdle that the Lord's word has to overcome. While we are speaking, we often feel that our feelings are not available to us. The highest price in the ministry of the word is the price of our breaking. The Lord has to break us into pieces before He can have a way through us. God's word has to touch us in a strong way before our reactions can be God's reactions. If a weeping Jeremiah could not make the Jews weep, a prophet who did not weep would surely not be able to evoke any tears from the whole nation of Israel. Jeremiah was a weeping prophet. If a weeping prophet cannot produce a weeping people, a prophet who does not weep will surely not produce a weeping people. In order for God's people to weep, the prophet must first weep. God finds special pleasure in brothers who let go of their feelings when they stand up to speak. When a minister of the word stands on the platform, he has to learn to match his feelings with the word.

WORDS BEING PLAIN AND HIGH

All ministers of God's word should learn from the Scripture the character of God's word. Once they learn this, they will know under what circumstances God will use them. Simply put, there are two characteristics to God's word. First, it is plain; second, it is high. God's word is plain. Even a blind man will not be lost and a lame man will not be put out of joint by God's word. God's word is very clear and plain. The parables in the Word are not riddles. If God's word were a riddle, it would mean that it was not written for man to understand. God's word is not a riddle; it is clear and plain. Therefore, every minister of God's word should learn to speak in a plain way. We must have the habit of speaking plainly and simply; we should not be wordy. We should take care that others understand our words. If others do not understand our words, we have to change our way. We should always remember that God's word is given for men to understand, not to misunderstand. Matthew 13 is an exception because the Jews rejected the Lord. Therefore, God's word was hidden from them.

A minister of the word has to be trained in his ability to speak. We may understand something today, and it may take us just five minutes to comprehend it. But we may have to spend five hours to contemplate on it. When we speak it, we should ask a brother whether he understands what we are saying. If he does not understand, we have to change our way. We need to speak in such a way that others understand immediately. We should never speak for half an hour and then find that only five minutes of our speaking were understood. Instead, we should speak for five minutes and make sure that others have understood those five minutes of our speaking. It is better to speak less than to waste twenty-five minutes of time. We have to learn to speak plainly. We should develop the habit of speaking clearly and not be tempted to become wordy. We should always use simple words and always consider how we can make our speaking understandable. We have to ask God to give us plain words that we can express. We may express our thoughts through a parable, but we still have to make our word clear. This is the very nature of God's word. If the nature of our speaking is different from the nature of God's word, we will surely encounter problems in our speaking. Those who have a problem with their speaking should forget about their "face." They should humble themselves and seek advice from other brothers and sisters. They should practice speaking to others for five minutes to see whether or not others understand what they are saying. They should be willing to accept correction so that they can speak longer the next time, perhaps ten minutes. Since we are here to speak for God, we have to learn to speak, and our words have to be uttered clearly sentence by sentence. The meaning has to be obvious, and the choice of words has to be suitable. We speak to make others understand. God does not want His word to become a riddle, like some parables in the Old Testament. God does not want men to have to spend a great deal of time trying to understand His word. A minister of the word should often seek advice from more learned and experienced brothers and should ask for their criticism concerning any part that is not clear. He should learn to improve his speaking and strive to make his words simple and plain.

God's word is plain, but His word is also high and profound. God never says anything shallow. He never says anything that sounds titillating but conveys no spirit. The speaking of the minister of the word should be like a hammer; in striking God's word, one should hit hard. If he hits softly, his word will not touch God's word. If our words are shallow, we cannot express God's word no matter how hard we try. Our speaking must maintain a degree of height and profundity. Once we change the nature of God's speaking, we cannot touch His word. Our speaking must be high. Our words must be high and profound because the Lord of hosts is coming through our speaking. Once our words become shallow, God will not be released. Some brothers speak in such a low way when they quote a verse that it is difficult to imagine that God's word can be released through them. Some brothers have such a childish way of exhortation that one wonders how God's word can come out of their mouth. We must take care of the loftiness of our speaking. As soon as our words become low, God's speaking diminishes or even disappears. When our words remain shallow, God cannot find any opportunity to thrust Himself out of the word. The more our exhortation stays on a low plane, the less others will touch anything. The more our exhortation remains on a high plane, the more others will touch something. This is a very strange phenomenon. Suppose a two- or three-year-old girl has just learned to understand words. We can say to her, "Tonight I will buy you a piece of candy. If you behave well, the Lord Jesus will love you." It is all right to say this to a child. But if we say on the platform, "Tonight I will give you all a piece of candy; if you listen quietly to my preaching, the Lord Jesus will love you," will this exhortation work? This is low exhortation, a childish exhortation; it is baby talk. Once our words become low, there is no more divine speaking. God wants His servants to always remain on a high plane. The higher we climb, the better our audience will receive our word.

We must realize that it is an important duty of the minister of the word to climb high before God. The higher we climb, the more divine speaking there will be. If we do not aim high, our teachings and exhortations will be low; we will be short of God's speaking. Once our words are low, God's word will not be released. God does not tolerate any low thoughts, low words, low exhortations, low parables, or low expressions. Therefore, our words have to be high yet, at the same time, clear and plain. This is the way to release God's word. Sometimes we have the light, the word, and the burden. We want to say the word in a plain way, but the pressure is great, and we cannot be plain. It is hard to speak plainly even when we practice. If we do not practice, how can we do it? We must learn to speak simply, plainly, and clearly. We have to make this our habit. At the same time, we have to aim our words as high as possible. We should never touch low things. Once we touch low things, God's word will not be released. This is a very important point.

ADVANCING ALL THE TIME

It is harder for us to speak today than for those who spoke one hundred years ago, and harder still than for those who spoke four or five hundred years ago. It is harder for us to speak than it was for Martin Luther, because the release of God's word is always advancing onward and upward. The more we speak God's word, the more profound it becomes and the higher it gets. Today God's speaking has reached the present stage, and we cannot go back to His former speaking again. We have to go on. The Lord said, "My Father is working until now, and I also am working" (John 5:17). God never stops working. He worked yesterday, and He is working today. His work today is more advanced than His work yesterday, and His work tomorrow will be more advanced than His work today. His work never diminishes; it only increases. His work is forever advancing and never retreating. Martin Luther saw the truth of justification by faith. But what men have seen in the last one hundred years concerning justification by faith is much more than what Luther saw. This is not arrogance. This shows that God's word is advancing. The best book Luther wrote was his commentary on Galatians. But believers today have seen much more from Galatians than what Luther saw. God's word has moved on, and it is impossible for anyone to turn back.

We must realize that all the truths are in the Bible. The basis of all our speaking is the Bible. Yet the discovery of biblical truth, the release of God's word, and the things that the church receives from God are advancing day by day. Every generation of God's children sees more than the generation before. For example, in the first few centuries, the church interpreted the kingdom to mean heaven, but in the last century, this matter has become very clear. The kingdom is the kingdom, and heaven is heaven; these are two different things. Today we are even clearer: The kingdom is not only a matter of reward but also a matter of spiritual reign and rule. We believe all the biblical truths were clear during the apostolic age. Later they were buried and then recovered little by little. Consider the example of resurrection. Our understanding of it has moved on. For years men spoke about resurrection in a limited way; they understood it only to mean to a certain sphere. But today some have seen what resurrection is. They have surpassed their predecessors in what they have seen. If God is merciful to the church, the word will abound more and more. When God speaks, His word always climbs higher and higher.

God's word is always advancing. He is always ready to give more to His church. In reading the best homiletics of the second and third centuries and in comparing them with the present ministry of the word, we can see how much progress has been made. The Holy Spirit has not held Himself back. The word is still advancing; it is not retreating. Although the church outwardly faces many obstacles, our God is still going on. God does not stop after He has accomplished one thing. He is still working, and He is still advancing. Therefore, the ministry of the word today should touch more than what was touched by former ministries. We should realize before the Lord that grace is pouring out in unbounded measure. In order for the church to grow to full stature and to touch the fullness of Christ, we believe that the riches of the ministry must increase. Do not speak with contentment and nonchalance. God wants us to touch something high. He wants to give us the high things. Perhaps God has not chosen us to be a pivotal minister, one who is a "joint," but I hope that we can still have a share among the ministers. Although we cannot build up the framework itself, we can at least fill in the gaps in the existing framework.

SECTION FOUR

THE AUDIENCE

CHAPTER EIGHTEEN

THE AUDIENCE OF THE WORD

Now we come to the fourth section, the audience. Speaking involves not only the minister but the audience, that is, those who listen to the word. Whether or not the ministry of the word is strong depends also on the audience. The minister of the word has much to do with the speaking, but the audience has something to do with it also. While the minister of the word bears more than half of the responsibility, the audience bears at least some of the responsibility also. Whether or not the word can be released depends largely on the ministers, but the audience has its responsibility also. The audience can become a hindrance to the release of God's word, and it can also become a strengthening to God's word. A few examples in the Bible show us how an audience should behave. We hope to learn something from these passages.

ONE

First let us consider Matthew 13. The Lord Jesus spoke in parables because God could not reveal Himself to the "wise and intelligent" (Matt. 11:25). The wise and intelligent cannot expect to see God's revelation. For the same reason, they cannot expect to receive supply from the word. A wise and intelligent man cannot receive direct revelation from God, and he cannot receive revelation from the ministers of the word. Whenever the ministry finds wise and intelligent ones among its audience, God's word is immediately frustrated. It can be so frustrated that it is completely blocked, or it can be frustrated to the extent that it is released only in a mild or weak way. The more a man considers himself to be wise, the harder it is for him to receive light from God. The more a man trusts in himself, the more God's word is closed to him. We should remember that, according to the Old Testament, God sometimes seals up His prophecy to men (Dan. 12:9). This shows us that the word can be opened up, and it can also be sealed up after it is released. We are not here to explain the meaning of sealing up or the number of years the word was sealed up. We are pointing out a spiritual principle. A man can hear God's speaking and yet find the word sealed up to him. A man can touch God's word and yet find this word sealed up. Daniel shows us the fact of the sealing, while the Lord Jesus shows us the reason for the sealing—being wise and intelligent. The Lord shows us how the word was hidden. God wants to hide things from the wise and intelligent so that they cannot get through. Once a man becomes wise and intelligent, the Holy Spirit, in accordance with God's counsel, hides the word from him.

The Bible gives us a basic principle: After man ate of the tree of the knowledge of good and evil, the way to the tree of life was blocked. From that time forward, the tree of life was sealed up by the cherubim and the flaming sword which turned every way (Gen. 3:24). Once man acquired the knowledge of good and evil, he could no longer touch life. This separation is related not only to man's own inability but also to God's prohibition. This is the meaning of sealing. It has nothing to do with man's ability. Even if man were able, God would seal it up anyway. This is a serious matter. Whenever man pays attention to knowledge, life flees from him. Whenever man boasts of his own wisdom and intelligence and takes pride and glory in himself, he has to remember that the revelation of God's word is hidden from him. He will not see anything; what he sees will only be clouded forms. This is God's sealing. The Lord said, "I extol You, Father, Lord of heaven and of earth, because You have hidden these things from the wise and intelligent and have revealed them to infants" (Matt. 11:25). God does this purposely.

In the ministry of God's word, we must pay attention to the condition of the audience. When we speak to new believers, we may not have to exercise our spirit that much; there may not be that much need for light and words. But in preaching the gospel, we find that we have to exercise much spirit and use many words. Sometimes we have to touch the higher revelations of God, things that are spiritually higher and more real. At these times, we find that we need more words, more light, and more spirit. Suppose a man thinks that he is wise and intelligent. God will hide Himself from such a man. He will not give him any direct revelation. When such a person is present, even the minister of the word cannot function properly. If the need for the release of the spirit is not too demanding, the frustration may not be that serious. But if the demand for the release of the spirit is great, the frustration is also great. If there is a big demand for the release of the spirit, such a person will become a great frustration to the ministry of the word. God's high revelations are blocked because God has hidden these things from such men.

In previous discussions we have seen the responsibility of the ministers. We must also see that, in addition to the qualifications of the ministers, there is the condition of the audience. If a man is in a condition that blocks God's blessing, his presence will bring the speaking down. It does not matter how strong the minister is; his speaking will be brought down. Even if the minister is very powerful before God, and even if he wants to impart revelation to others, his ministry of the word will be void of revelation in the presence of such wise and intelligent ones. At best it will contain little revelation. We are not altogether clear how the audience affects the speaking, but it is a fact that the audience does affect the speaking. Some people are never subdued by God. The intelligent ones are never subdued. In the presence of such ones, the speaking rarely can be high.

In learning to be a minister of the word, we have to remember that sometimes the problem is with us; the word is withheld in us. But there are times when the problem is not with us. We have dealt with all the hindrances, but the revelation, the spirit, and the word are still not released. During these times, the problem may be with the audience. When a man first learns to be a minister of the word, he does not have much revelation and light, and any hindrance probably is not related to the audience. But when a man has considerable experience in speaking, and he is called upon to release some strong and potent revelations, a mere brush with one or two unworthy or proud persons is enough to block off his delicate feelings; his words will not be released, no matter how hard he tries. The feeling of the spirit is very tender. One characteristic of the word is that it must be directed toward men. The word has to go out, the spirit has to go out, and the Holy Spirit has to go out. But when there is a person who thinks highly of himself or who is a critical bystander, the speaker cannot release the word in a pure way even if he has the word. Sometimes we have to lead a brother into God's light to know himself. At other times we have to lead another brother to the Lord to acknowledge the glory of the Holy of Holies. We should remember that in God's light there is pure revelation. There is no doctrine or teaching; there is pure revelation, nothing but revelation. This is a time of pure shining and pure breaking. If three or five brothers are just spectators trying to find out what is going on, having closed spirits, and feeling no need to touch or receive God's word or to prostrate themselves before Him, the word will be frustrated. It will be so frustrated that it will be bound completely. The more spiritual the things we try to impart to others are, the easier it is for our speaking to be affected by men. The less spiritual the things we have to give to others are, the less likely our speaking will be affected. The one thing that threatens the ministry of the word is an air of being wise and intelligent. The Lord will never bless the wise and intelligent. It is most foolish to think of oneself as wise and intelligent.

The Lord said in the last part of Matthew 11:25, "[You] have revealed them to infants." The gentler the audience is, the stronger the word will be released. The more humble the audience is, the easier it is for the word to bring someone to his knees. The more willing the audience is to receive the word, and the more obedience we find, the more light will shine through the listeners and open them to revelation. The harder it is for a person to receive help, the harder it is to help him. The easier it is for a person to receive help, the easier it is to help him. This is a basic spiritual principle. It is difficult for many people to receive help. They have resistance to the word, to the thoughts presented, and to the Scripture. As a consequence, it is hard for them to receive God's light. It is hard to penetrate all their criticism to reach their inner being. When the word suffers so much criticism, it is screened out and blocked. The more childlike a person is, the more he is ready to receive help from the Lord. The gentler he is, the less prejudice he has before God. The more he opens his heart to the Lord, the more his spirit is open to the Lord as well. God gives such ones a powerful supply of the ministry of the word. He gives them great revelations. God resists the stubborn. This is the reason we have to be seeking, humble, simple, and gentle. This is the meaning of being an infant. The more we become like an infant, the more grace we receive from God. The more arrogant and stubborn we are, the less grace we receive from Him, because God destroys the wisdom of the wise and sets aside the understanding of those who understand. The Lord has to bring us to the point of acknowledging the futility of our wisdom and understanding. If God leads us on for another three or five years and grants us mercy, we will look back and realize how much our own wisdom actually killed us. There will be times when we would have received grace, yet our own wisdom stopped us. Many people have not realized how their own wisdom has harmed them. When the Lord grants them mercy, they will see how much harm their wisdom has done to them.

TWO

First Corinthians 1:19 says, "I will destroy the wisdom of the wise, and the understanding of those who understand I will set aside." The purpose of doing this is that "no flesh may boast before God" (v. 29). Simply put, God does not want us to be proud. God does not want anyone to be wise or understanding. On the one hand, we have our own wisdom; on the other hand, we need power. Man has wisdom, but at the same time he is weak. Today God is turning things around. He is turning our wisdom into foolishness. The result is that our weakness becomes our power. This is a wonderful thing, and it is a very difficult thing to achieve. Man is wise, but he is also weak. Today the Lord is turning our wisdom into foolishness with the result that our weakness becomes our power. God is breaking man's wisdom. At the same time, He is giving us power.

This may be difficult to understand. What is the relationship between power and wisdom? Why is power established when wisdom is destroyed? How does a man become strong when his wisdom is destroyed? How does power come when human wisdom is removed? How does God destroy man's wisdom, and how does He give power to man? First Corinthians 1:30 says, "But of Him you are in Christ Jesus, who became wisdom to us from God." The Lord has become our wisdom. Following this phrase there is a colon, which indicates that this wisdom is "both righteousness and sanctification and redemption." This wisdom includes righteousness, sanctification, and redemption. How does God make Christ our wisdom? When our own wisdom goes away and we no longer hold on to any wisdom and understanding of our own, and when we become foolish instead, God will make Christ our wisdom. This wisdom includes Christ becoming our righteousness, Christ becoming our sanctification, and Christ becoming our redemption. Three manifestations of power are found in this. We need power to be a righteous man, we need power to be sanctified, and we need power to be redeemed. (Redemption here refers to the redemption of the body.) It takes exceedingly great power to do all these, and all of these are included in the Lord Jesus as our wisdom.

In other words, all of God's grace is given to us through revelation. God has made Christ our revelation. In the end Christ becomes our righteousness, Christ becomes our sanctification, and Christ becomes our redemption. We first receive the revelation, but as a result we get righteousness, sanctification, and redemption. Therefore, once the problem of wisdom is solved, the problem of power is solved. In other words, once the matter of revelation is settled, everything related to spiritual riches is settled. Spiritual poverty ceases, and poverty in the word also ceases. Everything in the spiritual realm involves our seeing; once we see, we have. If we do not see, we do not have. We cannot deal with righteousness directly; but we can see the revelation. Once we have the revelation, we have righteousness. We can only acquire righteousness through revelation. We do not need to find righteousness apart from God's revelation. This may explain the reason that the Lord does not want us to have wisdom. Once our own wisdom comes in, the Lord's wisdom leaves, and revelation leaves. Once revelation is cut off, all spiritual blessings are cut off. Once spiritual vision is gone, spiritual power is also gone. If we purge out all spiritual foolishness, spiritual power will increase. These two things are linked together.

A man cannot appropriate the work of the Lord directly; all of His work is preserved in the realm of revelation. When we have the revelation, we have everything. If we try to lay hold of the Lord's work apart from revelation, His work will be dead to us. Some sinners want to accept the Lord. They know that they are sinners and that the Lord is the Savior. Yet when they pray to the Lord, they do not seem to have understanding. They can even tell others of the teaching of salvation, but they are cold and unresponsive to the truth. This is to appropriate the Lord's work with the human mind. They do not have revelation. In another case, a man may be praying in his room or listening to a message in the meeting. When the Lord opens his eyes a little and he sees that the Lord has died for him, he receives the Lord's death in that instant. Once he touches revelation, he gets Christ. Without touching revelation, he can never have Christ. It all depends on whether or not he has received the revelation. This is a basic principle. God has kept His work in the realm of revelation. No one can be related to His work apart from revelation. A man can only be related to His work through revelation.

If we understand this spiritual principle, we will realize that the ministry of the word is very much affected by the audience. Once a man becomes wise and intelligent, God hides Himself from him. If we are like infants, waiting simply, humbly, and meekly before the Lord, spontaneously He will become our wisdom. Once He becomes our wisdom, all problems associated with power are solved. When we take Christ as our wisdom before God, we will easily find righteousness, sanctification, and redemption as well. If we do not take Christ as our wisdom, we will not be able to find righteousness, sanctification, or redemption anywhere. Spiritual reality is kept in the revelation of Christ. Once a man touches revelation, he touches reality. If he does not touch revelation, he does not touch reality. Righteousness in the past, sanctification in the present, and redemption in the future, which are all the power that our whole being needs, are kept in this wisdom. When the Lord Jesus becomes our wisdom, this wisdom includes these three things. God has put these three things—righteousness, sanctification, and redemption—in revelation. Once we touch revelation, spontaneously we touch these things. Spiritual substance and reality are all contained in God's revelation. If the audience of the ministry of the word is proud, self-assured, or closed in spirit, God will not be able to put any revelation into them. God will not give them anything. We have to learn to be humble, meek, and simple before the Lord. The more arrogant we are before the Lord, the farther we are from God's revelation. Even a minister of the word will not be able to do anything about us; even he will be frustrated by us. God hides Himself from the wise and intelligent and reveals Himself to the infants. This is a very serious matter.

THREE

Romans 11:8 says, "As it is written, 'God gave them a spirit of deep sleep, eyes to see not and ears to hear not, until this very day.'" This verse says that God has given the Jews a spirit of deep sleep. They have eyes, but they cannot see; they have ears, but they cannot hear until this very day. The situation in Matthew 13 is more serious than the situation in Matthew 11. In chapter eleven the Lord only spoke of hiding things. In chapter thirteen there is more than an ordinary kind of hiding; it is a hiding that is based on chapter twelve. It is an eternal rather than a temporary hiding. In chapter twelve the Lord Jesus cast out demons by the power of the Holy Spirit. The Jews who hated Him for no reason accused Him of casting out demons by Beelzebul, the ruler of the demons (v. 24). They hated the Lord so much that they closed their eyes and accused Him of casting out demons by the ruler of the demons. They clearly knew that the Lord Jesus cast out demons by the Holy Spirit, yet they hated Him for no reason at all. When they hated the Lord, they blasphemed the Holy Spirit and said that He cast out demons by Beelzebul, the ruler of the demons. They were prejudiced. They knew that the Lord cast out demons by the Holy Spirit, but they were determined not to believe this. They were determined to reject the Lord, and they insisted that He did not cast out the demons by the Holy Spirit, but by Beelzebul, the ruler of the demons. They were so hardened in their hearts. This is the picture in chapter twelve. These ones will not be forgiven, neither in this age nor in the one to come. Clearly, the Holy Spirit was working, yet they insisted that Beelzebul, the ruler of the demons, was working. The name *Beelzebul* means "the lord of flies." The Lord Jesus was casting out demons by the Holy Spirit, but they associated Him with "the lord of flies"; they accused Him of casting out demons by "the lord of flies." Such was the hardness of man's heart! This is the greatest sin in the whole Bible. No other sin is as serious as this one. Man commits many sins, but no sin is as great as this one. This sin will not be forgiven in this age nor in the age to come.

Then in Matthew 13, the Lord Jesus spoke in parables. The disciples asked Him, "Why do You speak in parables to them?" He answered, saying, "Because to you it has been given to know the mysteries of the kingdom of the heavens, but to them it has not been given" (vv. 10-11). They heard about the sower, but they did not know what it meant. They heard about the rocks, the birds, and the thorns, but they did not know what they meant. They also heard about the good earth, but they did not know what it meant. The Lord Jesus shows us a basic principle here: When men commit a grave sin, God closes up His word so that in hearing they would not understand, and in seeing they would not perceive. "For the heart of this people has become fat, and with their ears they have heard heavily, and their eyes they have closed, lest they perceive with their eyes and hear with their ears and understand with their heart, and they turn around, and I will heal them" (v. 15). It seems as if God was preventing them from repenting. Once a man has his own inclinations, prejudices, reluctances, and fault-finding attitudes, even God's light has to stop. Some people can preach outwardly, but they no longer have new revelations. What they see is passed on from one printed page to another mouth, and from that mouth to another printed page. The words pass on, but there is no new revelation and no new light. These ones are passing their days in darkness. We are afraid of committing sin, but we should be more afraid of committing sin without knowing that we have committed sin. Please remember that sinners could be saved at the time of the Lord Jesus, but the Pharisees could not be saved. God has a way to deal with the sinners, but He has no way to deal with those who are blind and in darkness. Seemingly, the Pharisees were not sinners. Actually, the Lord said that they were blind guides of the blind (15:14). The blinder a person is, the harder it is to deal with him.

Matthew 13 and Romans 11 show us a principle: A man can become so fallen that God's light is completely sealed off from him. We call this God's prohibition, or His sealing. Some people are in deep errors, not because they are foolish but because they are wise. A man who errs through foolishness is easily forgiven. But a man who errs through wisdom is not easily forgiven. Some people not only err; something is wrong with their heart. When a man errs through a deviation of his heart from God, God closes the door to him. This is a very serious matter. God has no desire for some people to see Him; He hides Himself from these ones. If God deals with us in this way, we are through. No loss is greater than the loss of vision! If God closes the door on us at any time, we are through. We should pray, "Lord, do not allow me to be so foolish as to say anything arrogant. Do not allow me to be so foolish as to reject the light. Do not allow me to fall to such an extent that there is no chance for me to repent." Without revelation, there is no repentance. The sealing off of revelation means the sealing off of repentance, and the sealing off of repentance means the sealing off of forgiveness. The Pharisees blasphemed the Holy Spirit; they could no longer repent, which meant that they would no longer receive any revelation. They heard, but they did not understand. They saw, but they did not touch anything. In other words, they only had words; they did not have revelation. Some brothers and sisters are unwilling to submit to others and to accept many things. When a person is prejudiced against something, he will say that it is wrong even when it is right. In order for a person to receive revelation from God, he must always be afraid of making mistakes. He dares not make presumptuous judgments, because he is afraid of being wrong. In order to receive light, one must not be presumptuous. When a man is weak and meek, it is easy for the Lord to grant him light and revelation; such a one receives the basic revelations as well as the extraordinary revelations. We have to learn to open our hearts to the Lord and to continually receive from Him. Once God seals up anything, we will not see any light. If a minister of the word encounters a person sealed from God, it will be impossible for him to release any light to that person.

FOUR

Light never waits for man! We should go to the Lord and beg like those who beg for bread. We should never presume that we have it already. This is a very serious thing. We have to see the seriousness of this matter before the Lord. We have to see that God has His work on earth today. The line of God's work has never stopped; it is forever going on. Those who have eyes will see the line of God's work; they will know what God is doing today. Once we stumble, we will fall behind and will not see. Once a man is prejudiced, he will not see. If twenty years ago we were behind in what God was doing then, we can only be further behind today. We should never allow ourselves to be left outside this line. This is the reason we have to humble ourselves. One thing is certain: God is going on now. He is going on step by step. We should be those who follow Him year after year. If the Lord will keep us in a spirit of humility and meekness, we will touch something. But if we are proud, arrogant, and self-justifying, we will find ourselves set aside by God. If we are willing to be a proper audience of the word, that is, if we are willing to receive the word and not give resistance to God's word, we will touch something in the ministry, and God's blessings and light will shine on us. Some, however, have already fallen by the wayside! May the Lord be merciful to us so that we will humble ourselves before Him.

Ephesians 4 tells us that the church will arrive at the fullness of perfection. It seems that God is raising up the standard of His own ministry today. Some have touched higher things; these are not ordinary things. But some have to wait for ten or twenty more years before they know or touch these higher things. Many things can only be seen after a period of time, and we are still quite a distance from them. We have to ask for God's mercy so that we will see something solid and real. May the Lord grant His church the ministry, and may we learn the lessons that we should learn.